PIECES OF THE TAPESTRY

This book is dedicated to all of our fathers:

Rev. John Walter Everett, Jr.
Samuel Goldstein
and
Irving Berkowitz

Pieces of the Tapestry

Read It Again...
of John's Creek
3630 Peachtree Pkwy.
Suwanee, GA 30024

PIECES OF THE TAPESTRY

May the Peace of the Perfect Valley between the Mountains of Faith, be yours forever.

Love,
Estatis Sowers
Elena Freemer

A GIFT FOR: _____

FROM: _____

DATE: _____

OCCASION: _____

Death releases spirit — which collides with other spirit — Through pieces of the Tapestry.
— DBYulin

The stories contained in this compilation are works of fiction.
All characters and events portrayed in the stories in this book are fictitious. Any resemblance to real people or events is purely coincidental.

PIECES OF THE TAPESTRY

Copyright (c)1994 by Elizabeth Bowers, Eleanor Freemer and Helen Tulis, as a compilation. Rights to individual works reside with each artist.

All rights reserved. No part of this book may be used or reproduced in any manner whatsoever without written permission from the authors, except in the case of brief quotations embodied in critical articles and reviews.

Library of Congress Catalog Card Number 94-74245

ISBN: 0-9644473-0-4

Published by Adept Publishing Association, Inc.
PO Box 87
Pine Lake, Georgia   30072-0087

Printed in the United States of America.

First Edition: December 1994

CONTENTS

CRYING IN THE BATHROOM	9
The Many Ways We Love	37
Singularly Human	76
Hot Coffee and Colorful Threads	174
Growing Out of Pain	151
Dream of the Future	218
Death & Survival	247
Index (Titles & Authors)	337
About The Authors	342

♓

Pieces of the Tapestry

Threads of time, like hands
Of hungry spider, weave full
Tapestry of life.

♓

-Elizabeth Bowers-

TAPESTRY
by
Elizabeth Bowers

Brave remembrances are
Tapestry covering vacuous souls;
Rose colored threads,
Warmth of early years,
Blend with blue and orange ties
To cooling elementary days,
And hours of knotted purple shades
Of tears and longing;
To restrain bright reds of
Frivolous moments, and
Give depth to earth tones of gladness,
So that green lows cannot hold still,
Golden threads that run
Forever through faith's tapestry of life.

♓

INTRODUCTION

We three have woven *Pieces of the Tapestry* with words as lovingly executed as the cartoons of Peter Rubins or Van Eycks for the Flemish weavers.

Watch the colors change; the woof and warp, like our moods, are vat dyes that make us so different, yet the same. Each strand, carefully placed, works into the main pattern, but never lets us lose sight of who and what we are. We are warm rich brown, blues and grays, pink like growing coral glints of gold. We are even deep purples for sorrows we have known.

It was our differences, the colored threads, that first attracted us three women to one another. The love of words, ideas and sharing, have been the loom that formed us. We have carefully plied our needles.

Pieces of the Tapestry weaves the experiences of joy and grief, challenge and prayer, comfort and disappointment, love and illusion, and despair and hope. *Pieces of the Tapestry* embodies our social conditioning, geographical differences, life span experiences, and value systems. Although our cultural diversity is evident in our works, no delusion is fostered as the varied colors blend, seeping through as one color.

With vignettes, essays, short stories, and poems the tapestry can be distinguished as it contains beliefs and thoughts. The reader can harbor the smell of the ocean as the adventurers see the California cost looming ahead in Bowers' story "*Pacific Reflections.*" Beginning with family in "*Kolk,*" and emitting pathos and disappointments, Freemer's thoughts carry the reader's emotions through developmental stages. Tulis' vignette, "*Greeting Seasons in the Cemetery,*" offers salvation in the sanctuary of the cemetery. Finally, the poems give recollections to immobilize memories setting them free to dance on the winds of commonalty.

The love which we Elizabeth, Eleanor and Helen share with one another is now yours through *Pieces of the Tapestry.* This is our gift to our readers, the universality of our lives and the secularism of our experiences. You may recognize in the multitude of our colors, some part of yourselves.

H

PIECES OF THE TAPESTRY
(A Montage of Short Stories, Poems and Vignettes)

by

Elizabeth Bowers, Eleanor Freemer and Helen Tulis

Edited by Elizabeth Bowers

Adept Publishing Association, Inc., Pine Lake, Georgia

1. CRYING IN THE BATHROOM

Rose sun shine down on
Weeping willow souls, grieving
For lost soil and seed.

♓

-Elizabeth Bowers-

Pieces of the Tapestry

WE WOMEN CRY IN THE BATHROOM
by
Eleanor Freemer

Where elsc can our tears flow freely,
Primal screams bounce off uncaring tiles,
Steady hearty smiles dissolve in pain
That stings our eyes like acid rain,
Ruining our makeup and the steely resolve
We vow not to let life get us down?

Behind locked bathroom doors we hide,
Reviewing the cruelty of the world outside,
Releasing frustrations, anger, despair,
Ones we can't talk about, ones we can't share.

My frail mother, faded like smoke.
I felt so alone,
Listened for her voice each time I answered the phone.
My father, my friend, was past eighty when he died,
Again I barricaded myself in, and cried and cried.

Children, they study our faces when things go wrong.
We play their game, pretend to be strong.
"Mommy, Mommy don't cry," they kiss away our tears.
So we sob under the shower where only God hears.

"God, why?" I pleaded, when our granddaughter passed away.
He gave me no answers, He had nothing to say.
I screamed about His choices for life, death and doom,
Where only He could hear me in my locked bathroom.

We women powder our faces, comb out our hair
With lipstick, paint on a smile, which we wear
Like a mask, to wash off with the tears we abhor,
Always in the bathroom, behind a locked door.

⚹

HOARDINGS
by
Eleanor Freemer

This drawer is like a hoarder's grave,
A crypt for pencil stubs and paper clips,
earless cups and plates with chips,
bits of junk I've always saved
for tomorrow.

My life too, is crammed with just such things;
broken promises, broken dreams,
shattered pieces from grandiose schemes
too heavy to soar on tattered wings,
to my great sorrow.

I've searched this wasteland on sleepless nights,
fingering chards
that need repairs,
hopes tangled in ribbons of past despairs,
shoved back into corners away from the lights;
Dark ancient sorrows.

I cry "Throw away these ancient relics of pain,
postcards wrinkled and turning to dust;
once shiny baubles now red with rust."
Alas, a fool, I bury them in this shroud again
to save for one more tomorrow.

)(

Pieces of the Tapestry

CHILD OF MY HEART
by
Elizabeth Bowers

    Child of my heart, like a morning glory in the night,
You hid the secrets of your soul's delight,
In the fullness of your spring flower;
You would not open your dreams to me,
But, like a dandelion, turned white with seed,
On the first breeze of spring, you took flight.
    Flesh of my soul, like a fire flaming hot to blue,
The whole of me, an open, burning wound,
Consumed with grief that will not heal,
A great emptiness chokes my essence.
Like unprotected reeds in the wind, my body wavers
On uneven space, a flower ignored by morning dew.
    Light of my sky, like a butterfly fleeing a dove,
The wild bird's song left with the dawn,
Chased by blossoms from the dogwood tree;
Autumn breezes blow dry, I cannot cry
And all my night visions are of sunken, barren trees,
Since the day you refused my gift, a mother's love.
    Shadow of spring, like a racing vessel in a lane,
The winds of sad misfortune bore you away,
Pushing you on into a mighty, rolling sea;
Your selfness hidden in the break of a wave,
Holding the whole of me to port in a strong head wind,
Full of thunder, lightning and gushing gales of rain.
    Dawn of my winter, though my arms, stretch out in love
Icicle glances pierce the heart of my soul
Like darts with sharp and poisonous tips;
My heart, like a fallen mountain stone to sea,
Shattered into a billion jagged pieces of raging pain,
When you slipped away in secret, like the winter dove.
    Child of my soul, you have put me to shore on an island
Where iron does not mix with miry clay,
And a mother's love is hurled far away;
The shadow of a strong and mighty glacier stands
In the mist of the raging sea, strong as an iron band,
Keeping you from the love I offer in my outstretched hand.

⁂

Pieces of the Tapestry
Lost baby breath blows
Scent of weeds of doubt and fear
From righteous garden.
♓

-Elizabeth Bowers-

KARA'S PATH

by

Elizabeth Bowers

    Kara Truitt took little notice of the painful pull of hot, sticky tar upon the soles of her bare feet. Frantically, she paced up and down the slender curb of the sparsely used stretch of asphalt highway separating Pleasantville from Absecon. On that late August afternoon, patches of red and pink impatiens bordering the road way shriveled up against a back drop of rain-starved shrubs and grasses. The air was thick with the scent of summer's fire but Kara, black kinky hair pulled back in a knot that matched the tightness of full lips pressed inward touching her tongue, took small notice.

    One thought held Kara's attention. "There is no end to this pain! Why Sheva? How could you hurt me this way?" Feelings stirred about within her like hot ash rising within an exploding volcano.

    Kara clutched at her churning stomach and stepped up her pace. "I've got to be the world's worse mother. Why didn't I see this coming? Such a child who could do this terrible thing! Damn it! Everything was going so well. She had to mess it all up again. What am I supposed to do now? Oh God, help me please!" She pounded the air with her fists and swore at the burning sun.

    Fresh tears, like a rolling river, filled her eyes as she remembered the phone call from LaVern Martin that morning.

♍♒♋■♑♏

Pieces of the Tapestry

"Kara, can you come over for coffee?" Lavern's voice held a cautious edge. "I've got something I need to tell you."

"Can it wait for a little while?" Masterfully, Kara bent forward and slipped her slightly muscular nut brown legs into royal blue shorts, while balancing the telephone between her head and right shoulder. "I'm still in my bare feet and I'm in kind of a rush today."

"Please Kara. This is really important." Lavern's tone was urgent.

"Look, it's already eight and Sheva has to be at the college by 9:15 for the Regency Exam this morning. I need the car, so I have to drive her." Kara righted herself, and slipped an arm into the short-sleeve blue floral blouse draped over her neck. "She's got to do well on the test this time. Whatever it is, tell me now so I ..."

"Kara, please listen to me" LaVern almost shouted, cutting her off. "Sheva called me about a half hour ago. From Brooklyn!"

Sunlight, like quivering streams of dazzling gold, poured through the double glass doors leading from the redwood deck outside to the family room where Kara stood leaning over the back of the oak stool next to the breakfast counter. "Brooklyn? What do you mean, Brooklyn?" She gave out with a loud, humorless laugh. "She's in her room still. I'm just getting ready to wake her." Nervously, Kara took hold of the telephone receiver with both hands.

"That's what I need to talk to you about. Sheva went to Brooklyn last night. After you and Garth went to bed, she left by bus."

"What?" Kara stood stiffly upright, her ear pressed hard against the telephone receiver. "Well that doesn't even make sense. Why in the world would she go to Brooklyn in the middle of the night?"

"She moved into an apartment with a friend who dropped out of college last quarter." Lavern's voice softened to a tense whisper. "She told me to tell you that she's not coming back home."

For an uncomfortable moment, there was silence as is felt before an approaching tornado blasts the airways with its freight train rattle, warning of death.

"But why?" Though her anger stood solid in her throat, Kara strained to keep her voice under control. "What you're telling me doesn't make any sense."

LaVern held her answer for what seemed like an eternal moment. "She's pregnant and she says she can't face you."

Pieces of the Tapestry

Kara flinched. "Pregnant!"

"Yes," LaVern whispered. "And she's having an abortion at 9:30 this morning."

Kara slumped down on the stool to ease the frozen heaviness of the blood draining from her face as a wash of outrage took over the whole of her being like a violent wave upon a stormy sea. "Tell me where." Kara's tone was thick calm.

"I don't know. She wouldn't tell me the name of the clinic. It's in Brooklyn. That's all I know," said LaVern.

"Brooklyn's a big place. Give me the address of where she's staying. That will help a lot." Kara, hand shaking, reached across the marble counter for a pen and writing tablet.

"I couldn't get her to give me her new address. I really tried but it was no use," Lavern's tone was apologetic.

Kara felt hysteria building up within her as she shouted into the phone. "Well did she tell you anything else?"

"Yes, one other thing. She asked me to tell you that she's so sorry." Lavern's words spoken in soft, soothing tones, were like horned vipers tearing the heart out of a jackrabbit already down and hurting.

Kara sat stiffly upright in her chair, free hand balled into a fist and resting on the counter-top. "Pregnant? Abortion?" Memories of the last time this happened were still painfully fresh in her mind.

"Well sorry just doesn't get it! Not this time," Kara shrieked. Her voice shook with unspent rage, as her hand gripped the beige princess phone tightly as though to choke out the vibrations of Lavern's voice.

With a loud sigh, Kara hung up the phone, buried her head in folded arms, and gave in to the turmoil building within her. Tears would not fall to cloud the vision that had formed in her mind. The image of Sheva lying prostrate on a dirty mattress somewhere, blood streaming down her bare legs as the tiny life within her was being sucked out ~ robbed of the chance to ever breathe the fresh scent of morning air ~ pulled at her soul. Kara sat perfectly still for a long while.

♍ ≈ ♋ ■ ♑ ♏

In the heat of the day, Kara lost all sense of time. Frantically, she searched for a burial ground for dead dreams. She brushed past patches of

Pieces of the Tapestry

salvia, their flowers drained of red coloring by hungry humming birds, and elder leaves yellowed by too much sun. Her company on that highway was a flood of agonizing thoughts rolling through her mind like a mighty tidal wave over unprepared land. Fresh tears rushed from her swollen eyes as stabbing pain held fast to her mid-section.

It had been her fondest fantasy to see Sheva, white satin dress against copper skin, ascending the long, winding staircase in the living room of their spacious home, her gloved hand upon the mahogany banister and the other looped through Garth's arm. In her fantasy, Kara was moved to joy when she saw Sheva's large eyes, obscured from the sight of a room full to over-flowing with family and friends standing in salute of the bride, glow like sable gems.

Kara fitfully paced up and down the same stretch of highway like a caged mountain lion in pain from a bloody wound filled with salt. "Damn it," she shrieked in agony. "I wish I knew what I'm supposed to do about all this! What God?" What?" She was drowning in waves of planted hopes that bear no fruit.

Nine o'clock had already come and gone. Now all that remained of the tiny life intrusted to her daughter was a legacy of bitter deception for worms to feed upon. "Sheva! Damn you! I am robbed! Robbed! How could you do this to me?" With her free arm held up straight, fingers grasping at air, Kara's tear-filled eyes raked the sky for an answer.

A large cloud formation, purple and shaped like a strutting peacock with wings outstretched, hovered in the distance. Kara stopped and studied it for a moment. There was no wind to give it motion. Still the cloud, like a feather kept airborne by gentle breath, inched its way closer to where she stood mesmerized and anchored to the wet tar.

The clouds changed shape and in the center she saw the perfect silhouette of a tiny man, skin the color of blue night and hair like silvery wool, peering down at her through thick glasses, an impish look upon his weather-worn face. He stood with hands on hips and legs astride revealing pink, rubber sole sneakers. He was clad in a green silk shirt with long sleeves, and a pair of bell-bottom trousers, purple like the clouds surrounding him. Bright pink gloves that matched a scarf tied about his unusually narrow neck, hid his hands.

In her mind, Kara heard a voice say in loud, penetrating tones, "You do not conquer a large dinosaur by watery means. You must swoop down upon it from the air." For a moment, the power of the words camouflaged the pitiful sounds of a heart being rent asunder by too great a loss.

Kara wondered if she was actually hearing the voice of the little cloud man. She could use a little magic in her life.

The sun rolled behind the cloud where the little man stood, and a gentle rain began to fall, cooling the ground beneath her feet. Kara breathed quietly as she made her way through a narrow section of roadway that offered no bike paths to walkers.

As she approached the edge of the road, a U-haul truck pulling a blue station wagon whizzed by, inches from where she walked. Kara lost her footing and fell flat, head hitting hard against the grainy asphalt. For a moment, she felt the sting of jagged pebbles cutting into her knees and the palms of her hands. The salty taste of blood upon her tongue did nothing to quell the tide of nausea welling up within her as she lay dizzy upon the highway.

Kara felt gentle hands mercifully gripping her shoulders and knees, lifting her up off the roadway as her eyelids fell closed. Blessed nothingness came before she could identify her savior.

♍ ♒ ♋ ■ ♑ ♏

Aroused by the persistent humming of a chorus of insects and fallen leaves gently caressing her face, Kara, like someone returning from a step back in time, slowly regained consciousness. She breathed in the acrid scent of rotting apples, and opened her eyes wide to take in her surroundings. Sitting up, she leaned backwards almost into the bend in the trunk of an apple tree, and looked to the West upon nodding sorghum growing wild in undulating rays of tempered yellow light. Perplexed, Kara felt as though she were standing within a wildly stirring tension between her own shadow and some other aspect of herself trying to make contact.

In a vain attempt to regain a sense of herself, she lifted her arms and stretched, breathing deeply. She felt a hand pressing firmly upon her shoulder. Kara glanced aside in amazement, to meet the smiling face of the little man whom she had earlier seen in the clouds.

"Tomorrows we'll see what we've broken and torn tonight thrashing in the dark." His voice was almost musical, yet stern. "I believe it was Rumi who said it first."

Still dazed, Kara stared into his charcoal gray eyes. "I've broken a lot. My life and my daughters." She turned her face away from his knowing gaze and was silent for a moment. "By the way, who are you?"

The little man stood in front of Kara and arched a bushy eye brow. A magnified twinkle shown through his bifocals, as a crooked smile played across his lips. "Actually I've been called a lot of names but you can call me Lopner. Lopner Pentrick."

He put a hand to his waist and bowed politely. "No matter though, dear heart. This isn't about me. It's about you." Lopner leaned back slightly, rummaged in his back pocket, and pulled out a long pink handkerchief. "Let me tell you something. I bet you didn't know that you've got an artist living inside you?" He removed his glasses, wiped them with the handkerchief, then carefully placed them on the bridge of his nose.

Kara glanced aside at Lopner. "No, I guess not," she whispered, shifting her gaze to a robin struggling to pull an earth worm from beneath a pile of damp leaves.

Lopner stuffed the handkerchief back into his pocket, as he shifted in close to Kara. He cupped her face in both his hands, his soft gaze boring into her ebony eyes. "That artist ~ It wants you to conquer the dinosaur. It's dying to paint a picture for you, one you'll love. But you've got it trapped in the jowls of the dinosaur. Can't find the proper canvass this way. You've got paint running all over the old canvass."

Kara sighed and shifted her gaze to the dying landscape and wilting leaves and bushes. She thought about her unborn grandchild. It would never have the chance to sit in spacious rooms with windows overlooking the budding life of springtime's glory or smell the scent of newly blossoming apple trees after a gentle rain.

"Artists inside people. What in heaven's name does that mean? All I know is that my life isn't a very pretty picture right now." Kara hunched forward and hugged her knees tightly, breathing heavily. "My daughter is out there hurting somewhere. And she's killing my grandchild. I am so angry! I'm helpless to do anything about it. I keep walking. Trying to decide what to do. But I'm getting nowhere fast. I hurt inside and it's like ~ I can't make myself think straight any more." Kara brushed a tear from her cheek.

Pieces of the Tapestry

She thought about her husband. "You know, it has suddenly dawned on me that I haven't even told Garth about Sheva yet. I'm afraid to think how he'll feel when he finds out." Kara put a hand to her mouth. "The last time Sheva did this, Garth nearly went crazy. He was so hurt."

Lopner's lips formed an enigmatic smile. "Sometimes when you grope along in the pitch black of the night, if you don't watch out, you might accidentally run head-on, into the rear end of an angry dinosaur and get the teeth knocked out of your soul." His look was penetrating.

"I feel as though I've been kicked all over. I don't even know who in the hell I am anymore. I guess it's my turn to be crazy. Look at me! My own daughter doesn't respect me enough to come to me with her problems. She confides in my neighbor instead. Then she runs away just like she did before. I have no control. I'm not the one she has ever listened to. My God, my God, my God!" Kara took no notice of the flood of tears streaming from her swollen eyes.

Lopner extended an arm and took Kara's slender fingers into his gloved hand in a comforting gesture of support. "If she had told you that she was pregnant and that she wanted to have an abortion, what would you have said to her?"

Kara shuddered visibly, as she tried to think of an answer. Pangs of jealousy hit as her thoughts turned briefly to her conversation with LaVern that morning. "Sheva trusted LaVern, not me. That hurts. Abortion is wrong." Her tone was emphatic.

Lopner's eyes held a questioning look. "Wrong for you or for Sheva?"

Kara shifted her gaze to the mulch covered ground and fell silent for a moment as she watched several small red ants pull a large green caterpillar across a dried leaf. "We're not supposed to take what we cannot give. This is what I've been taught all my life. So I guess I probably would have tried to stop her somehow." She reached out a hand to free the caterpillar but shrunk back when she realized that it was already dead.

"Kara, that artist in you that I told you about? Well, everybody's got one. None of them paint for other people. Maybe Sheva's artist is painting over a used canvass, covering up old stains. But whatever the picture, it has to do with her, not you."

Kara stared down into Lopner's gray, weather-worn face. "But she's only twenty years old. She hasn't even finished college yet!"

Pieces of the Tapestry

Absently, Lopner flexed the fingers on both his hands, removed the pink gloves, folded them neatly and put them in the top left pocket of his shirt. "Well, you know what the law says. A 20 year old girl is a women! Maybe her artist isn't interested in painting a college campus or a baby sucking at its mother's breast right now. Who knows, maybe some other subject suites Sheva's artist at the moment, like a dance party underneath the Brooklyn Bridge in the dead of winter or a hash house in Albany full of dirty dishes waiting to be washed. But that's Sheva's business. It's her life."

Kara winced at his words. "Frightening! I'm scared for my baby girl. I hurt for the baby she might have thrown out with the morning trash. God help her!"

"Hey, haven't you always been there to help Sheva out of trouble over the years?" Lopner gave Kara a long, penetrating look as he thumped his pointed chin with one hand. Then, without another word, he leaned down on one knee, his head bent toward a rectangular clump of dirt at the edge of a grassy bower. It was off-white and textured like a painter's canvas. Through its center, he drew an arrow, its head pointing to a dirt path through a virgin forest.

"Yes. At least I've tried my best." Kara hugged her knees tighter as she gazed upon Lopner's handiwork.

"Both you and Garth have tried hard. It couldn't have been easy for you but you never stopped cleaning up after her messes." Lopner's tone was sobering.

"Well, maybe it's time we stopped cleaning up after her. Maybe that's the best thing we can do for Sheva now. I won't go after her this time. I'll go home. Garth and I, we'll build a new life." Kara leaned back, head resting on the trunk of the tree, and shut her eyes.

♍︎ ♒︎ ♋︎ ■ ♑︎ ♏︎

A sound like the ambitious rustling of small animals sifting through dried leaves, brought Kara to alertness. She lifted her head slightly, and for an intimate moment, watched as two plump red birds playfully courted on the mulch at the edge of a nearby grassy bower. She thought of Garth and how she needed to be with him.

Pieces of the Tapestry

Leaves trembled as a flock of wild geese, like brisk wind, flew up from the tall oak trees forming the head of an arrow flung into flight. Kara pushed back away from the apple tree and extended her right hand across the front of her body, palm pressing hard into wet mulch. Slowly, she pulled her knee over her out stretched leg and on to the damp ground. Bracing herself, she struggled to her feet. Her sweaty palms raced over the wrinkles in her blouse and dusted twigs and pine needles from the backs of her legs and shorts.

The large bird flying at the apex of the arrow called loudly as though summoning Kara to the flock. She studied it for a moment. The flock passed above a seldom used dirt path leading straight through a virgin pine forest. Kara knew that a return down the old familiar highway would not be wise on foot at that late hour. By following the geese arrow, she would be in the comfort of Garth's arms in just a few minutes.

Kara's mood was lighter as she walked briskly up the dirt path toward the sun, now flaming in orange splendor, as it lay majestically upon the horizon, flanked by hues of purple, pink and blue night.

♓

Pieces of the Tapestry

STRAWBERRIES
by
Helen Tulis

Lusting for the
Red, red strawberries
Buried on my tongue
Eaten as if their potential Buddha
Hurdled their empyrean nectar
To usher in the discriminating
Awareness of life.
)(

ON VAPOR FLIES THE WORLD

Residue smudges
On vapor flies away my world,
As a plane scooping up horizons
On universal pathways,
Horrors!
Nobody home,
Neither searching ant nor howling coyote,
Only a box of empty humanity.
Stretched over a blanket of perennial love.
No voice,
No color,
No language,
No touch;
Just one simpering in,
The other, whimpering out.
No bright flare
To recoup the face of the meeting;
Only forever vapor.
)(

Pieces of the Tapestry

CONVERSATIONS WITH MY DAD
by
Helen Tulis

"Come, Chaikeh, take the phone and talk to your sister." Dad held the phone out to me as I stepped into the front room.

"No, Dad, please, I really don't want to talk to her now."

"Chaikeh, just a few words. They'll cost you anything?"

"No, Dad I'll talk to her when I get home. I just stopped by to leave this book with you. I found it behind some other books on a shelf in the school library. Can't imagine how it got there. I wanted to spend a few minutes talking to you about I. B. Singer. I wanted to unwind." I held Singer's book out to him. "Please Dad. Don't ask me to talk to my sister now."

My father held the phone tightly against his chest, so my sister would not hear the angry words. "Chaikeh, it will only take a minute."

"Dad, don't force me. I'm tired, and stressed out. I'm on my way home from school where all day I tried to teach kids who don't want to learn. Where was the Society Lady all day?"

I retreated back to the front hall. As I held the screen door open, I could feel my face contorting in pain. How could my father whom I loved so much think that I had something to say to my sister? I practically ran out of the door, my heart pumping angrily. Why should I talk to Mona? What did I have to say that she could understand? Sisters! We had the same parents, but that is all we had in common.

More is expected of you when you are the oldest. My life didn't take the same path as my sister. She married at nineteen. I married at twenty-six. One would think by then I was old enough and wise enough to make a perfect choice. Life isn't perfect. I loved Neil, my husband, but eventually I felt trapped in an impossible situation.

Did I unconsciously compare him with my professional brother in law? No. Mona's husband is a realist, a hard working doctor, who has allowed my sister to live a charmed good life. Neil, on the other hand was a romantic, a day dreamer, whose reach outspanned our means.

As I drove away from my parents house, I remembered times of pure joy, interspersed with days of irresponsible madness. Was I too practical to put up with Neil's hair brain schemes? I sighed as I pulled into my driveway. Resting my head down on the steering wheel, I could visualize the exact moment when our marriage unraveled. I knew right then, that for the sake of our boys and my sanity, I would have to break up what I believe God had put together. It was the day when Neil came home with a big smile on his lean face.

"Guess what I did today?"

Here was my tall handsome Don Quixote tilting another wind mill. A glow emanated from his very essence, and I could feel the heat from his excitement. I was afraid to ask.

"Come on Hon. Guess." I put my hand out to keep him from hugging me.

"Remember that plane I had when I first met you? Well I bought another one. This time it's for our business?"

"What business? Monkey business," I retorted, sarcastically.

Neil laughed, throwing his head back, his cowlick falling over his dark eyes. "The boys will love it. Next week we'll all take a spin, and find a perfect location for our second store. How's that, kid?"

I shook my head, trying to cool him down. "That's the whole problem with our marriage Neil. You always have to buy some kind of expensive toy."

"Not a toy Hon. You'll see. It's going to make us rich."

"Damn it Neil, I never said I wanted to be rich. I just need a sense of security. I don't want to have to worry whether tomorrow we'll have the money to pay our bills, or if everything we own will be taken from us."

"No one's going to take anything from us. When did you ever have to worry about your next meal?" A frost of anger tinged his words despite the smile.

Of course, even though I didn't say so, I knew we were heading for another disaster. That was the story of our marriage. We had our highs and we had our lows all along the way. Now I am a divorcee. How does this fit with being a nice, practical Jewish girl?

♍ ♒ ♋ ■ ♑ ♏

I unlocked my front door, and walked into stillness, past the phone, knowing I would not call my sister. What would I say? "Mona, dear, does it make you happy running from one good cause to another? Do you feel pious helping the needy, helping strangers. Do you ever sense that there are times in my life I could use a little compassion, a little warmth?"

However I walked back and did pick up the phone and called my Dad. I had to put a satisfactory end to our conversation.

"Dad, don't ever tell me to talk to my sister when I am not in the mood." My voice was husky with unshed tears. "Sure I love her, but the *talk* would only be surface. She can't understand my life, for hers is so totally different then mine."

I put my fingers up to my eyes trying to hold back my tears, like the little Dutch boy trying to save the dike.

"Chaikeh, you're the oldest you should show that you're a mench. What did I ask so much, just to say a word?"

"Sure Dad. With what kind of words would she have answered me? Does she remember? Does Mona ever think back to when we were young? I was the eldest, the one who taught her to tie her shoes, and button her coat. I held her by the hand and took her to school, made sure she crossed the street safely."

The tears flowed freely down my cheeks. "Now I need some one to hold my hand, but she talks down to me with her Society Lady voice, and uses words not used when you talk to a sister. She repeats those words she hears her husband say when he talks to his terminally ill patients."

My father was silent. The miles between us seemed to grow wider and longer. He sighed, "So, maybe if you talk you can tell her how you feel."

I matched his sigh with my own, "Good-by Dad. Enjoy the book I left for you. We'll talk about it another time."

I hung up the phone, went and washed my face in the bathroom, and put on some fresh lipstick. I practiced smiling in the mirror over the sink, and shook my head. Even Dad, the great peace maker couldn't understand.

My young sons, Dan and Mark stormed into the house. "Hey Mom, where are you?" I opened the door and opened my arms. Mona could wait for my phone call a little longer. I had better people to talk to.

⚹

Pieces of the Tapestry

LIFE
by
Eleanor Freemer

What did I expect to find
when I reached this
golden age in my life?
Trumpets sounding off stage,
the curtains parting to reveal me,
the star,
the grandam,
whose wit and sparkling mind,
like an iris, arches across a painted sky
to the accompaniment of applause and cheers?
I did not choose to be
chained to a rocking chair,
feeling the cold,
an ancient bouquet of pressed flowers
unraveling on my lap;
brown like rust,
bitter like alum,
poignant as memories and lost dreams
that will not be revived by my tears,
or by my faded smile.

Pieces of the Tapestry

I am hope's passion
Of running rivers in noon
Day's valley of truth.

-Elizabeth Bowers-

THE SURVIVOR
by
Eleanor Freemer

His knuckles tapped lightly on the bathroom door. "You Okay?"

"Yes." The word came out on the tide of a soft sniffle. He could almost see her wiping her eyes, blowing her nose, while she sat on the toilet seat, bent over as if nursing a stomach cramp.

"May I come in?"

"No."

"Are you coming out?"

"Soon."

He wanted to open the door that stood like a shield between them, and hold her in his arms and comfort her.

"It's over honey. No one was hurt. The kids are fine. It wasn't your fault."

"Go away. Please go away. Let me cry myself out. Please."

"Why must he sound so calm, so rational? Why can't he understand how I feel? How I can't talk now?" Linda needed time to be alone to relive what had happened just sixty minutes ago.

Sixty minutes ago? Had it only been an hour since the car had developed a mind of its own, pulling to the right and careening crazily across the width of the expressway before miraculously landing safely on a gentle curving shoulder?

Nausea filled her chest rising up to her throat. She clenched her teeth and let the tears flow freely down her cheeks.

Pieces of the Tapestry

"Oh God, thank you. Thank you. Thank you for saving the lives of my children."

Her children! She propped her head in her hands and sobbed. She had picked them up from their various schools as she did every Wednesday afternoon to take the two younger ones to the doctor for their allergy shots. Sherry, her budding teenager, had complained of having had a rough time in school. She was too tired to walk the three hilly miles home. Linda knew she really wanted to come along just to see if the doctor had taken her suggestion and brought in some more sophisticated magazines that were less than three years old.

Linda had eased herself onto the freeway after a ten wheeler flew past, and had driven along for no more than a few yards when her car started to shimmy and shake, and swerve out of control.

"Hurry. Get on the floor," she cried out.

She held on to the wheel with both hands, wrestling to keep it on the straight and narrow. The steering power was gone. Linda pumped her brakes and blew her horn to warn drivers on both sides that she was in big trouble.

As the car slued around, it smacked a vehicle on her right hand side, causing it to roll onto the verge like a tenpin. "Well, that's what he gets for not taking my warning seriously." She knew he was most likely thinking, "Crazy driver."

Her car finally stopped, nose pointing toward the road she had just traveled.

The children rose up like three specters from the floor. "Wow, what happened? Mom, you okay?"

"Yes," Linda whispered. Her whole body felt the aftershock. She closed her eyes and bowed her head against the wheel in silent prayer. Her legs were trembling like the weeds blowing in the wind alongside the road. Where would she find the strength to force open the door to inspect the damage, when the car was listing to one side like a drunkard?

"Please don't say anything," she told the children. "Don't open the doors."

The cars on the expressway were causing a traffic jam as the drivers slowed down to gawk, yet no one stopped to offer them any assistance. Linda looked across to the other car sitting on the shoulder of the road. Slowly, the door opened, and a young man stepped out. He moved around his red sedan, looking for damage, then stiffly walked toward them.

"You okay lady? What happened?"

"I don't know. I just couldn't steer the car."

He looked down and said, "Something's wrong with your tire." Like a doctor, he ponderously diagnosed that she must have had a blow out. Her wheel also seemed to have been damaged. "I don't know how you did it, but I don't even see a scratch on my car. You kids okay?"

They nodded like automatons.

"I'll get to a phone and call the police and your auto club if you give me your number."

Linda was actually able to smile and thank him and apologize for hitting him. He waved his hand and took off.

As they sat there, in a state of shock, a car finally did stop. It was their next door neighbor. He also examined the wheel and the tire, and told the children to get into his car and he would take them home.

Her heart still clamored, but she appeared to the whole world cool and contained, as she sat alone, along the side of the road waiting for help that soon came with sirens blaring. She had a book in her hand, trying to read, ignoring the ~ by now ~ four o'clock traffic. The officer looked at her, then her tire, and told Linda how lucky she had been.

In a quivering voice, she murmured, "Yes, thank God! I know."

Once the wheel and tire were changed, the officer held up traffic a little longer to allow her to turn around and slowly drive home.

Her husband, concern etched into his face, was at the door waiting for her. The ice around her cracked into tiny pieces.

"Oh God! I could of killed all our children." The enormity of what happened crumbled all of her defenses as she ran to the bathroom.

"What's the matter? Why are you crying now? You're home. It's all over." Her bewildered mate trailed after her to be stopped by the slamming door.

"Don't you understand? I could have killed them," she cried out.

"But you didn't," he tried to reason.

All Linda could picture was that huge truck plowing into them; her and her children's broken bodies spread over I-85. Her husband would be a widower. Women would come and cook and clean for him and lovingly console him over his loss. She sighed, hiccuped again, then washed her face and ran a comb through her tousled hair, hating him for remarrying so soon.

She put on some lipstick, revived, alive and amazed at herself. "Imagine! I actually drove myself home. After this, Linda thought, "I can survive anything."

She opened the bathroom door and fell into his outstretched arms. He enfolded her, then held her at arm's length to study her from head to toe. "You did all right kid. You sure did." He kissed her tenderly while she watched the eager widows quietly fade into the woodwork.

⛢

Pieces of the Tapestry

Butterfly sings tale
Of stalwert wolf, roming fields
Of winter ivy.
)(
-Elizabeth Bowers-

PLUMB DOWN TO EARTH
by
Helen Tulis

I didn't want to admit that the water I spotted dripping down from the ceiling of the closet spelled a small disaster. So I looked up at the drips making large yellow stains on the ceiling. I listened to the sounds of the drips and declared, "Uh, oh! This means I need a plumber unless I can see where this water is coming from."

I hopefully prayed that the sound of the drip would go away. Then, it would mean that I didn't need a plumber. Disaster would be over. But each time I sneaked into the closet to obtain a can of fruit or juice for dinner, I saw the evidence of water dripping. When I finally looked up at the ceiling, I saw huge puddles of wetness outlining the area into the shape of Russia. "Uh, Oh," I said. "I had better call the plumber, as this might get worse."

Even though I had been upstairs trying to find the source of the leak, I could not find the designated place. "I think this is a job for a plumber."

I called the plumber and he promised that someone would be over within thirty minutes. Sure enough, exactly thirty minutes later, the door bell rang and the plumber came in. He immediately said, "I'm Walter from the Drip Plumbing. What's the problem."

Walter was about thirty years old, brown hair and eyes. He appeared to be strong, as sometimes plumbers must carry heavy equipment. Yet, at the same time, they must be agile, as they might have to get into tiny spaces while doing their work. Walter looked like he could handle either situation. I ushered him into the kitchen where I opened the

Pieces of the Tapestry

closet so he could see the wet outline of a map of Russia as he peered at the ceiling.

"What happened here?" he asked.

"I don't know. All of a sudden, I saw this wet space and water running down," I replied.

"I'll have to get upstairs to take a look and see where it is coming from," Walter decided.

"I can't understand this. Do you think the commode is stopped up and overflowing in the pipes? I used some cotton balls, but some are made of rayon. Could that have done it?" I asked following Walter upstairs to the bathroom.

"I just don't know lady, until I check and take a look," he answered.

Walter took his time checking out the possibilities of a commode that leaked. He found that not to be the case. Then he took some instruments out of his tool kits and began tapping on various pipes. "Let's see now. Do you take a bath or a shower?" he asked.

"Oh, I take baths. But I have never used this third bathroom here. In the six years I have lived here, I never used this bathroom," I said.

"Well, that's got nothing to do with it. But we'll find the source. Don't worry," Walter announced.

I went back downstairs trying to figure out why I had a leak in the ceiling. What did I do to cause it? I decided I had done nothing.

Interrupting my thinking, Walter asked from the top of the stairs, "Do you want to come up here for a minute?"

I thought, "Great. He figured it out. It won't cost much because he knows where the leak is from."

"I think I am going to need your permission to cut a hole in this cabinet in the bathroom," Walter said, quietly.

"Why? Do you have to?" I inquired.

"Well, I don't want to but sometimes we have to do some surgery, like doctors," Walter professed, a smile on his youthful face. "It's not always that easy to locate the source of the leak, especially in one of these houses like yours," he said, apologetically.

Walter began sawing away the wood in the bottom of the cabinet as I finally gave him permission to do so. I could hear him whacking away as I had gone downstairs to get away from the noise. "Uh, oh. There goes the cabinet," I thought, closing my eyes.

Pieces of the Tapestry

Then silence. I heard only water running in the bathtubs. Quiet. Water oozing out of the tub was what I then began to hear. Steps. Walter's deliberate steps across the bathroom floor.

"Walter, what happened?" I asked.

"M'am, I have got to cut a piece out of the wall. Is that all right?" Walter asked.

"I can't believe you have got to do surgery on the wall in the bathroom. Why? Can't you find the leak without doing that?" I inquired.

"Well, you want me to find out whether that water is coming from this pipe or those? And the way these town houses were built, there is no basement. So, you have to tap into the wall to make sure," he informed me, looking like a real doctor with the scalpel like instrument in his hand.

"See, you've got to give me permission first before I can go ahead and work," he mentioned.

"I can't believe it. All this for a leak," I shrieked, shocked.

"Well, I can guess. But if it is wrong, I'd have to come back and you'd have double expenses. Right?" he asked.

"This bathroom is fine. The wallpaper is fine, too. I like this wallpaper," I stated.

"We'll have to get new wall paper if I cut through this wall, you know," Walter said, politely and with little alarm in his voice.

"I suppose I have no choice," I said, unhappily. I looked to the side when Walter started sawing through the piece of wall, letting the ivory wallpaper trail as if it were only toilet paper. Then, he stopped sawing and looked through the huge hole he had made. The sheet rock board crumbled and fell smashing into huge pieces that later turned into a sandy mess on the floor.

"This will tell us what we need to know. You mind holding the flashlight? You can look at the pipes to trace the water if there is any there," Walter pointed out.

I took the flashlight but could only see the innards of the wall. Slate gray pipes stood erect next to white thick pipes, while two other pipes were simply tied together. I said, "I don't see anything here."

"I don't think the leak is coming from here," Walter surmised. "It's from the other bathroom."

"What do we do now?" I asked, as if I were his partner, working beside him. "Finally, you give up. Right?"

"Oh, I know one other spot we haven't checked. And I'll bet that's it." Walter took the commode up, lifting it into the bathtub. Though he grunted, he set the commode straight up and stepped out of the bathtub without another sound. "That's what I hate about these kind of houses. It is so hard to work between two bathrooms the way they have been built," he complained.

"I can't believe you can't find that leak yet. How long have you been a plumber?" I inquired.

"Ever since I was eleven years old, I followed my uncle around. I even dug ditches. I have been plumbing all my life," Walter informed me.

I began to feel badly as if I had insulted him. But he quickly put that to rest.

"Yeah, my uncle taught me lots I know. Then I worked for this company since I married," Walter added.

I was skeptical about Walter's sawing down the walls and the cabinet. I ask, shamelessly, "So if you have worked there since you are married, how long have you been married?"

"Oh, I got married when I was seventeen," Walter admitted.

"Have you always worked this hard?" I asked him.

By now, Walter had found the source of the leak and was still looking at the pipe with his huge black flashlight.

"This isn't hard work. This is the last stop of my day. I can rest now. Come with me a minute and look in this wall space with my flash," he advised.

Again, all I saw were silver pipes and a long single pipe stretched along side the others. "Oh, there's water leaking out, lots of it!" I yelled.

"Yeah. I told you we'd find it. There sure is a leak. Probably been leaking for a while too. Then, when the floor boards were saturated, the water leaked through the ceiling. See?" Walter explained.

"What in the world am I going to do about fixing those two walls and that cabinet?" I asked. By this time, I was even counting up the bill for the plumber, too.

"How much is this going to cost me?" I asked of Walter.

"I can't tell you exactly, but when I finish in here, we can figure it out," Walter took out some tools and ran the water in the sink until it was full. By then, I was downstairs getting out the calculator, trying to run some numbers together, thinking I could determine the plumbing bill.

Pieces of the Tapestry

While I was downstairs, I thought to call up my insurance company. I recalled that I did have some insurance for flooding. Though this was not a real flood, there was enough water to damage the house. I wanted to check on insurance. I rang. Then, I listened.

"Oh, the water went through the ceiling. And what's worse, the plumber had to saw out portions of the walls and the cabinet. Yes. There is plenty of damage," I insisted.

The insurance man said, "You may possibly claim the resulting damage, but we cannot pay the plumber's bill."

When I heard this, I felt somewhat better. Now the sawed off cabinet did not look as bad. The huge holes in the wall no longer seemed so menacing. With new wallpaper, things would go back to normal.

Walter worked a long time fixing the leak. I heard his wrenches scraping on a long pipe, then hammering going on. Finally, he yelled downstairs, "I'm finished. You want to come up and take a look?" .

When I looked at the clock, I realized it was 6:30 p.m. Walter had worked through the evening hour, making it close to four hours on this job. As I turned to go up the steps I saw Walter standing at the top landing.

He called to me. "Wouldn't you like to take a look at the finished job?"

By now, I was exhausted from just worrying about the repairing of the walls, the replacing of wallpaper and the restoring of the cabinet. Besides which, I was getting hungry. So, I just said, "Walter, I am hungry. If you say you did the work, I accept that. If not, I'll just sue your company."

"Oh, no M'am. Everything ought to be replaced and repaired. I'll have all that stated on my ticket," Walter said, following me into the kitchen.

I asked, "Wouldn't you like a dish of fruit? You sure did work hard."

"Oh, yes M'am. That would be nice. I'll just sit here and write up the bill so you can sign it."

"I'm not signing it unless you admit you tore up the walls, Walter," I said jokingly.

"I tore up the walls because I don't really want to be a plumber M'am.

My mouth flew open. I could hardly believe my ears. "What? You've got to be kidding. Plumbers make good money. It's an honorable profession."

He looked at me. "My girl friend and I were talking one night about my going back to school.

"You mean to college?" I said.

"Yes M'am.

"To study what?" I asked, perturbed.

"I don't rightly know M'am," said Walter.

"Then what the hell are you doing here?" I asked.

"Well, aren't you a school teacher, M'am? You ought to be able to tell me what to study.

I said, "Hey, there is a college right up the street from here. Why don't you get dressed, not in your plumbing clothes. Go over to the college and talk to Ms. Curtis. Tell her I told you to talk to her. Get dressed up. Wear a nice suit," I glanced down at his muddy work boots. "And some clean shoes."

"M'am, I'm sure gonna do that," Walter said.

"I know you will," I said, encouragingly.

I watched as Walter walked down the cement walk day in front of my house and thought to myself, "Damn, now I have to deal with the sheet rock guy. I wonder if he wants to go to college too.

※

2. THE MANY WAYS WE LOVE

Dancing rock sing loud
To rising dark of sweet night
At birdland's offering.

♓

-Elizabeth Bowers-

Pieces of the Tapestry

Wings of love spread wide
As calm waters at rise of sun,
When strong breezes sleep.

☈

-Elizabeth Bowers-

LOVE, THE MASTER THREAD
by
Elizabeth Bowers

Love, sweet master thread
Weave's tapestry of season
In creation's joy.

Love, fire that warms all
Sons and daughters of sun;
Love, fine nimble fingers that
Move stalwart needle through faith's threads,
Weaving the beauty of eternal creation.

Love, spirit of life,
Weaving joy within every
Soul of creation.

Love, sweet food that fills the
Spirit of life, burning
Hot with passion of summer
Sun served up in every way,
Filling the longings of creation's faith.

Love, thread that holds tight
Flesh to energy of life
In season of souls.

☈

Pieces of the Tapestry

Cypress leaves wink at
Waking lacewings, when praying
Mantis lays new life.

※

-Elizabeth Bowers-

PACIFIC REFLECTIONS
by
Elizabeth Bowers

    Strained and tired from a busy day at the office, followed by lots of running around and rushing to get things ready for the trip to Cat Harbor, Tiffany Gilchrist bent down and breathed a sigh of relief, as she rested her red bucket on the fading asphalt at the edge of the marina parking lot. The high, metal security gate leading to the boat slips, was before her. She felt the tension of seldom used muscles as she pulled herself up. With an audible sigh, she reached a slightly damp hand into the side pocket of her light blue shorts and fished around for the gate key.
    "Thank God! I thought I left this thing at home," she muttered under her breath, wrapping long, slender fingers around the throat of the miniature blue and white buoy which served as a flotation devise for her keys.
    The marina key turned easily in the brass lock. As she pressed the full weight of her trim, scantily clad body against the heavy metal, hot to the touch, the gate opened effortlessly.
    The brilliant rays of an unusually hot July sun beat down upon the wall of rocks that lay in contrasting shades of pinkish-violets and vivid oranges toned with gentle touches of yellow ochre, separating the shore from the water line. Tiffany enjoyed the feel of its penetrating power upon her bare nut-brown shoulders as she stood for a moment, her free hand on the smooth railing, contemplating the angle of the ramp.
    "The tide is cooperating with me this time. The sea level is certainly a lot higher than it was two weeks ago. I can handle this a lot easier." Tiffany took a deep breath, enjoying the salty taste of the sea air. She

made her way down the long, gray ramp, grateful for its recently redone, non-skid surface.

Boats swayed rhythmically in their slips to the cadence of the wakes of passing vessels upon otherwise calm waters, reflecting the brownish-green wash of the fair Los Angeles sky. She was glad that her thick black hair was piled high on her head, out of the way. All that separated her upper torso from the full strength of the afternoon sun was a thin tank top decorated with delicate, light blue pansies.

She looked down at the gray, weather-worn dock. Its slight rocking motion made her feel as though she were already on her boat, the Ndoto Maru, well out into the great Pacific waters.

A moist, callused hand tapped Tiffany in the small of her back. The heavy touch was very familiar. She smiled and tilted her head up and to the side.

"Well lass, you're talking to yourself now, are ya?" The tall, burly man, skin beige and creased from many hours in the sun, playfully rubbed Tiffany's shoulders. His hazel eyes held a teasing glint as he gazed down on her.

She grinned up at him. "Brian O'Hara, you caught me again," Tiffany teased.

"Whaddaya say there lass! Here, let me help ya with that." Without waiting for a reply, Brian reached a well-muscled arm forward and relieved Tiffany of the bucket that was as rusty-red as his own thinning mop of curly hair. His brown sandals scuffed against the dock boards as he fell into step beside her.

Tiffany clapped him lightly on the back. She winked and threw him a grateful smile. Her ebony eyes peered playfully up at him beneath raised sunglasses. "Thanks a lot Brian. That bucket is a lot heavier than I thought it would be." She wiggled her shoulders back and fourth and flexed her fingers to loosen the kinks, feigning a look of helplessness.

"So what's a pretty lass doin' out here all by herself anyway?" Brian inquired, his Irish accent more evident than usual. "Where's that bull of a husband of yours and those two little darlin' rascals he hangs out with? Catalina awaits us lass. We gotta beat the party crowds." He tugged at the elastic waist band of his white shorts with his free hand.

She cocked her head to the side and gave him a teasing smile. "I told Forest I'd meet him and the kids here at six o'clock. I got here early

Pieces of the Tapestry

because I want to surprise him by getting the boat all cleaned up and organized before he comes. If I hurry, I'll have just enough time to load on the provisions and get it all done before six."

Brian glanced aside and saw that the smile had slipped away from Tiffany's chiseled features. Her arched eyebrows were drawn together. Several worry lines intruded across the middle of her forehead. Her full red lips were pressed tightly closed, as was her habit when deep in thought. He wondered if she might be thinking that maybe she set herself up for too much work. "Look. Tell ya what lass. I'll give ya a hand. Give me the keys to your van and my boys and me will do the tottin."

Tiffany's smile returned as she looked up into Brian's weather worn face. His eyes held a look of sympathy. Grateful, she reached an arm around his muscular frame and gave him a quick squeeze. "You're a good friend Brian O'Hara. I'll gladly take you up on your kind offer. Thanks a lot." With her free hand, she brushed back a stray wisp of kinky black hair that was obscuring her vision.

"That strained look on your face lass, says to me that you're long overdue for this vacation. What's been goin' on with you girl?" Brian's look was serious.

"A lot. I guess I really need to reorder my priorities." I seem to be running in every direction, getting a lot done for other people, but not giving anything to Forest and the kids. I missed Trinity's school play last week because of work. And by the time I got there for Brandon's little league game, he'd already scored the winning home run. You know, with the demands of our careers lately, Forest and I are having a hard time connecting with each other." It had been weeks since they'd made love. Tiffany ached to feel the touch of her husband's muscular body pressed against hers with only a fair sea and a tender sky as witness.

Brian squeezed her shoulders in a gesture of understanding. "Well, it's like this lass. Ya gotta hang in there. Forest is a good lad. The two of you'll have lots of time for gettin' close during the trip. But ya gotta remember to keep it up when you get back home." He smiled and winked at her.

The marina was alive with activity, as experienced boaters, separated into two categories ~ those who scurried about making ready to get underway to beat the crowds to Catalina ~ and those who were preparing for a long, lazy weekend of slip sailing. Several well-tanned boys sporting

Pieces of the Tapestry

white tee-shirts and cut-off pants, climbed over dinghies tied to the rock side of the docks. A tethered sabot, its single royal blue and white striped sail luffing in a gentle wind, rocked in the water behind a row of small cabin cruisers. The resident duck worked the swim step for bread crumbs. Nearby, several young children splashed about in the murky green waters. They were on the starboard side of a triple decked houseboat, white with cobalt blue trim. The houseboat, rocking to and fro in the slip next to it, was of a similar design, but hanging from its middle deck were bird feeders and large flower pots alive with blazing shades of reds, blues and yellows.

Tiffany enjoyed the salty taste of sea spray and the refreshing scent of fish charged air, as she and Brian negotiated their way down the busy expanse of docks, past a rolling ocean of titanium white power boats, trimmed in varying shades of blue and set off by polished chrome reflecting the ambient light. Sharing that part of the marina waters were runabouts and vessels with sails down and tied around booms. Weathered, hollow aluminum masts pointed toward a sky rich in varying tones of brownish-green tinged with subtle hints of pink and cadmium red. Along the way, Tiffany relaxed as a week's worth of tension oozed from every pore of her being. Caught up in Brian's playful mood, she greeted those they passed with a wave and a smile. On more than one occasion, she and Brian stopped for a quick chat with friends in common and to help sea-worthy captains, caught in unexpected puffs of wind, fend off from the docks.

♍ ♒ ♋ ■ ♑ ♏

Freshly painted in zinc white and trimmed in cobalt blue, the Ndoto Maru, rolled majestically in its slip. Tiffany felt a twinge of pride as she stood on the dock next to Brian gazing upon its solid, wooden frame. She placed a caressing hand gently upon its bow, as though feeling for life. Her eyes rested on the freshly varnished teak, while Brian set the pail down on the boat side of the chrome guard- rail.

Brian stood erect and stared at her in open admiration "You've come ta depend on the solitude of the boat like the rest of us wave watchers. Haven't ya lass."

She lifted her head and returned his gaze. "Indeed so." She turned her face toward the channel. "And all of this." She stretched her arms out

Pieces of the Tapestry

as though to encircle the whole of the marina. "It's as though it were a living, breathing thing sucking life into my veins."

For a moment, they stood wordlessly inhaling the rich tapestry of the marina. The old sailor's clock chimed the half hour as a strong gust of wind filled the air with the sound of clanking halyards.

Brian's reverie ended. "Well, I'll tell ya what lass. It's time for practical things now if we're to meet at the Isthmus for breakfast tomorrow like we planned. The boys and I'll load up for you now and then will be catching the wind and headin' on out to the island."

♍ ♒ ♋ ■ ♑ ♍

Tiffany waved good-bye to Brian as he boarded his forty-foot motor-sailor docked several slips down. Although she was more than grateful for all his help earlier, she was glad for the quiet moments to enjoy the flavor of the Ndoto Maru as she took care of housekeeping chores.

Catharticly, she emptied boxes and filled cupboards, forgetting all about the mirage of problems associated with her publishing company and the political intrigues of her community. Life on the Pacific for Tiffany was separate and apart from the mundanity of the outside world.

She thought about Dierdra and Brian's new motor-sailor. A smile came to her lips as she remembered how excited Dierdra had been the day they'd bought it. So far, they had not made it to Catalina under the new bright red sails. Maybe this time the wind would be kinder.

Tiffany hardly noticed the effort involved as she washed away two weeks worth of accumulated dust and mildew in the well appointed cabin and on the flying bridge. Happy thoughts destroyed tedium as they floated about, unchecked, in the undulating sea-reach of her inner sanctum.

For a while, her mind replayed the fun-filled hours that she spent in the spacious stern room with her daughter Antaria, two weeks ago. Then, they had enjoyed nibbling molasses pop-corn, telling stories and chatting about anything and everything. Together, they had cut out and hand-sewn the new, thalo blue and pink flowered curtains now hanging from the front and side windows of the forward cabin.

A smile played across her face as she thought about how patient Forest had been with the kids as they helped him polish chrome and sand

and stain the mahogany trim on the interior of all three levels of the well appointed cabin cruiser that would be home for the next two weeks. Forest did the painting of the exterior by himself, but Tiffany was proud of the way she and the kids had painted the interior without spilling any sizable amounts of paint.

Now all that was left to do was to get cleaned up and rested before Forest arrived with Brandon and Antaria. Tiffany licked her lips and tasted sweat. Needing desperately to cool down, she pulled the pins out of her hair, slipped into her swim suit and dove off the dock into the rolling waters of the marina. The shock of the water's chilly bit cooled her down in a hurry. Still, she was not moved to get out. She rolled over on her back and let the movement of the water shrink her long hair into a mass of black wool as she gave herself up to the cool liquid.

"This is so delicious," she said, as she slowly glided down past the gas dock and beyond the trimaran moored at the end of the pier, and out into the mouth of the channel.

By the time she had finished her swim and was climbing up the rope ladder onto the swim step she heard the marina clock chime six times.

"Well, I guess I'd better take a shower and get ready for the next stage. Forest and the kids will be here any minute and I don't want them to see me looking like a swamp rat."

Still chilly from the bit of the Pacific, she put on a rose colored sweat suit and dried her hair. She plunked herself down on the cushioned bench in the stern room, and sipped steaming hot cinnamon coffee from the fish-shaped mug the children had given her for mother's day, and awaited the arrival of her crew.

Absently, she played with the handle of the cup. Her mind was bombarded with thoughts about the raw beauty of the seascape of Catalina Harbor. Its protected waters offer a measure of security to the little ones moving about upon its shallow, brown waters in sailing dinghies. There, the air is fresh and it is no trouble at all to row to shore and cross the dirt path to the other side to swim in the blue waters of the Isthmus. There, the water is clear enough to see all the way to the bottom. Catalina is the only place she knew about in the Los Angeles area where stars could actually be seen dotting the night sky.

♍ ♒ ♋ ■ ♑ ♏

Pieces of the Tapestry

It was nearly eight o'clock when Forest and the children finally arrived.

"Sorry to take so long," Forest said, as he helped Antaria climb on board. "There were a bunch of things I had to take care of at the house. Then, I took the kids out for burghers and afterward, we stopped off at Beverly's House of Chicken to get this for you." Smiling the charming smile of a child trying to con his mother out a scolding, Forest handed Tiffany a large bucket of fried chicken.

A smile played acrossed her lips as the thought struck her that Forest had really bought the chicken in the hope that most of it would be left for him in the morning. Still, she accepted it as though it were a special gift of a precious stone. "Thanks sweetheart. This is so thoughtful of you." She looked up into his large, brown eyes, and smiled graciously. No mention was made about his tardiness.

"I'm tired mom," Brandon whined, his magicman pajamas already on. He got out his sleeping bag and unrolled it on the 'v'-birth.

"Me too," cried Antaria, following Brandon's lead. "But let's take turns reading this story first Mom."

"Yea Mom. I've got a great new ending for the story. Besides, there's no television. Dad wouldn't let us bring it," added Brandon, giving Tiffany a nudge.

"Why don't you guys let your mother eat first. You already had your dinner. It's her turn now," urged Forest.

Tiffany smiled at the exchange. "Oh, don't worry about it Forest. You go on and do what you need to do to get us ready to get underway. I'll take care of these two. I'm not that hungry right now anyway." She turned and hugged her children gently to her chest for a moment, happy to be with them. "Now, before we go any further, let's see what's inside the box underneath the 'v'-birth."

Brandon ran brown fingers through a tangled mass of black curls. His dark eyes lit up with laughter. "We already know what's in the box. "Daddy already showed it to us."

"Yea," chimed in Antaria, her dark braids bouncing about her shoulders as she skipped to the 'v'-birth and slid the box out. "Wet suits for Brandon and me," she squealed, pulling one out and holding it up against her small chest. "Purple wet suits."

Pieces of the Tapestry

♍︎ ♒︎ ♋︎ ■ ♑︎ ♏︎

By the time Brandon and Antaria were settled in for the night, and Forest had finished the thousand and one tasks that were a part of his customary ritual before easing out of the slip, the marina clock had chimed two bells.

"Two o'clock in the morning already! How does time pass so quickly," Tiffany wondered out loud as she eased her weary bottom down on the forward deck, glad for the moment of solitude. Nearly hypnotized from weariness, she stared at her long, slender legs, rich chocolate in the moon light, as they dangled from either side of the king plank, flanked by the shadow of her arms stretched out over the silver guard-rail. The big 360 diesel engine hummed smoothly as Forest made ready to cast off.

By the time he had done checking everything and was seated in his captain's chair on the flying bridge, Tiffany had already untied the mooring lines and was standing on the king plank, ready with the boat hook, to fend off at his command. The water was smooth glass and there was no wind. Still, she held her position until Forest edged the boat through the narrow channel leading out of the marina.

♍︎ ♒︎ ♋︎ ■ ♑︎ ♏︎

Tiffany smiled as she took her place in the First-mate's chair on the flying bridge. She inhaled deeply of the sea-scented air and snuggled up against Forest's warm shoulder.

"Well, the rest of the night belongs to us. Those two little sailors are fast asleep and everything's taken care of." Forest kept his face toward the restricted waters of the Los Angeles Harbor.

"Getting those two in bed wasn't easy. As tired as they were, they put up a good fight, especially Brandon. But I finally got them calmed down. We took turns telling that story. You know, the one you got Antaria for her 8th birthday last year."

"You mean the one about the peacock and the penguin?" Forest smiled remembering how much Antaria and Brandon loved to hear that story repeatedly. He'd read it to them so much that he knew every word by heart, as did they. "How many times did the peacock have to fly into the caves of the cold world before they let you escape?" he chuckled.

Pieces of the Tapestry

"Three. Plus I had to make up a different flight pattern every time, as usual. But, anyway, I checked on them again just before coming up here. You should see them. They look so sweet, all curled up in their sleeping bags on the V-birth. Just like two little innocent angels. I doubt that they'll wake up before we reach Cat-Harbor."

Tiffany pulled a blanket up around her chin to stave off the cool early morning dampness, as Forest maneuvered the boat through the inner harbor's maze of escort tug boats nudging tankers to their berths. She eyed him expectantly, as he stood to get a better look at a large Russian tanker that seemed to be coming into port under its own power. His tall, muscular frame, silhouetted against the moonlit backdrop, reminded her of the adventurous steersmen that she used to read about when she was a little girl. Of course, all of those story book sailors always had beards and long hair, but Forest's hair, hidden beneath a wide-rim straw hat, was short, and his walnut colored face was clean shaven. Still, the look of adventure in his dark brown eyes reminded her of the way she thought the characters in her sea tales must have felt when they were about to conquer the savage seas of make believe.

"Blasted! What in blazes is wrong with those guys?" yelled Forest as a Russian tanker sounded one short whistle as it rounded the bend. "Don't they know they're supposed to cut their engines and wait for an escort. They're too blasted big to be under power this close in."

Holding the wheel of his vessel hard to starboard with his right hand, Forest angrily raised the middle finger of his left hand at the on-coming tanker, in a gesture of contempt. Alas, it fell on empty eyes. The crew on the tanker was too busy getting the mooring lines ready to dock to notice a finger raised in the semi-darkness of the early morning.

Tiffany eyed him, laughing to herself. She knew he loved this part of sea-life more than any other. The challenge of making it through tight waters was what provided the gravy on the rice for him. "Forest, don't get so worked up. They're doing it right. See, they've got the tugs helping," said Tiffany, pointing to the two tugs at either side of the vessel's stern that had previously eluded Forest's sight.

♍︎♒︎♋︎■♑︎♏︎

The clock on the panel board said 4:44 a.m., as they made their way under the Vincent Thomas Bridge. Already, the inner harbor was like a giant maze, filled with water-born vehicles of every type bobbing about in all directions. Yachts held to their slips in neat rows casting their lights upon rippling waters, while runabouts crowded with day fisherman rocked on the wakes of work boats, and early morning sailing vessels put out to sea. A couple of trimarans made their way through the narrow mouth of the channel, barely missing the Russian tanker.

As Tiffany stood to get a better look at the harbor, the boat rocked suddenly, as it was hit by the powerful wake of a passing speed boat, knocking her back into her seat. "How soon do you think it'll be before we clear the break water," she asked, out of breath from the fall, and a little on edge from the busyness of the harbor.

"Well, there is an awful lot of traffic. It's holding us down to about three knots. Crawling speed. I'd say at least another hour at this rate." He looked down at her and read the familiar tight-lipped expression on her face. "Hey, come on. Nothing to worry about. Look, the kids are asleep, we've got a full moon, and I've got everything under control. All you have to do is just relax and enjoy it." Forest put his arm around her. He squeezed her shoulder in a gesture of reassurance.

The full moon poured its reflected light down upon the expanse of the harbor, but Tiffany almost missed its magic as she struggled hard to keep her eyes open. She did not want to sleep now. There was too much to see. She turned her attention away from the moon and looked instead, upon the shimmering harbor lights. Stifling a yawn, she reached beneath the panel box on the flying bridge for the thermos. She poured herself a cup of cinnamon coffee. Holding the cup with both hands, she sipped the hot liquid, letting it warm her as she longingly looked out upon the early morning collection of lights that turned the seascape into an enchanting story-book land, complete with castles and dancing fairies. In the semi-darkness, even the well-lighted barges looked like expensive palaces fit for noble ladies and kings.

♍︎ ♒︎ ♋︎ ■ ♑︎ ♏︎

As they made their way to the mouth of the harbor, Tiffany could see the light house at the edge of the breakwater. Beyond that, the open Pacific lay as a solid sheet of sparkling crystal.

The majesty of the moonlit harbor was intoxicating. She snuggled in closer to Forest and spread her blanket over his lower torso.

Pieces of the Tapestry

Affectionately, she rubbed the inner hardness of his bare thighs with her open palm. "Sweetheart, there's nothing like this, is there." Tiffany fixed her gaze on Forest's angular face.

Forest sighed longingly as he turned and looked into her dark eyes filled with unmasked want. He drank in the sculptured beauty of her high cheek bones and prominent brow. He feasted his eyes upon the rich chocolate of her skin, smooth as the calm Pacific in the soft yellow light of the full moon. "Let me have your mouth," he murmured.

The tender fullness of his open mouth upon hers was exhilarating. She parted her own lips slightly, inviting him in the way she had done on their wedding night fifteen years ago and many times thereafter. Her hand, now resting on his lap, vibrated to the feel of his rising passion. With each insertion of his tongue into the waiting warmth of her mouth, it seemed as though it was the first kiss all over. The luxurious feel of his probing hands upon her needing body made her want to feel the full expanse of her body up against his maleness. Instead, she settled for the feel of his free hand upon the tender warmth of her breasts, as he maneuvered the boat out of the protected waters of the Los Angeles Harbor and pointed the king plank toward the broad expanse of the open sea.

♍ ♒ ♋ ■ ♑ ♏

Tiffany sat, head resting on Forest's shoulder, in comfortable silence, as sea and sky came together in early morning splendor. The California shore line had disappeared several miles ago and the horizon of Catalina Island was not yet visible. A smattering of sailboats and yachts kept their distance as Forest guided the vessel through the open waters of the calm Pacific. Together, Tiffany and Forest tasted the sweet dew of the morning and languished in the soft majesty of its potent music as the hum of the diesel engine blended into harmony with the rippling sound of the ocean waters caressing the planking along the boat's hull. Occasionally, the distant warning signal of an unseen tanker added a whistling chord to the morning song. Sea and sky blended in the music of the awakening day. The sea gulls and the leaping scowls of porpoises that followed their wake united with them in the oneness of the morning.

)(

Pieces of the Tapestry

Sunshine in my heart
Fills sweet morning with all that
Breezes share with God.

-Elizabeth Bowers-

SWEET MORNING
by
Elizabeth Bowers

In the hour of first light,
Comes wild, opened winged sight,
On mercy seat of honeysuckle glory,
Calling all sweet breath of earth and sky
To the chorus of proud sun's best delight.
Sounds like heaven's great choir
Fill morning breezes with music
Born of spring's desire.
Blessed trees hold branches high
In welcome to sparrow's need
For calm in the pause from soaring about.
Sweet melody of morning fires
Dew kissed flowers to open wide
Their waking petals before rose briars,
As wild asters splatter purple shades
In great season of life.

Pieces of the Tapestry

Thread of season's light
Molds seas and sand dunes into shapes
Of Heaven's great plan.
※

-Elizabeth Bowers-

COUNTESSA FOR A MOMENT
by
Helen Tulis

The tryst took place in a drab, small hotel room in Lisbon Portugal. The Roma Hotel on Avenida da Roma was selected as the first meeting place after a hiatus of twenty-seven years.

The little brunette remembered the Portuguese Count very well. They had met at Syracuse University where they were both students. In the mind of the little brunette, the Portuguese man would still be the charming, scintillating, carefree and warm friend she had known at the university. He had informed her then that he and his family were very rich. They owned vast lands and grew grapes in the vineyards of Porto, which was the wine-producing area of his country. Even though he was a student twenty-seven years ago, he would inherit all the wealth of his family upon his college graduation. He would even have a title; the Count de Vallois.

Now, twenty-seven years later and almost 4,000 miles from the American university where they had been students, the two friends met. The brunette wondered how she would feel when she saw the count. She thought she might not even recognize him.

Finally, after peering down the long corridor of the Roma Hotel, she saw the count, a stocky man, wearing dark glasses. He made his way down the hall with deliberate steps, waving his hand in the air, trying to catch the brunette's attention. Jose`, the count, gave the middle-aged brunette a long and tight hug. She smelled the aroma of tobacco in the room, as he hugged her closely, repeating her name three times, softly.

Pieces of the Tapestry

She was suddenly overcome by his presence, as she took his hands into hers, staring at him in silence.

A time capsule. The twenty-seven years melted into one year, one month, one day. Quickly, the brunette flashed back to their first meeting when she was twenty-one. Jose` had said, "Wait until you come to Portugal. You will be the Countessa de Vallois, because I am the Count de Vallois."

"How silly," she had thought then. "A Countessa? I'll never even go to Portugal." But here she was with the Count, in this small, drab hotel room in Lisbon, Portugal.

The American had brought her friend a travel clock with LCD numerals as a welcoming gift. The clock was as light as a feather and Jose` remarked how much he liked it. Then he reached in his pocket and pulled out a tiny green box. Smiling, he handed it to the little brunette.

She opened it, and was delighted to discover a jade and gold pin in the shape of a cat with delicately crafted whiskers. "What a coincidence," remarked the American. "Neither of us knew the other would bring a gift."

Jose` had always been thoughtful. At college, he had taken her to dinner and had hired a violin player to serenade her. Once, he brought fresh rolls and bread to her dormitory and they had breakfast together.

After exchanging gifts, the two friends showed one another pictures of their respective families. The American noted that Jose` had six children, three boys and three girls. She had two sons. His children attended universities in London. Her sons attended colleges in Georgia. He had married a diplomat's daughter and had remained active in Portuguese politics. She was divorced and pursuing a career.

Soon the tryst would be over. The little brunette looked at the man whom she had not seen for twenty-seven years. He sat on a chair; then quickly jumped up and sat on the edge of the bed.

"Something is wrong," thought the brunette. "He is rather jumpy."

Jose` admitted that he was tired. After all, he had driven over 200 miles from his home in Porto to Lisbon. The once jovial man was now subdued and serious.

"So, you live in Georgia?"

"Yes."

"Always, since we met?" he asked.

Pieces of the Tapestry

"Yes, My family has lived there since I was born. What about your family?"

"Oh, my family is very bad." His English was halting and speckled with Portuguese words.

"What do you mean?"

"Oh, you don't read the news? The revolution with the government, with the people, is very bad"

"So what happened? What happened to you?

"It's very bad. Party politics, just terrible. I had very strained life for several years. I had vineyards, lots of healthy grapes. Revolutionaries thought I was a Fascist. They took everything away. Millions in the bank. The revolutionaries took it all. I was even in prison for 183 days. Thank God my family escaped to Spain."

"In prison?"

"Oh, I been in the prison. You don't see." He held his jaw with his hands. "Here, even in prison, they knocked out two teeth." He opened his mouth, pointing to the empty slots in his gums. "The revolutionaries wanted to kill me. Everything was so bad. Even my daughter tried to kill herself. She hate I been in prison."

As the little brunette listened attentively, Jose` spoke of politics, revolution, hunger, pain, greed, and hate. She thought to herself, "No wonder he is no longer jovial. No wonder he doesn't laugh like he once did."

Soon the tryst would be over. The little brunette, for a brief moment, had finally become the Countessa de Vallois. As she deliberated on this idea, the Count gently pulled her towards him.

⚹

Pieces of the Tapestry

Broken sky holds gleam
Of sunshine's golden promise,
In faith's sweet rainbow.

ι

-Elizabeth Bowers-

SPRING CLEANING
by
Eleanor Freemer

Who cleans the woods?
The garden spider
black and gold,
tatting a web
of Belgium lace
that stretches across the
dogwood leaves
to sift the dust
out of the April sun,
And knit an errant fly
into his grand design.

Who cleans the woods?
The fat bumble bee.
I hear him humming as he
vacuums with his slender hose,
the delicate nectar
from day-lily and rose.
and brushes the pollen
from the dandelion's face.
When done, hangs high his
shiny honey cone.

Pieces of the Tapestry

Who cleans the woods?
The wind and rain,
a busy pair,
washing and sweeping away debris
that collects on mossy pillows
'neath barren trees;
brewing a heady potpourri
from sodden leaves
and skeletal limbs
of last years blooms.

Who cleans the woods?
I clean the woods.
I rinse out every lily pod
and polish the mist from
the minnow's pool,
making them shine so I
can catch your reflection
when, like the sun,
you sail into my sky
and bring spring back to me.

♓

Pieces of the Tapestry

ESSENCE OF LOVE
by
Elizabeth Bowers

In the wind, and in every leaf
Upon each dogwood tree,
Is the elusive essence of love,
Moving through sorrows and joys,
Renewing the souls of creation.

⚛

WHEN IVY DANCES
by
Elizabeth Bowers

When lilies rise to meet wild clouds like tides
Pushed forward by brisk breezes at sun's gate,
The rock of my longing rises up as
A lion in the midst of a swollen
Volcano at its end time of rising,
And leaves a fiery caress upon
Sweet mouth of heaven's gate thrust open wide.
When ivy dances with warm drops of dew
To bright notes, as clear shinning after rain,
The light of my desire rises up
Like a tender breath of spring, sweeter than
Gardenias planted in rich fertile soil,
And stands not as prickly thorns thrust away,
But with full flower raised in praise of sun.

⚛

Pieces of the Tapestry
ON MY MOUNTAIN
by
Elizabeth Bowers

On my mountain,
A hidden place in the distant sky,
I do whatever I will;
It is a wonderful thrill
To sometimes be a red bird
Flapping my wings as I fly
Through tops of trees
And clouds so high;
Or drill for my supper deep
In sun-baked ground or wonder,
Soaring, floating up into clouds,
As the worker bee,
Pollinating flowers before resting tired wings
Upon a bending twig
Dangling from a mulberry tree.

I do whatever I will;
It is a wonderful thrill
To roll along flowery paths
Or ride breezes above
Roses and marigolds until quietly,
I stop to mill about and
Contemplate the fullness of love;
Friends and things I need and want,
I have right now,
Each, regardless of the form it takes,
Is my good and faithful pal.

)(

Pieces of the Tapestry

I walk in peaceful
Meadows filled with glory of
New day of true faith.
⚥

-Elizabeth Bowers-

THE GAME
by
Eleanor Freemer

"Grandmom can I come over to your house today." I could see my six year old grandson's deep blue eyes under the canopy of long black lashes as he pleads with me over the phone.

"No darling, not today Grandmom is busy."

"But grandmom, I won't bother you. I'll play by myself."

"Oh sure." I wasn't going to be trapped into that familiar, unreliable promise.

"You know Aron, Grandmom spends the morning at her computer. Besides," I said, using rear guard tactics, "You're all coming over to spend the day on Sunday. I have a surprise for you. So I'll see you then, love."

"Okay Grandmom." The voice still bore a pout, but he ended as he usually does, "I love you. Bye. See you Sunday."

Did I feel guilty over putting him off? Just a little. Did I lie? No, I told him the truth. I was busy at my computer, but not working on the *great American novel* that I have been struggling over for the past three years.

Being a grandmother, with four young ones living within walking distance, has been a pleasant distraction, but a distraction none the less. I also find it quite debilitating, being married to a grandfather, who has been retired for the past three years, with too much time on his hands, which he uses grousing about my sloppy housekeeping; while he has lost all sense of adventure and romance. Therefore within the secret confines of my computer, lives a dashing mature woman whose life exists vicariously for me through the adventures I plot.

While cruising through the local discount store, a few days before, I wandered into the computer department, and found some out of date computer games marked down, "$5.00 each." There was not much to lose at this price, and they looked like the kind of things boys six and ten would like.

The game the clerk recommended highly was the Dinno Game, which joined two others in my shopping bag.

Now I am not a real computer whiz, although the processor I use has a hard disk, A and B drive, windows and color, I seldom wander past the word processing program. Carefully reading the instructions, which were "easy enough for a six year old" to follow, I found out they were also comprehensible to one over sixty. To my delight, there were sound effects, and plenty of color action, just like at the arcade. Tentatively I moved the figures across the screen, seeing how the program worked, so I could show the children. This, my own new found addiction, was the surprise I had bought to keep the two boys busy while my daughter and her husband went off for the day.

By late afternoon, I knew all four protagonists and had watched in horror as they were vanquished by the scurrilous Beast because of my lack of dexterity. I only had two hands and ten fingers, and the action seemed to call for using more digits then nature had supplied me. However my mind was busy also. While learning the complexities of this game, another story line emerged where Andrea, my heroine waits for her rescuer under the streets of Los Angeles. I hear her plea, "Save me." I am trying an almost impossible maneuver, when my husband calls up, "Aren't we having dinner tonight?"

What a time to want to eat!

The next morning I was trying to get myself through the 2nd level, and rescue Donna DeSepto tied to the subway tracks. You can see why I would not have time to play with the little one. He would come over and want to take full control. Come Sunday, I would challenge them both to a duel of wit and action. Sunday, we trooped up to my "office" and I inserted the disc into my computer. "Watch out kids," I told them. "Here comes Grandmom. We're going to Play Dinno. I may even give you all a turn at the controls."

Pieces of the Tapestry

They brushed this aside. "We'll take turns Grandmom. We know what to do. We won't fight."

"Now boys, just a minute, let me show you."

"We know grandmom. We know." Zeke's voice rose impatiently. "See."

To my astonishment, Zeke put in the disk, typed in the prescribed letters and the picture flashed on the screen. His little fingers flew over the keyboard, page up, page down, enter, shift. The figures jumped and fought their way just up to the final destination where the heroes collapsed in defeat.

"Here," I moved another chair in front of the computer, "Let me try."

"Grandmom no! You can always play. It's our turn now. You go downstairs with Grandpop. Please!" he whined.

Reluctantly I relinquished the chair to Aaron, who couldn't sit on it for long.

Laughter and excitement gushed down. The floor vibrated as the younger one jumped up and down when his big brother discovered a new move, a new setting. The sound effects were not enough for them. They added their own. "Beep, beep," they called. "Bang, bang," they shouted. Peeved, by being left out of the fun, I could hardly concentrate on the Sunday paper.

I'm happy to report they never rescued Donna from the minnow Rex. So far, neither have I, but I'm not worried. Just you wait and see. I'll destroy Minnow Rex before they come back next week. For I'm older and smarter then they are ... I think.

☿

ODE TO A MONARCH BUTTERFLY
by
Elizabeth Bowers

In the quiet of the early morning sun,
Like a weed standing in currentless space,
Held captive by colors of orange and black,
I watch proud Monarch stop its migration
And dance on the backs of rose scented breezes;

Butterfly wings, like royal gems, hovering
Two breaths away from a red wood fence
Separating somber rows of corn, wheat and barley,
From sun drenched fields of milkweed delight.

In the quiet of the late afternoon sun,
I watch as fluttering wings, like waving rainbows,
Catch the power of spring's last breeze
And glide like sweet angels into summer's light;

Then on across a thousand miles of day and night,
To reach a Gulf front Hide away
As autumn colors settle in Northern trees.

)(

Pieces of the Tapestry

Sweet Source of wind and Rain, give abundant harvest To struggling vine.
)(
-Elizabeth Bowers-

A REAL BUTTERFLY
by
Helen Tulis

The open field commanded the presence of a delicately colored yellow butterfly. It danced in the gentle breeze of early fall. Up and away it flew as it barely missed the low lying long tree limbs heavy with leaves. One could barely see the butterfly as it became a speck in the blue sky.

Just then, a small girl was running through the fields, carrying a green pail with her. She was wearing a white ruffled pinafore covering a red dress. Her shoes, strapped across her feet, were worn as she had played in them all summer long.

Though her hair was not long, its brown curls covered her neck. She kept on running while looking into the sky. She asked, "Where is that butterfly?"

Paula was very perceptive. She had her eye on the yellow butterfly long before she began running from the house. Paula held up her pail and continued, "I want that butterfly."

Her Mommie who thought Paula was in the yard, began calling, "Paula. Paula." When she got no answer, she dashed out of the house and ran after little Paula.

"I want that butterfly. Get him. Get him," she cried.

"No, Paula. I cannot get him. He travels a lot and has flown away," said Mommie.

"But I want him," wailed little Paula.

"Butterflies will be back. If this one does not fly back, he will send his friends," Mommie consoled Paula.

Pieces of the Tapestry

They both walked back into the house. Paula was disappointed because Mommie couldn't catch the butterfly.

♍ ♒ ♋ ■ ♑ ♏

The following week, Paula went shopping with her grandmother in the mall. Paula was getting tired, because they had walked so much, looking for a toy in all the shops.

"Grandmother, I want to rest," Paula said.

"All right. Let's rest here," said Grandmother, selecting a place to sit near some indoor garden area in the mall.

Just as Paula turned around, she spotted a beautiful black and yellow butterfly amongst the greenery and flowers. She was almost afraid to look, as she was afraid the butterfly would fly away just as the yellow one had done. She gazed at the butterfly as it sipped the juice from the leaves.

Grandmother noticed the butterfly, too. She said, "Paula, if you will be still, you will see a big beautiful butterfly right there." She pointed to the closed in space.

"Grandmother, will it bite me?" Paula asked shyly.

"No," said Grandmother. "It doesn't bite."

"Will it hurt me?" Paula inquired as she clung to Grandmother's skirt.

"No, little Paula. The pretty butterfly will not harm you."

"What does it do, then?" asked Paula who was almost three years old and very inquisitive.

"Oh, it drinks juice from leaves and flowers. Then it flies to other flowers and does the same," answered Grandmother.

"Could I have it?" Paula asked.

"Well, we could just look at it, because it will want to fly away," replied Grandmother.

Grandmother took Paula closer to see the big winged butterfly as it sipped nectar from the flower. They both walked cautiously so as not to frighten the butterfly. They tip-toed to the indoor garden, being careful to stand a distance from the butterfly.

As they approached the butterfly, Grandmother noticed the satiny black sheen of the butterfly's wings. It had a grand design of orange as if paint had spilled from a pen onto the black wings. The wing span was so large it appeared as a small plate on which one could eat, especially when the full span of the wing was evident. Both Grandmother and Paula walked around the open garden space, careful as not to disturb the butterfly as it had lit on its nourishment source.

"Sh, sh," said Grandmother as they took small steps back to the bench where they had sat before.

"I want that butterfly," said Paula.

"No one can have a real butterfly," said Grandmother. "They go to special places all over the world

"But that is a pretty one," said Paula.

"Yes, but after it eats, it will fly away to another flower. And we might not see it again," Grandmother warned.

"We can go to see it," said Paula.

"Butterflies go 1,000 miles sometimes. This one may visit South America. That is a long way away, Paula," said grandmother.

"What do they do there?" asked Paula as she jumped along the way.

"They make people happy there because butterflies have such beauty," said Grandmother.

Paula tip-toed to the garden again to admire the huge butterfly's satiny wings as it remained silently on the leaf. She put her finger up to her lips. "Sh, sh. I don't want the pretty butterfly to fly away," whispered Paula.

♍ ♒ ♋ ■ ♑ ♏

Grandmother Helen remembered how much her own mother Grandma Rose loved butterflies. Once when she visited her mother she noticed a picture of a blue butterfly. Grandma Rose had cut it out of a magazine. She had placed it in the corner of a frame that stood on the dresser. When sunlight would shine on the dresser, the butterfly almost came alive, sparkling as if it were still flying in the fields. Grandma's daughter, Barbara, had caught a grayish brown butterfly and had placed it in a frame so grandma could hang it up in her room. It was not unusual to find butterflies and replicas of butterflies in Grandma's house.

On a trip to Brazil, Grandmother Helen discovered an unusual butterfly for Grandma Rose. In the hotel gift shop was a silver frame in which a metallic blue butterfly lay. "Oh," she thought, "that will make Mom happy because she loves butterflies." Though this butterfly was

Pieces of the Tapestry

expensive, it seemed to be the perfect gift for grandma Rose. Encased inside this silver frame, the metallic blue butterfly showed its expansive wing span, highlighting its rarity.

"Wrap this up. I'll take it," said Grandmother Helen as she took the delicate butterfly back to the hotel. "Grandma Rose will love this."

Grandma Rose showed the Brazilian butterfly to Paula. She let Paula play with her jewelry box in which lay butterfly pins, black and coral colored, butterfly earrings to match, and one big butterfly pin that looked as if it could fly away by itself. Grandma Rose, when sitting on her open deck outside, would call Paula over to her, as she pointed to the various butterflies nipping flowers in the garden.

When it was time to leave the mall, Grandmother Helen called to Paula, who was intent on seeing if she could catch the butterfly. The butterfly rose and slowly began to reach higher zones as it catapulted again towards the earth. Finally, as it began to disappear, Paula asked, "Where is the butterfly going?"

Since the two of them had to go home, Grandmother Helen quickly said without thinking, "Probably to Grandma Rose's house."

"Then I want to go too. I want to go to Grandma Rose's house," said Paula as she ran a little faster, trying to catch up with the swift butterfly.

"Okay. Let's go," answered Grandmother Helen as they scampered away.

)(

Pieces of the Tapestry

Midnight road, lead me
To sweet world of dreaming trees
High on your mountain.
 ℋ
-Elizabeth Bowers-

LOVE FOOD
by
Eleanor Freemer

My mother never visited the family without bringing an offering of love. As my parents were in the shoe business, almost all my life, I can not look at a man's size twelve shoe box without smelling my mother's savory knishes, hot from the oven, bursting from this unique container.

When she planned a visit, Momma was up early in the morning, and hurried to the neighborhood Kosher butcher's shop for a slice of liver and something she called meltz. This was a disgusting looking organ that came from some unidentifiable part of a cow's anatomy. The two pieces of meat stayed under the broiler until they resembled shoe leather. They were chopped, then mixed with chicken fat, celery salt and pepper, then put into the refrigerator to cool and for the flavors to blend. While it sat waiting for the chemistry to make its magic, she made the dough, measuring the dry ingredients by the handful, stirring in oil and water, kneading, then rolling it out into a thin sheet.

By ten o'clock, the magnificent stuffed dough would be ready to taste. "Ah, delicious," our mouths salivating, cooled the burning knishes, which were always the best ever.

"No more," she'd admonish, with a slap at our hands if we tried to sneak another one from its berth in the shoe box. "You'll have when we get to the Tante's."

On Friday, she made soup nuts (mandelen); rolling long tails of dough that she sliced, then put in the oven to dry as compliments for the chicken soup. Momma braided challah, which would accompany the roast chicken and the home made wine. The wine was put up every year,

Pieces of the Tapestry

months before Passover. The large jugs sat wrapped in a blanket on the kitchen radiator like a baby incubating through the winter. It was decanted for Passover, then sipped throughout the year on Friday nights until a new batch was started again after the new year.

Momma also made cinnamon buns. Fresh from the over, they exuded a warm yeasty smell that greeted one as soon as the front door was opened. I would unroll them like a Torah Scroll to pick out the nuts and raisins like words of wisdom, then devour the sweet cake.

A cook book in the kitchen? Recipes written down and handed from one bride to another? I had never heard of such things. My mother's hands remembered what her mother had taught her. The texture, the weight, the very way the fingers moved, were the skills I observed.

Her secrets were never to be shared with her daughters. She had no time or patience for us to weigh and feel and learn ingredients from her. When I was married, I bought cook books, asked for recipes from friends and copied them out of the newspaper. I tried to add a teaspoon of love in everything I cooked, but nothing I made ever tasted as my memory savored my mother's treats.

Years after she died, I found the courage to make a batch of knishes. With trepidation, I asked my father to taste them.

He put one in his mouth, and closed his eyes and sighed. "They don't taste exactly like Momma's, but they're good. Yes, they're very good."

We shared a smile, a new memory, a taste of my love.

※

Pieces of the Tapestry

Impatiens' spirit
Rides morning sunbeams, drenched in
Angel's shiny dew.

ι

-Elizabeth Bowers-

TALKING ABOUT MIRACLES
by
Helen Tulis

"I've promised too much" I thought, as soon as I had hung up talking to the rabbi.

He had asked, "Would you come to Havdalah service Saturday night? We will have a discussion then some refreshments. It would be good to have you join in the discussion."

For the past three Fridays I had not attended services; either I had been out of town or had been baby sitting. Once, I had not gone because the weather had been bad and I knew I could not see to drive in the rain at night. I was however, anxious to go to this Havdalah service, as the topic was myths and how we got there. It sounded provocative. So without thinking it over I said, "Yes Rabbi, I will surely come."

That Saturday I picked up my Mom and brought her to my house for dinner. I had concocted a meal especially designed to tempt her waning appetite. At the blessed age of ninety-two, she doesn't eat well when home alone.

I had set the table with new place-mats, floral designed, and my best silver and china. The food was laid out like a painting; sliced broiled filet mignon, chopped salad with homemade dressing, fresh corn, small red potatoes with onions, rice, squash and a fresh fruit salad. I even made some chocolate pudding, because Mom said she loved it. I was really happy having made this evening meal special. Then Mom looked around and said, "This is too much for me. You shouldn't have done it. Don't give me too much food."

A little disappointed by her reaction, I smiled "Eat as much as you want mom," and sat her down at the table, where we said the prayers before breaking bread. As we were eating, Mom insisted, "You take me home after the dinner, because I don't want you to drive home in the dark."

I did not answer but just refilled my glass with tea.

Mom persisted, "Let's go back to my house on time so you won't have to drive in the dark."

At first that sounded reasonable, but as time flew by I noticed that I could not get Mom home then return to this area to arrive at the beginning of the Havdalah service. My mind began to click off, "Time. Time to take Mom home. Time to come back here. Time to drive another ten miles to the Temple. No time." I panicked.

Heartily I suggested to Mom that she could come with me to the Temple, enjoy the service, which would only last an hour, then I would take her home. She looked out at the fading light, then back to me. "How will you drive me home?"

Again I went over my plans, while she shook her head, consenting only if I hurried to leave on time.

It was then that I noticed that Mom did not have on an appropriate sweater or make up to enhance her appearance. I wanted her to look her best when I introduced her to the rabbi, whom she had never met. So I suggested, "Mom, you can wear my new scarf and that pretty pink sweater. They would look good on you. O.K.?"

She sighed and thought out loud, "I am an old woman. I don't need to look so prettied up."

"But Mom, you would look so pretty in that new sweater. See, it is more attractive than this old dark one. I'll make up your face. You'll look wonderful," I said leading her into the downstairs powder room, and grabbing for the make-up tray.

"Here, put on the sweater, then sit on the toilet and I'll make up your face."

Pieces of the Tapestry

She put her face up to the light, and quizzed me while I tried to put some lipstick on. "You never liked doing this when you were younger. I'm surprised you know how to do it now."

"Well, I'm not so good," I laughed hurrying to accomplish this self appointed task, "But you are looking real good already, if I must say so myself."

Within forty minutes we were both dressed and ready to go. I opened the back door, and saw that night had already enveloped us; and a covering of fog was developing. Mom had difficulty seeing clearly, and did not notice the light fog that was rolling in. Cheerfully I said, as she stepped into my car, "We'll make it Mom."

Her reply was, "Be careful. Be careful when you drive."

I heeded my mother's advice, as I rounded the curve into an embankment of fog. I kept up a patter of conversation, centering on her attendance in religious school when she was a child in Poland.

"We had a big rabbi, the main rabbi from Warsaw who also taught us about myths, religious laws, menhugin. He came from a distance just to teach us children."

"Did you go to religious school everyday?"

"In my tante's house we had our own tutors. I learned too much religious practices. I could not even comb my hair on Saturdays. My tante was very strict and religious" Mom added.

By this time I had driven five miles. The fog was sitting on top of the houses, not even moving, as I drove past the main highway. Finding the small streets near the temple was becoming a problem. I slowed down, looking carefully and closely out of the front windows. I even resorted to putting on the blower, trying to wipe the fog away. I felt I was blind folded. Once I came so close to a black car in front of us I had to quickly and suddenly stamp on the brakes to avoid a collision. Fortunately Mom wasn't aware of the situation and talked on about Europe and her religious background when she lived with her tante. My arms and legs were shaking from tension, as we finally approached the road on which the temple was located. I could barely see the golden lights sitting far up on their posts in the midst of the parking area.

"Mom, we're here." I shouted. I looked around hoping someone else had come early, but saw no one. Only the circle of fog that swirled around the golden lights was actually visible. No one else had arrived yet.

Pieces of the Tapestry

I became rather anxious as I checked my watch. We were fifteen minutes early, but the place looked desolate.

"What kind of place is this?" Mom asked. "No one here? We are the only ones? In our shule we have a special man, the shamus, who comes early to let us in. Who lets you in here?"

I saw her wriggling around in her seat, still tied down by the seat belt. I said, "Mom let's just wait a minute."

"Oh no. Not by me. We wouldn't wait. You could get killed here in a minute and no one would know it. It's dangerous." Her voice took on a sharp edge. "Let's go on the main highway to see people," she commanded.

Having read just that day about someone being held up on a lonely desolate road, I agreed. "OK, I can make it up to the main highway as it's not too far from here. Then, we can turn around and come back. By then, more people will be here."

Turning down the dark road, I pointed out lights, businesses, and some cars to Mom, trying to placate her anxious feelings, and I must admit now, my own. "You see Mom, there's the main street."

"Well to me, this is too far out of the way. How far is it from your house?" Mom asked.

"It's not that far. In the daytime, you can see better you know. It just seems far tonight." I stammered.

After turning around and heading back I found myself completely confused, not knowing in what direction I needed to go. The fog was heavier now. Even the gas station appeared to be an igloo up in the Arctic. Nothing looked familiar on either side of the street. I was lost.

"Don't just drive around and use up gas. Go inside and ask directions. Anyway I think I had enough." Mom insisted.

"We'll get back fine." I reassured her.

Sheepishly I went into the nearest gas station, "How do I get back to the main highway?"

"Oh you ain't but three blocks off of that. Just go up here one block, turn left." He waved his skinny arm around. "Then, go two more blocks. You can't miss it," the young attendant said.

"I don't want to get lost again." I almost whimpered, "I have my elderly mother with me and she is worried about our making it home."

"Well, you ain't far from the main highway. I come down it a different way, but I told you the easy way, so you won't get lost." he promised me.

"OK. Thanks again. You are so nice." I added, as I walked out, still unsure of what I was to do. It was a scary world out there. Mist was clinging to all the cars, and hung as a coat of film on the traffic lights.

"So, can you go back?" Mom wanted to know.

"I can go back. Yes. I can go back," I announced confidently, "But I am not sure I really want to now. It's so late."

"Yes you're right," Mom agreed. "The best thing is to go home."

She's right, I realized. I laughed; you should always listen to your mother. "Yes Mom, it will be safer to go home."

By this time I was headed in the right direction, following landmarks that I recognized. Down one long residential road, and then another long street meeting at the highway, would get me home. Finally, I was on familiar territory. The young attendant had indeed given me the right directions.

Mom looking around and sensing I was relieved said, "You should take me home, too. I can't sleep in your house, you know, I like my own bed. When you're old, you'll like your own bed. Wait, wait, till you get old. You'll see I am right." Mom insisted.

"Fine, Mom. That's a good idea. I'll drive you home." As I said this I felt calm, as if a fog had lifted. I could see Mom's point of view. I needed my own bed tonight too.

We drove in silence. I kept thinking about the promise I had made the rabbi. "Yes, I'll surely be at Havdalah service, where we will talk about myths."

I thought, as I drove my mother home; I wanted to ask the rabbi to talk about miracles in his next discussion group. There was no myth in our driving through the fog, getting lost and finding ourselves. We had experienced a miracle. The rabbi once wrote, "God saves us many times. That is His miracle."

During the following week, I wrote the rabbi a letter and made a donation to the temple, thanking God for His miracle.

⚸

Pieces of the Tapestry

Black bird, at first light,
Lays great wings upon golden
Joy of heaven's breath.

ι

-Elizabeth Bowers-

BEAUTIFUL BLACK
by
Elizabeth Bowers

Beautiful black is my rich soil,
Like round trunks of Georgia Pine trees,
And clouds that give up precious ran
To make things grow for you and me.

Beautiful black are my good shoes
Worn on favorite dress up days
Like Sunday brunch at Grandma's house
Or graduation day at school.

Beautiful black is Mother's hair,
Curls soft like sweet baby lamb,
And shinning bright as raven wings
Soaring in summer sun at noon.

Beautiful black are all good nights
When eyelids close in peaceful dreams,
Or stare in wonder at the moon
Shinning down on sleepy earth.

⚥

Pieces of the Tapestry

Garden of faithful
Souls blooms in sea of heaven's
Everlasting sun.

ι

-Elizabeth Bowers-

SEASON OF THE HAWK
by
Elizabeth Bowers

My wings burn like dry ice upon flesh,
As I soar through heavy clouds upon
The back of a mighty blowing wind,
Rushing to embrace the one who sits
With folded wings atop the sleeping
Tree that caresses the source of light
Above, waving dreaming leaves to heaven.

No creature living in the land of
Four seasons has a head and neck so
Thickly feathered and glorious as his;
His wings are broad like falcon's feather
Dress, bold and have the look of leaves
That hang on trees until cold breezes
Turn warm as my burning desire.

Within his eyes, fierce as the gleam of
Lightening in the season of new life,
I behold the strength of rushing wind,
Moving through bowels of clashing clouds,
And I hear his longing for me in
His song, an agonizing whistle,
That matches the cruel scream of my want.

Pieces of the Tapestry

I am larger, stronger and bolder
Than my mate, still he mounts me with power
And I feel the fire of his life
In the roundness of my wings as a
Burning heat moved by rushing liquid
Wind, mighty in season of plenty;
Hypnotized, I am alive with need.

We cover the proof of our joining
With the warm strength of our wings until
Full orb that lights the dark sky goes and
Returns again in glowing brightness,
Rendering to us our cherished ones
Helpless, dressed in softness like the cold
Wet covering of sleeping forest.

I fly as wind, with their chattering
Calls as my banner, hypnotized by
Scent of living prey as I roam sky
And forest bed in search of breathing
Flesh fit for sharing with my delights;
With speed of lightening flashing through a
Stormy sky, I pounce upon my prey.

Our wings are empty now, we stand in
Burning heat of season of plenty
Watching as the proof of our joining
Lay their wings upon gentle breezes,
And glide swiftly from our nest to race
Faster than eagles above steep cliffs,
Until their season of mating comes.

)(

3. SINGULARLY HUMAN

Hold to thriving root
Where elements of all life
Emerge in season.

♓

-Elizabeth Bowers-

PRIORITIES
by
Eleanor Freemer

My friend, was widowed at age sixty-three.
Overnight her hair turned
from midnight black to blonde.
Her tight size 16 skirts now end
just below her knees, to swish like water
against a rock, as her wide hips move
rhythmically when she walks.

My dear friends'
full red lips smack in sad disapproval
when she looks at my gray hair.
Though fond of me, she honestly must say
it makes me look so old.
She pats her own gold crowning glory
preening; she would never let her
hair get to look that way.

More's the pity.

I have to laugh for she still
thinks like a girl in her teens'
whereas there are other things that mean
much more to me then the color of my hair.
I am comfortable with these gray tresses,
each silvery streak I wear,
like a medal of honor, earned
on the battlefield of life.

See me for what I am, a woman
celebrating forty four years of marriage,
a wife, to one good man whose
three babies I have pushed

Pieces of the Tapestry

up and down the city's dusty streets
in an old fashioned baby carriage,
singing lustily over the sound
of city hawkers and city traffic.

I was the nurse, who tenderly, lovingly,
tended elderly sick parents,
mourned the death of a young grandchild,
watched loved ones die, and others born.
Together we have climbed the heights of joy
dropped into the deep abyss of sorrow,
Learned all broken dreams
cannot be pieced and pasted back together.

Dear Friend, look, see
these deep wrinkles around my eyes?
They are from searching beyond the horizon
for a child, always the last to slowly wend
himself home from school.
My ears are now attuned to the slamming
of his car door when he finally
drives home by the light of the stars.

Nothing changes, different times
bring different worries.
Children grow up, leave the warmth
of our feathered bed
to feather ones of their own.

My friend has a lot of cheek
to think I could care to look
as she does for I am ME, a woman
who loves running in the rain,
flying against the wind
chasing colored balloons, or floating
across the grass wearing a wreath
of soap bubbles in her graying tresses.

Pieces of the Tapestry

My long loose dresses give me freedom
to sit spread legged on a wooden step
beside a loving grandchild who carefully
combs these unmoussed hairs with
her warm sticky fingers.
Warm~ warm hugs, warm breath, warm kisses
flutter across my face,
carrying whispered messages of love.

Down through the passageway of years
I've heard them all before, each circles
around and around my heart like a toy boat
sailing in an overflowing tub.
Old friend, I need no blonde hair
to make me feel young, as I will always be
as young as I feel, and despite my gray hair,
I know I am still very much loved
and very much a woman.

)(

Pieces of the Tapestry

REAL MEMORIES
by
Helen Tulis

Childhood is walking to school,
the only white girl in an
all-black neighborhood.
Childhood is waking up early on Sundays to read the
Ralph McGill editorial in the Atlanta Constitution
while Dad stood nearby to explain it.
Childhood is taking a flashlight to bed to read Little
Women under the blanket,
Childhood is walking to the library with my two sisters
to check out our limit of books, then cooling
off in a washtub and spritzing my sisters with the
garden hose.
Childhood is singing verses to my friends, on the yellow bus
weaving its way to the Hebrew school, where my
teacher challenged me with "aleph beth" and lessons in morality.
Childhood is starring in the play called the Dybbuk, playing
baseball in the school yard, going to picnics and swim
parties, but also getting my first kiss.
Childhood is playing that card game called "go fish" and
riding a boy's bike before I owned a girl's,
Staring at my sister's photo of Van Johnson on my wall,
Because he was a popular Hollywood star.
Childhood is hearing my sister saying: "Bet you can't walk to
school without stepping on the cracks in the sidewalk."
And I would take her up on the bet.

א

Pieces of the Tapestry

Flax blows in threatening Winds, as blue bells struggle to Feed on golden rays.

✷

-Elizabeth Bowers-

SECOND CHANCE
by
Eleanor Freemer

It was a cold, blustery Friday morning in November; when Sue Ellen Parish, a tall, slim woman of thirty-five, disappeared. She was last seen running across the Red Apple Super Market lot, laughing in the wind.

Jimmy Joe, the young and a little overweight bag boy, tried to keep up with her as he pushed her loaded grocery cart to where her rusted brown 1979 Station Wagon stood. Sue Ellen waited breathlessly for him to catch up, and set the bags into the back of her station wagon. He watched for her lips to part into that perfect smile that ran right up into her blue eyes; then her, "Thanks Jimmy Joe, you sure are a big help," as she rewarded him with a generous tip.

"You sure look happy today Mrs. Parish," he said after thanking her. "You have a real good day."

"I will Jimmy Joe," she assured him. "I sure will. I wish you a real good day too."

He turned around and rode the empty basket, like a scooter, back into the store out of the cold. He never looked back. However, three hours later when he went out again to the then crowded lot, he was surprised to see the station-wagon still sitting there. He looked into the back window and was puzzled to see it was empty.

That evening, when questioned by the police, his round face crumbled with fear. J. J. (which is what he really wanted to be called), couldn't remember if he had said anything to Lally Perkins, the check out clerk, about Sue Ellen's car being there all day. However, Friday was a busy day, and there wasn't much time for talk. He guessed by late afternoon, he had forgotten, but he did remember how happy she looked.

Pieces of the Tapestry

"Happier then usual?" Sgt. Copes asked suspiciously. Jimmy Joe looked bewildered by the question. He said he thought she always looked especially happy since she had been working for Ms. Mabel in the beauty salon. "She'd tell me she was going home first, put her groceries away; make Mr. Parish's lunch ready for him when he got hungry; then return to the mall, ready for work. Mrs. Parish said she loved working for Ms. Mabel," He smiled over at Mabel.

Sue Ellen loved her job. After twenty years of marriage to the taciturn Tom, the warm noisy place with its occasional off colored jokes, the talk, the laughter and the gossip, became her haven. Ten months ago, walking on the strip mall, she saw the notice on the front door for a receptionist and general handy lady. Feeling daring, she had walked in and had been hired on the spot by Mabel Markey.

This morning, Mabel told Sally, her one operator at Hair to Stay, she knew something was real wrong as soon as she opened the shop. Sue Ellen wasn't at her heels.

"She's always right here. If I'd take a step back, I'd tread on her toes. That's how close she is to me coming in." She gave a smoke filled cough, and glared at Sally who never came in on time.

"Why, I missed my breakfast this morning too," Mabel ran on, feeling deprived of the thermos of fresh coffee, and the big bag filled with ham and biscuits Sue Ellen brought from home every morning.

The two women would share breakfast while Mabel would talk and Sue Ellen would listen, an arrangement that suited them both. Mabel liked to talk. To everyone's satisfaction, Sue Ellen was a good listener. Whatever was mentioned during the day never got beyond the front door with her.

Mabel looked at her watch for the fifth time. "Sue Ellen knows Friday's my busiest day," she muttered.

"Ain't like Sue Ellen to be late," said Sally, popping a fresh piece of gum in her mouth.

"That's a good worker there. Sue Ellen don't only wash heads around here. She sweeps up the floor and keeps the wet towels picked up. If I need anything, she goes and gets it for me, and does all the errands and answers the phones," Mabel told Sally.

"Yep! A real asset." Sally smacked her gum in between words.

Pieces of the Tapestry

"She's gettin' a lot of good experience here too. You don't never pitch in Like Sue Ellen does." Mabel grabbed a rag and started wiping down the front counter.

By ten o'clock, Sally was getting on Mabel's nerves.

Sally's chewing gum popped to the accompaniment of her fast moving hands and tongue. "My gad, ain't that the truth." Sally let out with a hardy laugh; splintering the air, redolent with shampoo, hair spray, lotions and lady's perfume.

"For God's sake, stop with the popping all ready. You sound like a bee bee gun. You're getting on Louella's nerves." She turned away quickly from two accusing pairs of eyes in the mirror.

Later Mabel apologized to both Louella and Sally, for she really liked the girl who was a young version of herself. They both loved a bit of gossip, that broke the monotone of the day. They both fed and shared with one another their clients' secrets, some which Mabel thought should have been reserved for the confessional.

"No sweat Mabel," Sally laughed good naturedly, blowing a big bubble in defiance.

Mabel joshed the ladies with a laugh, "I'm like a psychiatrist, and you only pay me for hair style but get some real good therapy for the same cost." Even her most reticent clients let their hair down as they close their eyes under her gentle hypnotic massaging fingers.

It nagged Mabel that Sue Ellen never gave out a thing about how she was feeling or her problems at home. It was times like today when Mabel could have used a clue as to where she might be. She knew Sue Ellen had plenty of problems at home.

♍ ♒ ♋ ■ ♑ ♏

Mabel had known Sue Ellen's mother. She remembered all too well when Mary and Louie were killed in a motorcycle accident one icy night.

"Sue Ellen was just fifteen years old at the time, homely little thing." She reminisced out loud. "The whole town felt sorry for the child. She had no kin folks to take her in. The neighbors whispered how it was a pity she never had a real home life. Her folks being so wild, living, then dying like irresponsible kids. Had no right to have kids of their own."

Pieces of the Tapestry

Mabel shook her head, but her stiffly sprayed hair didn't move from its curls. "Folks said, the apple doesn't fall far from the tree, so maybe that's why they all acted afraid to take in the pitiful scrawny looking child." Mabel gave Louella's hair a rough brushing as she remembered the evening she saw a threat in Sue Ellen's sapphire eyes that looked at the world in innocent bewilderment.

"Only Tom Parish, said she could come live with him. He was her daddy's best friend, you know. He'd never married, which made some people think he was a little strange." She stopped to look at Louella's hair, and gave it a little pat before gusting it out with some hair spray. "The town's keepers of morals and law frowned on that arrangement, but they didn't stop him. So he married her and made sure she finished high school, he said, before moving into her bed." Her shoulders moved dramatically.

"She's always sweet. Never complains." Louella got the last word in as she opened the door to leave.

Mabel roughly washed Martha Prime's hair.

Martha just closed her eyes under the onslaught, and remembered those years. "People in town never saw much of Sue Ellen until after she had the baby," she said. "She came in town to do shopping and to show off the little baby girl."

"Once she came in to have the baby's hair cut, cause she was afraid she would cut the sweet little thing if she tried to do it herself." Mabel had Martha on the chair, quickly rolling up her thin brown hair. "I asked how they were getting along, how Tom was doin.' She said they was doin' real fine. She was real comfortable with Tom because he was so much like her Daddy." Mabel put Martha under the dryer. "A young girl shouldn't feel comfortable with a man because he's like her Daddy."

"Well," Martha said before ducking her head all the way under the dryer, "Tom and Louie both were crazy about motorcycles, and hunting, and like my Joe, they'd come back red eyed and smelling of beer. Tom treats her good though, that I know, even if he ain't what a girl would think as a romantic figure. You know yourself Mabel, there are worse kinds of men than that. You hear me?"

Sally looked at Martha's wrinkled face and sagging body, and thought to herself, "What would such an old biddy know about what a young girl wants." She ran her hands down her hips, and smiled into

Pieces of the Tapestry

Joanne's knowing eyes in the mirror. They went dancing at the roadhouse together on the weekends, where strapping young guys knew just what young girls wanted. She popped her gum again, and leered wickedly over her friend's head. "I think we both need a little more sunshine in our hair. Remind me next week."

Only Mabel was ever invited over to visit with the Parish's. She saw how Sue Ellen kept his house clean, learned to cook the things he liked, and was a real good mother. She'd been tickled to watch Sue Ellen play with baby Mary Louise like she was a little doll.

Tom had a "fix it up shop," in back of their little cottage where he brought to life anything from a toaster to farm machinery. His hands were always black and smelling from grease, and his brown teeth carried the message left by three packs of cigarettes a day. He coughed up phlegm more then words. Living so far out in the country with Tom and her baby Mary Louise, Sue Ellen almost forgot how to talk, and the older she became, the quieter she grew.

When Mary Louise was seventeen years old, with no more sense than an old boot, she became pregnant and married a boy from high school. By the time the baby was a year old, Mary Louise was fed up with married life. She came into the beauty parlor to get her hair done one day and told Mabel that she was going to leave her boy husband and move back home.

"His mom and dad looked as if it's my fault," Mary Louise said with a giggle, "that he spends all morning in bed. He works for his poppa, and will never be anything but a gopher. The baby and me need things. If I get a job it will be for me, not him. Fix my hair real pretty, will you Mabel. I'm going looking for work this afternoon."

When she left, Mabel laughed, and told Sally, "I hope she leaves that boy before she becomes pregnant again. If she was my daughter, I tell you, I wouldn't take her back."

Sue Ellen must have felt the same way, for that first spark of rebellion flickered in Sue Ellen's eyes when Mary Louise came over that night and said she had taken a job at Belk's. She told her mother that it wouldn't be any problem as she would leave Jacquie with her. "She loves you so much Mama, she'll be happy staying with you forever."

Pieces of the Tapestry

The next day Sue Ellen came home and said she had taken a job at Mabel's salon. Mary Louise and Tom were shocked. "Why do you want to do that?" Tom protested, "don't I make enough money for you?"

"It ain't the money Tom. I raised Mary Louise, but I don't intend to raise our grandchildren too. I saw the sign in Mabel's window. I went in. It was so nice and friendly in there. It's like ..." She smiled wistfully at Tom. "Like belonging to a club and getting paid for it." She walked over to him where he sat at the kitchen table and put her hand on his shoulder.

"I never did anything in my life except stay in this house, and it's time I ventured out. I'm like Jacquie, a baby who ain't ever learned to walk or talk."

Tom looked at her, puzzled. What could those gossipy women have to say that could interest his wife. He fought in his non-violent way, but Tuesday morning she was dressed in her best cotton dress and was out to the mall. Mary Louise came to drop off the baby and was shocked and angry to find her mother had really gone. She left in a huff.

"You tell Momma how much the baby cried that she wasn't here," she said, as she put the dry eyed Jacquie in her car seat and drove off in a cloud of dust.

After several months, Mabel told Sue Ellen, "You have a nice gentle touch. My ladies tell me they sure enjoy when you wash their heads, darlin." Sometimes the ladies would shake their curls and look at Sally, with raised eyebrows, saying Sue Ellen didn't hurt them when she pulled out the rollers.

That was enough for Sue Ellen. She decided after three months to attend classes at the Continental Beauty School. Mabel knew one day Sue Ellen would want to be her own boss. Then where would that leave Mabel? "I should never have encouraged Sue Ellen. It's all my doing," Mabel muttered to the head below her.

Subtly, slowly, Sue Ellen created a new image. She had her hair cut and permed at the school. The ladies who saw her every week likened her to a fall chrysanthemum, as her hair took on a golden glow. Lipstick emphasized the lushness of her lips and a bit of gray on her eyelids made her blue eyes sparkle like they held a happy secret.

Even Tom couldn't completely ignore the change. The long earrings dangling from her ears, tinkled like silver bells as she glided around the house. Her drab, cotton dresses were replaced with bright skirts and tops,

Pieces of the Tapestry

and even tight pants crept into her wardrobe. He heard her hum under her breath as she did the dishes and scrubbed the kitchen floor. Tom would sometimes feel her staring at him, studying him, looking at him as if she had never seen him before. Sometimes she would come into his shop, talk to him some nonsense, and touch him as if seeing if he was real.

When he asked her, "Ain't you tired from all that woman talk, and standing on your feet all day?" she only smiled.

What would she have said if just once he would have raised his eyes and encouraged her to speak, he now wondered. He was afraid she would have spoken of lonesomness, longing for more than she had. If they had talked, would she have been content to stay with the grandbaby while their daughter went back to work? Would she have still taken the job with that woman?

"What's she hiding?" Mabel wondered, as the morning dragged on. "This sure ain't like the Sue Ellen I've known. If I didn't know better, I'd say it was a man."

By 10:30, Mabel was getting a little upset, wondering why Sue Ellen hadn't shown up, or even bothered to call. She doubted that Tom would know anything but got on the phone with him any way. Who else could she call, Mary Louise? Maybe she was a little tart with him, but he also got on her nerves.

"Sue Ellen too sick to use the phone?"

"What do you mean Mabel? She was feeling the same as she feels every morning. How come you think she's sick?"

"Well, you tell me why else she didn't show up this morning. This, my busiest day?"

"I don't understand what you're saying Mabel. Sue Ellen did what she does every Friday." In his slow drawl, he explained, "We ate breakfast together, then I seen her put the empties in the back of the wagon. She waved, then drove off like she always does every Friday."

Mabel could almost see him scratch his head with his greasy fingers. In a querulous tone, he went on about his routine of going out to his shop, which was still in his back yard. "I don't see her when she comes back with the groceries. She never asks me to help her. Never! She left me my lunch as usual. I ain't expecting her back till supper time."

"Well, don't wait supper for her old man," Mabel screamed at him, as if trying to shatter his placid demeanor. "Her station wagon is standing

Pieces of the Tapestry

empty in the Red Apple parking lot since this morning, and she never showed for work. Do you hear what I'm saying? She's gone off some place. Ask your daughter if she knows where her mamma is. Then give me a call back." She slammed the phone down in his ear.

Mary Louise became hysterical. She didn't know where her momma could be. What could she do if anything happened to her? Maybe she had been kidnapped.

By nine that night, the sheriff deputy's spiral note book was filled with all kinds of squiggles. He had questioned everyone who had seen Sue Ellen that day.

No one had a recent picture of Sue Ellen. Tom carried a wrinkled one taken when they were first married twenty years ago. He couldn't say what she was wearing that morning or remember if she mentioned going someplace before or after work. Jimmy Joe and Lally remembered a beige raincoat that enfolded her like a blanket.

Sally shook her head, trying to recapture the morning. "It was like any Friday Morning. I could set my watch by her. Mrs. Parish coming in at seven o'clock on the dot, waving her hand with the shopping list. Why she needed a shopping list, I don't know. She always seemed to buy the same things. I could have done her shopping for her."

She closed her worried eyes as if visualizing all the items in the shopping cart. "Sometimes she had coupons from the Sunday paper, cut real neat, and her check from Mabel, all ready to go. Mrs. Parish, was always sweet. I can hear her sayin, 'see y'all later. Have a good day,' as she went out with Jimmy Joe." By then, tears had inched down both sides of her pugged nose.

His cronies at the ELKS had teased on how Sue Ellen was getting younger and Tom was getting older. They gave him a friendly punch on the back and warned, "Watch out Tom. Somebody's gonna steal her away."

"No, she ain't kidnapped," Tom thought, "it's something worse then that." He hadn't watched out and now she was gone. His shoulders became more rounded with each question, and the baby's crying added to his burden. Mabel sat twitching across from him on the relic of a sofa that Sue Ellen had recovered with a bright flowered print.

"What about the folks at the beauty school?" Mabel asked, wanting to take over the investigation herself.

Pieces of the Tapestry

She was told by the deputy that Sue Ellen had come in on Monday, Tuesday and Thursday, as always. "The director, well he had gone to visit his Daddy in Florida, and couldn't be contacted either."

The deputy went on to say, "Oh, he did, did he?"

A picture formed in Mabel's mind, but she said nothing. Maybe they would figure out the scenario for themselves.

The local television station pitched in with a shot of Tom holding his old unrecognizable picture of his wife. Tears poured down his wrinkled cheeks as he pleaded for her return. A few stations in Florida said they would show it during the news. The Reverend Wheeler from the Baptist church said they would all say special prayers for that special lovely lady.

♍ ♒ ♋ ■ ♑ ♏

Sue Ellen sat on a wooden porch that faced the warm blue waters of the Gulf of Mexico. She was far from the turmoil and the wintry blast of cold wind that tore through her home town. The morning sun warmed her body through her thin nightdress and she imagined it was the loving touch of Porter Harris that had burned her naked flesh yesterday and all last night. This was the first time she had seen the ocean. This was the first time any man had touched her that way.

She heard the screen door close and rested her cheek against his hand which he placed on her shoulder when he walked out, then moved down to her full breast. Her face flushed. She was almost ashamed of her reaction to this man who had so recently come into her life. Here she was another man's wife, a mother, and grandmother, acting like a cheap young girl from a modern romance story.

As she returned his kisses, she slipped out of her gown and followed his strong, tall, nude body into the water. They splashed and rolled like dolphins in their private beach, until he laughed, "Come on kid, I need some real food. Let's go eat."

Porter played music on his father's record player, as she sat on a stool listening, watching him cook. She had never heard anything but country rock. This, he said was Beethoven describing a day like the one they had shared yesterday, today and would have tomorrow and tomorrow. She was always learning something new from him about him.

Was it only yesterday that she had been born again? She had felt this rebirth the moment they drove up the sandy beach to this old house that belonged to Porter's father. She was like a child at her first birthday party, laughing as they emptied the trunk of food and the clothes he had bought for her on the way down to Florida. She could hardly wait to put her perishables away, slip into her tiny bikini and race Porter into the ocean.

He carried her out and floating under a perfect sky, he made love to her for the first time. Her heart and body pounded like the surf as they rode each other and the breakers. Later, exhausted, they lay together in the cool bedroom with only the sound of the breeze whistling through the half-closed louvers.

When she opened her eyes, the world beyond the window looked all purple, pink and gold. The colors seeped into the room, splashing across the bed as Porter's fingers stroked her arms. When she stirred, his lips against her ear poured out a litany of how he had fallen in love with her that first day when she had stepped hesitantly through the door of the beauty school.

He had taught her more than the art of hairdressing. He had become her mentor, courting her with words, a gentle touch, laughter. His eyes would crinkle up when he teased her about being an old granny.

It amazed Sue Ellen how Porter listened, making sense of whatever she said. Patiently, he explained the mysteries of life that she had never encountered before. He laughed at her jokes, but never at Sue Ellen. Those emerald eyes, his touch, told her how precious she was to him.

"Tell Tom you're going away with a friend. He won't mind," he had coaxed her, after she had been at the school for three months. "Tell him about my father's house at the beach. Just don't mention my name," he grinned. "Take something for yourself Sue Ellen. One weekend in paradise, just one romantic weekend."

At first she had been shocked by his proposal, and had brushed his suggestion away. As he became more persistent, she began watching Tom, talking to him, touching him. He never seemed to notice. So she never told Tom. She truly believed that he would never miss her. She could never talk about such things to Mabel.

Only to Porter could she talk. "Talk to me, Porter. I love you talking to me. Tell me some more about your folks. Tell me about when

Pieces of the Tapestry

you were little and those stories about when you were in the army," she sighed with contentment. "You know, I guess that's why I love working in the beauty parlor. All those ladies are so free with words, saying things I never heard before. They tickle me with their talk." Her lips curved into a smile. "They're like you, not ashamed to say the most secret things out loud, and when they say it, it sounds just right." She turned in his arms to look at him.

"Tom never talks much. It's like living in a desert." She slowly picked out words to describe her life. "He planted me some flowers against the kitchen wall, and they're shaded by the roof. They never get enough sun or rain, and I have to go out every day and water them, but it never seems to help. They wilt, and die. I cry for the poor flowers," she sighed softly. "I cry for me."

She ran her hands across his face, feeling his strong hawk like nose; her finger lingered in the cleft of his chin, and caressed his strong lips. She wanted to keep an imprint of his high cheek bones burnished from their day in the sun; and his deep set dark eyes speckled with yellow. Her palms brushed his close cut curls that felt crankily under her hand. She longed for the very feel of him to stay with her, to cherish when he would be just a memory. Sue Ellen felt tears prickling her eyes.

"You're like the ocean," she whispered, "pouring into me, with words and touches that make me blossom like my flowers do only after a storm."

♍︎♒︎♋︎■♑︎♏︎

Sue Ellen woke the next day to Porter's cheerful whistling from the kitchen as he put on the coffee and scrambled eggs. She stretched and smiled, then followed the sounds to where he waited for her. She put bread in the toaster, then turned on the television that sat on the counter.

"I never had a TV in the kitchen." Her laugh caught in her throat like a fish bone as Tom's face broke out on the screen.

Tears ran down like runnels on Tom's face, and his voice crackled as he begged, "Whoever took my beloved wife, please bring her back safe to me."

Shocked, Sue Ellen listened as Tom told the world something he had never told her, even in their most intimate moments.

Pieces of the Tapestry

"I love you Sue Ellen," he cried. Tom pulled out a picture of a fifteen year old girl that no one would recognize as Sue Ellen.

Mary Louise's face swam next to his, clutching her crying baby. "Momma, if you hear us, please come home."

Guilt growled at her like a hungry dog as she listened and watched her family plead to her. Sue Ellen had always felt invisible around Tom. A woman wants to be noticed, not just needed. Mabel must have called him to ask where she was. Mabel was more like her mother than her own mother had been.

"I guess she was worried," was Sue Ellen's first thought. Sue Ellen pointed a trembling finger at the television set. "Porter, that's my family. I must call them, let them know I'm well and alive. Oh God, so alive. "

"Sue ..."

"Hush," she said sadly as he started to speak. "Tom's a good man. He's always been kind to me, even when everyone else turned their back to me."

She moved into Porter's arms, clinging to the man who had taught her about love. "This has been the best weekend of my life. No one has ever given me such a gift. I love you Porter, but I must first talk to Tom. If he wants me back, then I've got to go." Her voice was shaky. "If it's all right with you, we'll stay as long as we planned. It's just till tomorrow." She laughed wistfully, "I'd hate to drag all these groceries back home again."

⚥

Pieces of the Tapestry

Sparkling waves entice
Speckled dancers to purple
Fury of white sands.
1

-Elizabeth Bowers-

ONE WATER WAY
by
Elizabeth Bowers

Delica Imoudu's eyes were dim lights shinning through the tinted glass doors of the Gantry Inn. July sun caressed the eastern horizon, but the lobby was already a buzzing hive of activity. People of varying sizes and skin tones, dressed in the pale green uniforms of the Bhontu Rangers milled about in clusters.

"Goodness, I didn't know we were supposed to wear uniforms," she whispered through clenched teeth. Delica smoothed out the wrinkles in the floral sun-dress clinging embarrassingly to her medium frame. She stepped to the right of the automatic opener and walked through the big glass double doors, her green and gold regulation briefcase in tow.

Smiling broadly, Delica showed her Bhontu identification badge to the two guards standing at attention near the entrance. She decided not to worry about being out of uniform and held her head erect as she made her way down the plush burgundy carpet.

A tall, slender woman with nut brown skin like Delica's, in a loosely fitting uniform, stood behind the registration desk. Her soft black eyes flashed as she cast a glance at Delica. "I thought you said the other day that you were going to be here by first light. Everybody else managed to get here a while ago," she snapped, head shaking and right foot tapping impatiently.

Delica smiled broadly and winked at the woman. Gold hoop earrings dangled as she tilted sideways and set her briefcase on the carpet. Righting herself, she patted her long black hair into place. "That was my intention Sharna Banks. But half way around the bay, I realized I forgot my briefcase. Plus, I had to check on my luggage. I had it shipped so I wouldn't have to sail over here with it. A whole week without a change of clothing is a bit much ... even for a Bhontu Ranger, wouldn't you say? By the way, why didn't you tell me everybody was coming in uniform. I feel a little silly dressed like this." She tugged on the hem of her sun-dress. "Did my bags arrive yet? What about Tony? Have you seen him around?"

Laughing, Sharna ran a hand through tight curls dyed to match the morning sun in autumn just before rain clouds come to hide it. "Oh, I would have mentioned it but I thought you knew. Besides, you wore that outfit to impress Tony. Well too bad. He's got patrol duty today." Her modestly endowed lips curled up in a full face, knowing smile. She shoved an open book in front of Delica and handed her a pen that looked like a blue feather duster. "Your bags arrived hours ago. They're in your room, #544. What did you do about your briefcase?" Her laugh held a hint of mock sarcasm.

"Well, you know how the wind is in the morning. Nothing blowing and I'm stuck in my sailing dinghy." Delica absently flipped through the pages of the registration book. "My engine was down, no gas. I had to row all the way back through morning fog."

"I'll bet that took a little bit of time," Sharna interrupted.

"When I finally got back to my apartment, I had to fidget around for my keys. My briefcase wasn't in my room where I thought I'd left it. I had to go to the security office for help. Tanika Henry was on duty."

Sharna tossed her head aside. "Was she able to uproot herself from her perch long enough to be of any help?" Sharna feigned a laugh.

"Of course. We split up to look for it. I looked all over the complex and the grounds." Delica's tone was serious. "No luck."

Sharna leaned over the counter top and peered down at Delica's briefcase. "Well, I see you've got it with you."

Thin lines formed across Delica's forehead. "Yes, thanks to Tanika. She found it about a half mile into the woods that ..."

"The woods bordering One Water Way?" interrupted Sharna.

"Exactly. Whoever stole it, apparently couldn't get the lock opened.

"So they just tossed it on to a grassy bower, " Sharna finished.

Delica put a hand to her brow in exasperation. "How do you know what I'm gonna say before I get the words out of my mouth? That is so annoying! Did Tanika call ahead?" Three extended fingers tapped protectively against the gold security lock protruding from the front side of her briefcase.

Sharna raised an arched eyebrow. "Something strange is going' on around here," she said with an air of mystery. You're about the eighteenth ranger that's been hit this way today. The other briefcases were recovered from the same woods. Nothing apparently missing." She leaned forward, a hand cupping her rounded chin, eyes staring intently at Delica's suitcase.

Delica stepped in closer to the desk and placed the palms of her hands on the counter top. Her high cheek bones sagged, giving way to a worried frown. "Strange." Her tone was thoughtful.

Shrugging her shoulders, Sharna slid the registration book in front of Delica. "You haven't signed yet."

Delica's dark brown eyes narrowed slightly, as she studied her friend. "By the way, why is my partner working the desk? Where are Derrick and Kevin? They usually handle the desk for these training sessions." Delica's long, slender fingers gripped the pen as she moved with exaggerated quickness, precisely and efficiently, then signed with a flourish, on the last free space.

Sharna shrugged indifferently. "Derrick went home sick yesterday."

"Well what about Kevin? Where is he?"

"He hasn't reported in yet. Maybe he's sick too. Must be something going around. Anyway, Chief Taylor asked for a volunteer to work the desk." Sharna stood up straight, both arms raised toward the marble ceiling, and eyes shut tight.

"You volunteered?" Delica looked openly surprised.

Sharna let her hands fall onto the counter top and opened her eyes wide in mock indignation. "No. I got volunteered. I was in the restaurant trying to wake myself up with black coffee and a sweet roll, minding my own business, when it happened. So here I am." A looked of exaggerated fury spread across her round face.

Delica rolled her eyes at Sharna, then laughed. "Well now that everybody's here, you're no longer needed on the desk. Come on with me. Since you're so eager to volunteer for things, you might as well help me unpack. Oh, by the way, I wore this dress to keep cool, not to impress Tony," said Delica.

"Sure you did," Sharna said with a laugh. I'll believe that the day the sea turns to sulfur."

♍︎ ♒︎ ♋︎ ■ ♑︎ ♏︎

Delica spent the better part of the morning in the lobby mapping out strategies for besting the other teams during field training while playing bid whist with Sharna and other members of her watch patrol. Delica's mind was only half way on the game. Between making books and adding up game points she kept an eye out for Tony Philips. She thought about how much she liked him and how nice it would be to sip fruit coolers alone with him on the beach before the training week was up.

The blue owl clock nestled between the limestone statue of the Hindu goddess Durga, and the imposing presence of the Greek God Poseidon, chimed eleven times. The card game broke up and Delica turned and headed for the staircase.

She looked up and saw a burly man in an officer's uniform, waddling down the stairs. "Good morning Chief Taylor." Delica held her position at the foot of the stairs while he squeezed past her.

"Morning Imoudu. Good seein' ya again." Chief Taylor rolled his fat walnut colored fingers into a pudgy fist, and gave Delica a friendly tap on the side of her face. "Not time to go to your room yet. I've got an important announcement to make first."

With an affirmative nod, Delica ducked out of his way and retreated back into the main lobby. She watched as the Chief took his place behind the long registration desk. He reached out a flabby arm and picked up a silver gavel. His dark eyes formed into a squint as he tapped it loudly three times on the marble counter.

Chief Taylor gave the patrol rangers a stern look. "All right, listen up." He pulled out a long scroll, unraveled it with great fan-fare and read out loud, in piercing tones, the long list of training rules.

The rangers stood at attention, feet together and arms down straight at their sides, as he spoke.

"Remember now, I'm counting on each and every one of you to be on time for every exercise. I want your best efforts during training." The Chief rubbed the woolly, salt and pepper beard framing his pudgy face.

"We're doing something a little different this year. Need to strengthen public relations so the Council has invited the citizens of One

Water Way to come and view some of our training exercises. This means each patrol's gonna have to compete publicly as a team against every other patrol. I think the big thing everybody in town is talking about is the Hunt. You all know the rules. You start at first light. Check the bulletin board in the main lobby for team assignments. It'll be posted by then." He walked from behind the desk and stood directly in front of Delica, his eyes boring sternly into hers. "Everybody in field uniforms. Understand?" he said through clenched teeth. We gotta get going with this thing."

The Chief's serious expression evaporated. A teasing smile took its place. "But, in the meantime, you all get on to your sessions." He eased back behind the registration desk and picked up the silver gavel. "Then this evening, I want all of you out on the beach behind the inn for a big bash. It's gonna be a beach party. Beer and barbecue."

A roaring cheer went up from the rangers. It was quickly silenced by the hard tapping of Chief Taylor's gavel.

"Hey, wait a minute rangers, listen up! You need to be in field uniforms in time for the first session." He glanced around at the clock, then turned back around. "It begins in exactly fifteen minutes. Get to it." His voice boomed loud and brassy, as though aided by a microphone.

♍ ♒ ♋ ■ ♑ ♏

In the mellow afterglow of the day, Delica enjoyed the comforting feel of the warm beach sand on her bare feet as she made her way to the water's edge. Purple night rose like a delicate bird in full flight. Orange sun hugged the western horizon, its brightness fading. "What do you want to do first Sharna?" she asked, stopping just short of the water line, legs wide apart, eyes fixed on the sparkling waves caressing beige sand.

A spray of water carried by an untamed puff of wind, landed on Sharna's tongue. "Hum. That's odd. The water has a strong taste. I don't remember that being the case before." She held her tongue out in the hope of getting another drop of water from a kindly breeze.

Concerned, Delica bent down and reached a cupped hand into the warm, shallow water. She straightened, tipped her head forward into her hands and breathed deeply. "Ugh, it smells like rotten eggs." She stuck her tongue into the water and grimaced. "Your right Sharna. This stuff doesn't tastes like any sea water I've every had. Something's wrong! It's as though somebody poured a whole bunch of chemicals into it." She squinted

Pieces of the Tapestry

against the glare of the fading sun as it sent shimmering orange speckles dancing in splashing little waves upon purple waters. The smell of freshly popping corn, and roasting beef ribs, filled the air with enticing aromas, hiding the potency of the chemicals.

Sharna's eyes widened. "Great Durga! I was only kidding this morning when I made that crack about the sea turning to sulfur ... I've got an idea," she said excitedly, folding her arms into a cross upon her chest. "We're not on duty now. Let's not make a big issue out of the river water just yet. Chief Taylor told us to party, and that's exactly what we should do. Come on. There's a sand sculpting contest going on right now. You're the best at that. What do you say we build one together. Guaranteed first place. Greek or Roman gods and goddesses only."

In need of a diversion from the intensity of the day Delica gave in to Sharna's pleading. Her reflective mood changed into one of playfulness as she reached a well-formed, arm up and tapped Sharna gently on the shoulder, her feet digging into wet, gritty sand. "Great idea. Let's do it." Smiling, Delica squatted and maneuvered herself beneath a nearby beach umbrella, red with black stars, like the one piece swim suit clinging to her slender frame.

"First I'm gonna go get something to drink. Do you want anything?" Sharna asked, taking a step backward in readiness to leave.

"If they've got any strawberry crush ... I'd like some of that." Delica squatted and let her fingers play in the sand as she watched Sharna race off to the refreshment table.

She arched her back and stretched the tension out of her neck, glad to be sitting on sand made tolerably warm by the sun's retreat. The thought of the Hunt scheduled for morning didn't go well with the intense heat of the season. At that moment, Delica did not feel like being an efficient ranger. Her mind was on Tony's warm smile. She wondered what it would be like to feel his arms around her waste, his lips pressing against her own.

♍︎♒︎♋︎■♑︎♏︎

When Sharna did not return right away, Delica decided to get started alone. She went to work near water's edge, molding beach sand into the shape of the goddess of victory as the cooling spray gently soothed her hot flesh.

Pieces of the Tapestry

Six men, faces covered with a tangled rainbow of thick stage makeup, came dancing up the beach. They were dressed as grasshoppers with green wings opened wide. A seventh man joined them. He wore the plumage of a giant blue jay over a hefty frame. He stood to the side of the others and strummed an old fashioned lyre, as they sang along. "A merry old owl sat in a tree with a base guitar upon his knee ..."

Delighted, Delica gleefully joined in the singing in full voice.

"And sang a silly song about a bumblebee ..."

After they left, in the soft light of the half moon, Delica put the finishing touches on the five foot goddess. A warm hand pressed the small of her back sending a shower of luxurious tingles racing to the pit of her stomach. She titled her head around and smiled into warm dark eyes.

"Tony Philips. Good to see you but you shouldn't sneak up on me like that." She wondered if he noticed the blush building up on her face. "I might have decked you," Delica said, fluttered. "What's with the uniform? This is supposed to be a beach party."

Tony's pouting lips stretched into a broad smile. "True, but everybody can't play. Besides, something's going on. It's pretty serious." His look was contemplative as he surveyed Delica's handiwork. "Nice calves," he said, awkwardly smoothing the sandy leg of Athena. "Delica, you've really got a knack for this sand sculpting business."

Tony's face was like almonds touched by the favor of the sun in late fall. Delica blushed more from his nearness than from his complement. "Thanks Tony. I've been doing this forever. It's fun," she replied.

In the half light of the moon, Tony's eyes flashed like large black pearls in full sun. Delica shuddered as his hot breath teased the pit of her stomach. She turned her head aside and looked to the vastness of the shimmering horizon instead of at him. "Are you going to be on duty for the whole week?" she asked, her eyes still surveying the water to hide her desire for him.

Before he could answer, Sharna came racing back from the refreshment table. "Sorry it took me so long. Guess what? There is a sign posted on the far end of the pier saying NO RECREATIONAL SWIMMING. Delica, maybe we were right about the water." Sharna's voice was brimming over with excitement. She eyed Tony, waiting for his verification.

Pieces of the Tapestry

The peace of the night was broken by the angry sound of a woman shrieking obscenities. Delica turned in the direction of the noise. There, bent over the ramp leading to the wash-house, was a heavy set woman in a dress that looked gray against the backdrop of night sky. It was the cook who worked in the main dining room of the inn.

Tony's thick brows came together as he tugged on the edges of his uniform jacket. He stood to his full 6'2" and made ready to investigate the cause of the cook's distress. He put a hand on Delica's bare shoulder. "Before Sharna interrupted, I was going to invite you to have coffee with me when I go on break but it doesn't look like I'm going to get a break now. I'd better go see what's wrong with cook." He flashed an apologetic smile at her, then turned and started walking toward the ramp, one hand holding tightly to the stick at his side.

"See you later," called Delica. Her shoulder still tingled from the magic of his gentle touch. A delicious feeling engulfed her as she watched him make his way to the ramp. "I hope the fates will be good to me in the morning and assign you to my Hunt team," she whispered too low for Tony to hear.

♍︎ ♒︎ ♋︎ ■ ♑︎ ♏︎

Delica and Sharna made their way through the crowded groups of beach partiers. They took the long way around under the pier leading to the boat docks. The flood lights from the pier were strongest there. A sound like the loud bickering of birds, made them stop in their tracks.

"Isn't that Derrick over there?" Delica pointed to a figure standing near a runabout at water's edge. "Oh my gosh! Kevin is with him. Delica crouched behind the wooden trusses, out of sight, and peered through a crack in the planking of the pier to investigate the ruckus. She nudge Sharna to get down beside her. "Look. I think that is Derrick over there."

Sharna squinted her eyes for a better look. "Great Durga! If I'm not mistaken, that's Kevin with him," she whispered, "loading boxes onto that runabout." She put a hand to her mouth.

From out of the fog, came a man who stood like a Georgia pine waving in hurricane force winds, blood dripping from his face. "Gimmi one of dem clips man. I gotta git dis thang ta work or we ain't gonna make it." The man's accent was thick southern country, and his voice was slurred as though he were intoxicated.

Kevin reached into a box and pulled out something that looked like a stainless steel drapery pin and handed it to the man. Then the man disappeared into the fog. Derrick and Kevin dragged the runabout into the water.

Sharna pulled on Delica's arm. "For sick people, they seem to be getting on just fine. What do you suppose those two are up to?" she asked.

"I didn't recognize that guy they were with. I doubt if he is from One Water Way," replied Delica. She kept her eyes glued to them until they sped off into the foggy river.

Further down, Delica heard familiar voices. She surveyed the way ahead. Dr. Rainier, the head of the Bhontu research team, was standing under the pier like an aged penguin. Surrounding him, were six old men who looked like a gathering of whining seals. Their faces bled with outrage as they pointed pudgy fingers and waved plump hands in his face.

"Now look here, Rainier," yelled a short, fat man, bald except for a half ring of silver wool, extending from ear to ear around the back of his apple shaped head. "That was a stupid idea. Attaching those sensors to the bottom of the ranger's brief cases without letting them know about it."

"Yes," came a baritone voice from the crowd. "Every single clip is missing from the cases. You were the one with the stupid idea to put the clips on the cases in the first place. You were the one who said the rangers didn't have to know about them. Now they're gone. We've got to get those clips back before it's too late." The man's beak-like finger pecked away at Dr. Rainier's chest.

"And that's not all," yelled a tall, bearded man with coarse black hair growing out of his nose and ears. "Now on top of everything else, the river is polluted. Chief Taylor's got all the rangers laying around on their behinds on the beach. He doesn't have a clue about any of this. You'd better get it under control before he finds out." The man's voice held a menacing edge.

"And don't forget the caves in the lee of One Water Way," yelled the short, fat man, poking out his massive stomach to pen in Dr. Rainier.

Sharna shifted nervously. "Let's get out of here before anyone sees us," she whispered.

Delica hesitated. "Okay ... but ... wait a second. That clip Dr. Rainier's holding up to the light. It's just like the one Derrick gave that man." She stretched forward for a closer look.

"Great Durga, Delica. What's the big deal about a clip that acts as a sensor? If they catch us spying on them, we'll be in real trouble," Sharna urged.

"No," said Delica, squinting. "That's no ordinary clip. You heard the man. It's important to them that they be found. Look how it shines so bright. We've got to find out what it is."

"But there is nothing we can do ..." Sharna's voice faded. Her head was cocked to the side as she stood at the edge of the water-line. "Listen," she whispered. "Sounds like a snake wriggling in very dry sand."

"Quiet," Delica whispered, putting a hand to her lips. "Somebody's coming ..."

A hand covered Delica's mouth, startling her. A burning sensation in her neck made her wince. She struggled to put a hand to the spot but fell to the ground, unable to stop the flood of deep night consuming her essence.

♍ ♒ ♋ ■ ♑ ♏

Delica opened her eyes and quickly covered them with the palms of her hands to block the strong light streaming down from the overhead light. Through the cracks between her fingers, she surveyed her surroundings. A wave of nausea hit her as she lifted her head. "My God," she cried out. She lay on the blue carpet of her room in the Gantry Inn; swim suite still on, and blood trickling from the side of her head.

She forced herself to her feet and looked around. The bronze statue of Zeus that had sat on the mahogany table in front of the gray couch, now lay upside down near the closet. The mattress was split open, cotton everywhere. Blankets and sheets lay in a heap on the floor near the double window and every drawer was pulled out. The clothes that she had hung neatly in the closet, now lay strewn about the room, pockets turned inside out. Her regulation briefcase was gone. A blue feather lay where it had been.

Delica put a hand to the side of her face. "Good Athena! What happened to me. Her emotions soared like the tide at full moon.

Pieces of the Tapestry

Delica felt as though she were standing eyebrows high in a pool of hot water as she walked into the lobby and realized that she had barged into a meeting between Chief Taylor and his senior officers. "Sorry Sir," she said, eyes darting about the assembled group. She did not expect anyone to be roaming about so early. The sun would not be up for several hours.

By the serious looks on their faces, their eyes fixed on her, Delica judged that whatever they had been discussing was important enough to make them give up the balance of their night's sleep. She stood rigid, heals together, arms at her side, several feet away from the circular conference table that had been hastily set up in the lobby next to the marble statue of the god Zeus dressed in full battle gear.

Chief Taylor smiled slightly, nodded and waved a hand to invite Delica to join the meeting. "At ease Imoudu. We were hoping we'd get to you before you left for the Hunt."

Delica clicked her heals together and raised her arm in salute. "Sir?" She wondered if, somehow, they had found out about the robbery of her room last night. She had not had a chance to tell anyone about it yet.

Chief Taylor cupped his beard in his hand and sighed. "Afraid were gonna have to pull you off the scheduled Hunt. We got bad trouble here in One Water Way." He looked long and hard into Delica's eyes, a serious expression on his weathered brown face. "Lotta reports about rooms being ransacked last night while everybody was at the beach party. Briefcases and personal items were stolen, including mine. Only clues we got are a couple of blue feathers. We need you on a different kind of hunt. I'm pairing you up with Philips. Puttin' both of you in charge of heading up this special Hunt. Y'all gotta get to the bottom of this thing fast before there are any more robberies." With a fiery look in his narrow eyes, the chief scanned the assemblage through thick, brown rimmed glasses, as though searching their souls for any hint of disagreement with his decision to put Delica and Tony in charge of the special Hunt. "Banks and Fisher will assist."

Pieces of the Tapestry

When the meeting ended, Delica went straight to the coffee shop adjacent to the lobby. She was relieved to see Sharna seated at a table with Tony and Morgan, holding an ice bag to the side of her head. "Sharna, I'm so glad you're all right." She leaned forward and patted Sharna's shoulder affectionately.

Morgan Fisher sat with broad shoulders hunched forward, elbows resting on the table, a cup of steaming black coffee before him. "Imoudu. Haven't seen you in a while. What's going on?" He half rose from his seat.

Delica took the seat next to Tony. "A lot. The Chief just told me he wants us to handle a special Hunt." She turned to Tony and handed him a manila file with his name typed on it in red lettering. "We get to work together on this one." She smiled up at him, blushing.

Tony winked at her as his hand brushed up against hers. He opened the file and was silent for a moment as he read its contents. "You're right. Special orders for the Hunt." He looked at the orders and then at Delica. "I've been wanting to spend some time with you. This is my chance." He smiled at her and gently squeezed her arm.

The heavy-set Shop-keeper sauntered up to their table and handed Tony an envelope that smelled as though it had been dipped into a vat of lilac perfume. "Some guy just delivered this. He told me to give it to you."

Tony sat with his chair tilted back, and legs spread to either side of the table revealing high topped black boots that were at least a size twelve. His brow furrowed as he studied the contents of the envelope.

Delica and Tony exchanged pleasantries, as the shopkeeper waddled off. When he was out of earshot, she filled Tony and Morgan in on the events of last night. "So, what do you propose we do first Tony?" She glanced aside at him.

"You know the cook had me chasing down this guy she said stole her purse, then fled off in her car. Now this strange note. I wonder who it's from?" Tony shifted his gaze from Delica, back to the note in his hand.

Morgan had a look of adventurous excitement on his well defined features. He sat with broad shoulders hunched forward and elbows resting on the table. "Well what's it all about? Does it have anything to do with the Hunt?" His eyes, the color of pecans still on the tree in early fall, were fixed on Tony. His square jaw, held fast by large hands, was the color of sun-streaked beach sand.

Tony feigned a laugh, shaking his head. "It's a poem, believe it or not." He started reading it. *"While making my approach to the inn, I flew low over damp, dark caves. At the mouth of One Water Way River, Men dressed like gulls road high waves. I cut my engines in mid flight when I saw that they had broken the law. Stolen briefcases piled high in the stern, befouling the water with sin."* Tony shifted his gaze to Delica, a crooked half smile on his face. "What do you make of it?"

"If you ask me," interrupted Morgan, "it sounds like a lot of nonsense. Must of been someone trying to play a convention trick on you Pal." Morgan reared back on his chair, a look of irritation on his face.

Excited, Delica shifted in her chair. "I disagree. Obviously the author of the note knows about the stolen briefcases."

"Yes, as does everyone else in town," said Morgan, sarcastically.

Ignoring his comments, Delica went on to say, "I suspect that everything in the note is accurate. That part about befouling the water with sin, most likely has to do with the heavy concentration of sulfur in the river water ... also our drinking water."

Tony shifted in his chair and turned the note over. "And here it says ..."

"Oh for the love of Zeus! Give me a break," chimed in Morgan. "What kind of a nut writes stupid notes? Get over it Philips."

Tony sighed. "Come on Morgan." He read the other side of the note. *"Come fifty feet beneath the sea and be with me forever in my secrete paradise ... Silver clips and manta rays weave limestone future at my floral gate."* Tony surveyed Sharna and Morgan for a reaction before shifting his gaze to Delica. A crooked half smile played on his bronze face.

"We've got serious business here," said Delica.

Tony put an arm around Delica's shoulder and scooted his hips in close to her. "Tell you what, we're going to need to follow up on this. I say we go back to our rooms and change into sailing gear. Then we can meet down by the docks in half an hour and start checking things out."

The feel of his arm about her neck sent delicious tingling sensations up and down her spine. Delica forced a professional demeanor. "The only thing wrong with that is that the criminals don't work during the day. All of the thefts have occurred after moon rise. We'd be better off spending the day down at the marine sanctuary investigating the last part of that note. Later we can check out the water front," Delica replied.

♍︎ ♒︎ ♋︎ ■ ♑︎ ♏︎

As the afternoon sun melted into the horizon, Delica and Tony began scanning the marina area for clues. Sharna and Morgan followed close behind as they walked along the wooden docks to where the power boats and small sailing vessels trembled in breezes that drove wakes from ships under power rippling through waters.

As they were rounding the bend, Sharna tripped. She grabbed a hold of the wooden railing to break her fall. A green cosmetic bag lay on the dock next to her foot. She reached down and picked it up. "This is mine. I had it with me last night at the beach party," she said, alarmed. "How on earth did it get all the way out here?" She opened the gold clasp. "Rats! . Everything is gone. Even my new burgundy lipstick. Who'd want that?" She stepped in closer to Morgan and tugged on his shirt tail. "Let's go get those crooks."

With an admonishing look, Delica turned to Sharna and whispered, "Talk softly. We have to be very quiet. Can't risk being overheard." Delica could feel the grain of the wooden planks through the soft rubber of her sandals as she ambled along. "We're going to have to take a trip down river to the caves after we've had a look at the marine sanctuary," she said, eyes straight ahead.

Tony casually wrapped an arm around Delica's waist. "Yes, I believe you are right," he said in husky tones. "Sharna's cosmetic bag must have been tossed when whoever attacked the two of you made their get away, probably in a power boat."

♍︎ ♒︎ ♋︎ ■ ♑︎ ♏︎

Tony stood guard, rooted to the sticky wooden deck, as Delica skillfully attached the blue sail to the mast and boom and untied the mooring lines of the blue and white Bhontu motor-sailer. He watched as Morgan went off to help Sharna check the engine. "How long do you think it will be before we can take off?" Tony asked.

Delica threw the mooring lines into the sack in the stern of the boat, then turned to Tony. "There is a good wind blowing now. We'd better get underway before we lose it. "

The breeze grew strong beyond the delta, giving power to the sails but causing the vessel to heel mightily as Delica struggled with the wheel through the wind-chopped channel. The blood rose hot in her face. She caught sight of what looked to be a boat load of giant sea gulls in green caps and orange life vests. They zoomed by in a 26 foot speed boat; its true colors obscured by the fog. She was certain that they were the same group who serenaded her on the beach last night. She strained to see the vessel's CF numbers ... 3784.

As the wake of the speed boat rolled beneath it, the motor-sailor began to wallow vigorously. Sharna grabbed the handrail on the bow to keep from falling into the churned up frothy waters. She felt her stomach rise to meet her face. "Great Durga! Don't you know there are laws against speeding in protected waters fellows," she shrieked angrily, waving a hand in the air as though to drive the point home. "You almost knocked me off the boat!"

Morgan shook with quiet laughter as he watched Sharna rant and rage at the speed boat. He was an old hand at boating and did not feel the slightest bit of annoyance as the port side of the vessel where he stood, leaned into the water. He made his way around the outside of the boat and joined Sharna on the king plank. "Come on girl, get a hold of yourself. We'll have a lot bigger things to worry about on this trip. No time to be concerned about a little thing like a speed boat's wake," he whispered.

A blue feather like the ones found in the inn, landed in Sharna's hair. Morgan bent an elbow down and untangled the feather from her tight curls. His expression was serious as he twirled the feather in his hand. "We'd better go join the others and let them see this. You go on through the hatch and I'll go around like I came." He held her below the shoulders and guided her as she lowered herself into the mouth of the hatch, then made his way back around the outside of the vessel to the stern. "What do you guys make of this?" He handed the feather to Delica.

She sat low on the floor of the stern, mulling over the significance of the blue jay feather while at the same time, concentrating on the business at hand. Traffic was heavy on the river. Another wake came rolling in, much larger than the first. The motor-sailor heeled and rocked mightily. Delica grabbed the tiller and pulled back on it. "Morgan, grab those ropes and pull in on the jib. Sharna and Tony, I need your weight on the high side now." She shouted orders to her crew with a confidence born of early years on the high seas maneuvering through rough ocean waters.

Pieces of the Tapestry

Once the wake passed, the wild rocking subsided and Delica regained headway. "Wow, that was a rough ride," she said, wiping spray from her face. Excited, she smiled and her face glowed like freshly polished bronze in the filtered sunlight.

"I'll say. Great sailing Delica," said Tony genuinely impressed. "We almost toppled but you knew exactly what to do to keep the boat from tipping over. Even I am not that good under these conditions. How did you get so good?" He shifted his position onto the floor, facing away from the bow, establishing eye contact with her. The souls of his shoes butted up against hers and he felt the heat of her excitement.

Before Delica had a chance to answer, Morgan, chest puffed out, feigning modesty, chimed in, "I taught her, of course. I've been sailing all my life ... ever since I was a baby. She was a great student."

"Oh, is that so?" said Tony, in teasing tones. He glanced aside at Delica for a hint of verification.

Delica returned Morgan's teasing look. "Its true. Morgan taught me how to sail when we were kids. We grew up next door to each other, you know. Joined the patrol together too, right out of college, but that's a long story and we don't have time to get into it now." Her expression became serious as she leaned against the tiller and pointed the bow toward the open channel.

♍ ≈ ♋ ■ ♑ ♏

The sixty feet dive in full scuba gear through the coastal waters gave new energy to Delica as she swam among the colorful tropical reef fishes. Although she had visited other marine sanctuaries many times before, none could compare in beauty to this. Sea turtles followed swarming schools of fishes through brilliant corals as giant manta rays eyed the colorful colonial anemones. She felt at one with the universe as she feasted upon the beauty of the teaming biological diversity of the live bottom shore reef.

Several clusters of species that she'd never seen before, swam past her nose piece. The silver clips protruding from their tails were just like the one she'd seen under the pier. She maneuvered toward them and opened her specimen case, gently guiding a few of them inside.

Pieces of the Tapestry

Tony was just up ahead, wriggling past butterflies and angels browsing among the sponges and corals. Clusters of sea urchins surrounded him. He took a few samples, then turned and signaled to Delica to surface.

Darkness fell like a velvet blanket, hiding the crimson sky. As they headed back toward the channel, Delica felt little cause for comfort. Heavy fog rolled in making visibility a thing of the past. Not wishing to take unnecessary risks, she turned on the running lights and added power to the sails by turning on the engine. She was grateful that Morgan had fixed the compass light while she and Tony were foraging the sandy sea floor and the limestone reefs in search of clues. Now the compass heading was all they had to guide them down the cost to within a safe distance of the caves.

♍ ♒ ♋ ■ ♑ ♏

The full moon, half hidden by clouds, was the only light they allowed themselves as they quietly groped their way through the glade near the edge of the rocky shore-line.

"It's kind of spooky out here, don't you think." Delica's voice was a hushed whisper.

"You got that right," Morgan said. "The fog is so thick that I can hardly see the compass heading"

"Why would anybody want to hide stolen property way out in this God-forsaken place?" Needing comfort, Sharna let her hand brush slightly against Morgan's bare arm as she walked close at his side.

"Too bad we can't turn on a flashlight," Tony commented. "Can't give away the advantage."

As they climbed a steep hill, Delica thought she heard a sound, like that of a crane being raised to its highest position. A somber mood engulfed her as she turned in the direction of the noise. She stumbled over a rocky incline. Off balance, she reached out and grabbed Tony's hand.

Tony squeezed Delica's hand in a gesture of affection and forced himself to a lighter mood. "It seems to me that we're getting close. I've an instinct for these things, you know." He strained his eyes against a light, like that given off by a one-hundred-watt bulb, glowing up ahead.

Pieces of the Tapestry

"Come on you guys, lets follow that light." He gave Delica's hand a squeeze before releasing it.

They followed the light along a path through the gorge and down a hill. There, the power of the fog diminished. The night air wreaked of sulfuric acid mixed with choking smoke and another scent akin to body sweat from a team of athletes after a 26 mile run at a fast clip in the full strength of summer sun.

Sharna tugged on Morgan's shoulder. "Look Morgan. Over there." She pointed to a 26 foot speed boat on a trailer, hitched to a sports utility vehicle. Its color was kept secret by the absence of sufficient light. "Isn't that the speed boat that almost knocked me off our boat with its wake when we were still in protected waters?"

Delica put a hand to her forehead as she strained to get a good look at the vessel. "It sure is," she interrupted. "I memorized the CF numbers and those are exactly the same ... 3784."

"Somebody's bent over behind that tree." Morgan pointed to the tall oak tree to the right of the sports vehicle.

Delica pulled up the pair of binoculars that hung heavy about her neck, and peered through them for a look. In the clearing in front of the truck, she saw the familiar figure of a man, average in height and build, yet distinctive in mannerism. He was talking to a tall, thin man whose skin tone blended in with the night like purple softened by burnt sienna.

"All Right! It's Spencer and Youngblood. And that man we saw them with last night is standing over there." She pointed to the stern of the boat. "Look, they are loading boxes off the boat and into wheelbarrows. Aha! A couple of the boxes have come loose. One is open. Looks like its full of regulation Bhontu briefcases. Oh, and silver clips, too." Delica handed her binoculars to Tony. "Check it out."

Tony put the binoculars to his eyes. "You're right. Looks like we're in business. There is some kind of building cluster at the end of the path. That's where they are headed with the boxes." Morgan looked around cautiously. "They probably have weapons, so we'd better be on our guard."

"We're going to have to get inside that building somehow. I seriously doubt whether they'll invite us in, so we've got to find our own way," said Delica.

Pieces of the Tapestry

Sparse grass tickled her ankles as she led the way, out of sight of Kevin and Derrick. They moved with cautious precision through the protection of thickets bordering the dirt path leading to the rear of the building. Men in wet suits, carrying large specimen containers, crossed a wooden platform that served as a connecting link between the main building and a dark area behind it. Delica guessed it was an entrance to a cave. The lights dimmed before she could get a good look.

Tony moved in close to Delica and placed a hand on her back. "Looks like some kind of major operation. There are many more of them here than I thought," he said.

"Yes. I think you're right." Delica looked at the many dark forms moving about like shadows on a child's bedroom wall at night. "But so far, the only thing we can prove they're guilty of is stealing our personal items and brief cases and ransacking our rooms," replied Delica.

"Listening devises, I understand. But what kind of operation needs lipstick and used hair brushes?" put in Sharna.

"A lot of the tropical reef fishes have tiny silver clips like the ones we saw under the pier, stuck through their tails. We've got samples on the boat to take back to the Research lab. Dr. Rainier knows something about the clips because, remember, he had one in his hand last night." Delica wondered just how much the good Doctor knew but kept her suspicions to herself.

"Great Zeus! They've got all kinds of guards along the bridge," said Morgan.

"It doesn't matter. We still have to get in there. It's the only way to collect solid evidence and find out who is behind all this. Morgan, you and Sharna stay here out of sight and keep an eye on what's going on. Tony, come on with me," said Delica.

"Right. We'll keep in touch by radio." Morgan scooted in close behind the thick hedge.

Sharna knelt beside Morgan. "We'll call for backup if we see anything conclusive."

Pieces of the Tapestry

Delica and Morgan made their way through the thick woods to the right of the building and down the glade near the rocky shore line. They sloshed through pools of water and mud as they grouped along through the dark haze.

"Great gods, visibility is terrible." Delica looked over her shoulders. I feel like I'm walking on the edge of a star ship in a sunless part of the galaxy. What about you?"

"It's rough. We gotta go on though," replied Tony.

As they climbed a steep hill, Delica thought she heard a noise like rushing water. An odor, like that of rotting eggs, was sickeningly strong. She put a hand to her nose and turned toward the sound. Something rough and hard hit her foot. She stepped backwards, stumbled, and fell to her knees. Her left knee burned like fire as it met a jagged rock in a pool of murky liquid. She forced herself to hold back the scream rising in her throat.

Tony rushed to her side. "Are you all right Delica?" he whispered.

"Yes, but my knee isn't. I've got to rest for a little while." Delica groped around her immediate area. The feel of muck caressing her hand made her pull back and look. Near the edge of the slime, she saw a familiar sparkle. "Tony, look. That's one of those clips." She lend sideways and fished the clip out of the slime.

In her excitement, she accidentally touched her hurt knee with the clip. "Well for goodness sakes." Delica looked at her knee in astonishment. "This clip seems to have healing properties. The minute I touched my hurt knee with it, the burning sensation went away."

"Let me have a look at that," said Tony. "It looks like it's made of silver but it doesn't feel exactly like any metal I've ever held." Tony rubbed the clip over the calluses on his palm. He gave out with a slight laugh. "Well it can't cure calluses. They're still here."

Delica reached into her side pocket and pulled out a handkerchief. As she whipped the slime off that had accumulated on her knee, a thought came to her. "Maybe it only works with the slime. Might be that there's an alloy in the clip that, when acted upon by something in the slime, has a beneficial effect on skin." She took Tony's hand and rubbed the handkerchief full of slime over his calluses. "Now rub the clip over it and see what happens."

Pieces of the Tapestry

"Wow! You're right." Tony held out his hand to Delica. "The calluses are all gone. This is great stuff."

"The clips must have something to do with that top secrete underwater project involving pharmaceuticals. Obviously somebody found out about it. That must be why Dr. Rainier and the others were so upset under the pier last night." The thought held tight to her mind.

Tony wet his lips and drew in a deep breath. "Well, that ties in to what I overheard last night when I was making my rounds. I didn't think much about it then because it was just some of the guys who work in the kitchen talking about it."

Delica's curiosity was peeked. "So what did they say?"

"You remember when the cook had her fit on the pier?"

Delica laughed softly. "Yes. She was pretty upset about something."

"Anyway, I walked her back to the restaurant to take her statement. Just as I was getting ready to leave through the rear exit, I heard a couple of the kitchen helpers talking. They said that a group of our top scientists have been conducting experiments to determine how environmental changes on shore are affecting sea life. In the process they accidentally discovered an alloy that, in the presence of specially treated silver, becomes a healing agent with ten thousand times the power of aloe."

Delica's look was serious. "So many of the reef fishes had clips attached to their fins. That must be part of what they're working on down there. But whoever has stolen the clips probably has no idea about the slime. This place is full of that stuff. If they knew its value, it certainly wouldn't have been thrown out like bad garbage."

♍︎ ♒︎ ♋︎ ■ ♑︎ ♏︎

The interior of the cave was artificially lighted, revealing an underground landscape filled with colorful, strangely shaped rock formations. A giant waterfall emptied into a well-lighted salt water lake teaming with life that rivaled the marine sanctuary Delica and Tony had visited earlier.

Green slime oozed through a copper pipe propelled by a nuclear powered engine. Delica followed the flow of slime to a dimly lighted

Pieces of the Tapestry

chamber that had the look of other caves in the area. The rotting eggs smell was stronger here than on the beach.

"Come on Tony," she called, "let's see what's going on back here."

Tony looked around, then scowled. "It's a lot to cover. Maybe we should call Philips and Banks. Let them know where we are."

Delica reached around and pulled her radio out of her back pocket. "We're going to need extra teams out here to investigate what's going on."

As Delica turned to press the call button on her radio, she heard an anguished cry, like that of a wounded animal. "Tony, did you hear that?" She teetered and stretched her hands to break her fall, palms firmly on the damp marble floor.

A moving pile lay prostrate on the floor against the wall in front of her. Delica let herself drop to her knees. She placed one hand over her mouth and pointed to the heap before her with the other.

Tony reached out a hand, and helped Delica to her feet. "Let's go check it out," he said.

Tony pulled back the blood soaked blankets. His eyes flashed horror. "It's Tanika! She's been in a blaze of a fight. Somebody really did a job on her face. It's pretty messed up."

Blood oozed from her chest. "My God! Looks like she's been shot in the chest. Look at that." Delica pointed to the puncture in Tanika's shirt below the breast pocket. "She's been shot but she's still breathing."

Delica felt her heart racing as she tore open the front of Tanika's shirt to expose the wound. "Quick Tony. Grab a fist full of that slime and hand it to me. Maybe we can save her life with this clip."

Tony stuck a finger in the slime and held it for a few seconds. "I don't know. This is not like it was with your knee. She's bleeding pretty bad."

Delica acted on blind instinct, first smearing the wound inside and out with the green slime, then moving the silver clip inside the open flesh. As Tanika's breathing became steady, Delica looked aside at Tony. "I think she's going to make it."

Tony's answering look was one of astonishment. "That's some powerful stuff we stumbled on," he whispered. "Here, let me try some on her face." He rubbed slime gently over Tanika's face, then the clip.

After a short while, Tanika regained consciousness and sat up. "Delica. Tony. Boy am I glad to see you guys!"

"Who did this to you?" Delica asked.

"Derrick and Kevin. They're the ones!" She covered her face with her hands and sobbed softly.

Delica put a comforting arm around her shoulder. "Looks like they've been really busy. Got any idea what it's all about?"

Tanika moved her hands from her face, chestnut in the dim light. She fixed her dark eyes on Delica. "I had rounds third shift. I found you and Sharna under the pier last night, out cold. I went for help. Derrick and Kevin were hanging around down by the docks. I told them what happened. They offered to help so I let them"

Delica raised an arched eyebrow. "I wondered how I got back to my room."

Tony rubbed a hand across his throat. "So how did that lead to this?" he asked.

"As I was leaving Delica's room, I saw them rushing down the hall with arm loads of regulation brief cases. I tried to question them but they pushed me aside. They were too fast for me. I went into the coffee shop to use the phone to call the chief. I couldn't believe my eyes when I saw the cook trying to stuff a green purse into a box full of stuff, like tubes of lipstick and used hair brushes, and other stuff that looked like it might of come from the rooms."

Tony's eyebrows shot up. "The cook? I thought something was funny with her last night. I had the feeling she was faking that robbery business."

Delica looked aside at Tony. "A lot was going on under the pier last night. She was probably trying to create a diversion." She looked back at Tanika. "So what else?"

Tanika clasped her hands together and pressed them against her chest. "Anyway, the next thing I knew, I was lying on the floor of a speed boat. Derrick was at the helm and Kevin had his knee in my stomach, waving a gun in my face."

Delica scooted in close. "Did you get a look at what they had in the boat?"

"Yes. When they stopped near the end of the pier to pick up the cook." Tanika stretched her neck. "Boxes. Ranger brief cases. I couldn't see what else."

Pieces of the Tapestry

Delica got to her feet and peered into the stream of flowing slime. "I can believe that the cook and those two are capable of pulling off these burglaries, but I'd be willing to bet they're working for somebody else. Much more than robbery and attempted murder went on last night."

Tony helped Tanika to her feet. "Where did they take you in the boat?"

"I couldn't tell you how to get there exactly because I was on the floor the whole time. I couldn't see. But when we got off the boat, they drug me down this wooden draw bridge and into a building that looked like some kind of heavy manufacturing plant. A tall, dark guy greeted us. I couldn't really see his face because my eyes were very swollen, but I could tell that he had on a white smock over dark colored trousers. To tell you the truth, his thick Jamaican accent sounded a lot like Dr. Rainier. Anyway, he asked them if they got all the clips. They said they did, but wanted the ten million dollars he'd promised them first. He told them to get rid of me and then they'd get paid. The last thing I remember is Derrick pointing a gun at my chest." Tanika shudder visibly, and put a hand to her chest.

Delica patted Tanika's back supportively. "This is all we need to close in on that place." She pressed the voice activation button on her radio. "Sharna. Delica here."

"Hey. Did you guys make it to the caves? Sharna's voice was an excited whisper.

"Yes, and we got everything we need. Better make that call for backups now." Delica spoke softly into the mouth piece.

"Done. They already wired us a search warrant. Everyone's in place."

"Great," Delica said. "Move in now. Take the lot of them into custody and search the place. I think you'll find the stolen items in there along with some other very interesting stuff."

♍︎♏︎♋︎■♑︎♍︎

Later that evening, Delica and Tony reported their findings concerning the clip and the green slime, to Chief Taylor and his senior staff. The chief said he learned that the clips were a part of a secret scientific tracking experiment. Every Ranger brief case had a clip attached to it so they could be tracked and visually observed by computer. Certain species of fishes living in the new marine sanctuary also had clips attached to them for the same purpose. Dr. Rainier had been involved with the project from the beginning. Somehow, he discovered that he could substantially alter species of fishes using the clips in combination with sulfur and human DNA.

Delica stood, legs astride, arms behind her back. "Sir, there's one other thing. It seems the clips, in the presence of a green slime that is a waste product from Dr. Rainier's lab, have incredible healing properties. I used it to heal my knee, and Tony's calluses, but more importantly, Tanika's gun shot wound."

Chief Taylor opened the blue spiral notebook in front of him and studied it for a moment. His brown-rimmed glasses moved up and down on his broad nose as he peered first at Tony and then at Delica. "I see. Great job Rangers. You did good."

"Thank you Chief." Delica found her emotions and tensions running down and clenched her hands together behind her back, bracing herself.

"Rainier got the DNA he used from the personal items his thugs stole from my Rangers." Chief Taylor looked back at his notebook. "Y'all gonna have to ..."

"He was using all of us as guinea pigs," interrupted Delica.

"Yes. That makes me blasted angry! This stuff is top secret, Imoudu. Forget about it, both of you." He eyed Delica and Tony up and down. "Can't discuss it with anyone."

♍︎♒︎♋︎■♌︎♏︎

As Delica walked into the lobby the next day, she heard Chief Taylor's voice booming over the loud speaker, "First class job last night rangers. You all did good. Now to other business. The first place winner of the sand statue building contest is Delica Imoudu."

"Nice going Imoudu" Smiling, Tony winked at Delica. She looked like a modern day bronze statue of Athena, standing against the backdrop of brilliant sunlight streaming in through the double glass doors. The floral sundress clinging to the sumptuous curves of her body bought tingling heat to his mid-section. He slipped an arm around her waist. "Let's go to the beach and make a lover for Athena."

Pieces of the Tapestry

Delica glanced aside at Tony, blushing. "I'd love to."

Tony held her hand in his as he drew courage from the comfort of warm, wet sand upon his barefeet. "I've been wanting to say something to you for the longest time Delica." He drew in a deep breath of air filled with the scent of Delica's intoxicating perfume.

Delica smiled up at Tony. "You seem nervous. What's wrong?"

Tony stopped and pulled her to himself, a hand on each of her shoulders. "Delica, I think I've fallen in love with you," he whispered, sheepishly.

"I don't have to think. I already know that I am in love with you. I have been for a very long time." Delica's tone was full of spun sugar.

The honeysuckle smell of her hair and the pressure of her arms about his neck and waist nearly drove him wild with wanting her.

She tilted her face up toward his and met the fire of his passion upon her soft lips as he pressed his lips to hers for a long, delicious moment of forever.

)(

Pieces of the Tapestry

Cold wind steals my light
When day turns to quiet night,
Birds fly out of sight.

-Elizabeth Bowers-

DONNA'S ROOM
by
Helen Tulis

Donna's room was always Donna's room, even though Ruth, her younger sister, had use of the other bed. Twin beds were the trend in the 30's and 40's, for children.

These twin beds were special. The bedspreads were blue decorated with flowers and circles that resembled a highly ornate birthday cake. Mom always removed the spreads, washed them, ironed them, and recovered them when company visited on Sundays. The spreads always looked new and hung daintily over the bed.

Even the furniture in Donna's room was a treasure. Donna herself, when she was eight years old, used to polish the light mahogany beds. She was careful to dust the high dresser which held her momentos on top. Mom would inspect the room after all the polishing to give approval that the job was done right. She once complimented Donna and said, "You see, if you take care of your possessions, they will last you a lifetime."

Donna was proud of her room. Her Van Johnson pictures gave it the finishing touches of a Hollywood scene. She saved several of Van Johnson and Robert Walker's photos from movie magazines only to be in conflict as to which ones she had room to hang on her walls. Mom said, "Don't make a stable out of your room."

Meanwhile, Ruth, who was four years younger, could only take directions from Donna. "Don't bring all your books in my room. It makes it messy," Donna directed her.

"I'll sit on the rug and keep my books where I want them," retorted Ruth.

"You are a pest," Donna responded. "Move your things into the closet."

Pieces of the Tapestry

"I'm going to tell Mom that you are mean. And you are selfish," yelled Ruth.

But Donna's room was Donna's room. She always came home from school and hung up her clothes, like mom taught her. Her school books were kept in the hall out of the way. She even began polishing her shoes in the long hall so as not to spill polish in her room.

Ruth never gave up reporting on Donna. She once said, "Daddy, Donna took my space in the closet."

That was a serious remark because each of us had a special space in the closet for her clothes. The room was not spacious, just adequate. So each person had to cooperate and use space wisely. Dad just looked around in the room, inspected the closet and answered, "Zai a mentch (be a human being). Try to get along with each other. You put your dress here and Donna puts her two dresses on this side. Isn't that better?"

Though Donna was not satisfied, she grumbled some words and continued cutting out pictures of her favorite movie star, Van Johnson. When she looked up, she was annoyed and said, "Ruth, you are the biggest tattle tale."

Mom, who was listening, said, "Zoll zein "Sha. Let it be quiet."

♍︎ ♒︎ ♋︎ ■ ♑︎ ♏︎

As the years swept past, several grandchildren were diapered on those beds. The blue spreads were no longer there. Mom had made sure to protect them. She had placed them inside a plastic cover and hidden them in a huge closet. Furthermore, the family had moved to a different neighborhood in a house that had several bedrooms. Yet, one bedroom was still labeled Donna's room, where the twin beds still rested.

Here, the furniture from Donna's room still looked new. She still polished her dresser and beds. At times when the sun would shine through the lace curtains, the light picked up the beautiful sparkle of the rich woods.

Mom would take down the blue bedspreads and say, "Now, how do you like that? Still beautiful." She would then place them on the beds before company came.

Dad would say, "Close the doors to Donna's room," as if it were an alluring site that would vanish if the air touched it. When company came, many times guests would place their winter coats on Donna's bed. I remember once Donna jumped on top of the pile of coats, furs and all. She exclaimed, "I'm on top of a mountain. Look at me."

Dad heard her yelling and opened the door only to reprimand her. He said, "Vos tit zich dah? Donna, don't act like a monkey. Zah a mentch."

Ruth squealed back, "You are a monkey. You are a monkey."

♍︎♒︎♋︎■♑︎♏︎

Donna's room changed when Dad put my old desk in it. Of course, by now, Donna was married and so was I. The desk had been another treasure because Dad bought it for me on my sixteenth birthday. It actually did not match the reddish brown mahogany furniture in Donna's room. Contrary to the finish of the beds, the wood in the desk was dark brown, almost a light black. The handles, curved and made of metal, were a contrast to the other pieces of furniture. Dad used the desk often, making it a permanent collection of Donna's room.

After Daddy died, the desk was put into the den. There, no one used it. It just sat and collected dust. It was never moved back into Donna's room because Donna's room became the Russian's room.

About a year after Dad's death, Mom acquired a boarder through a Jewish agency. Of course, Mom herself, agreed with her doctor that it would be best not to live alone. By this time Mom was over ninety years of age. Her eyesight was not good as she had macular degeneration. Even walking was a strain as Mom had arthritis in both knees, making it difficult for her to get around. Therefore, having a boarder sounded helpful. At least someone would be there at night, in case Mom needed assistance.

Welcome Kenneth, the Ukrainian. Yes. He would inherit Donna's room. That was the only room available to him.

First, Donna's furniture had to be moved before Kenneth moved into Mom's house. Mom thought about this and quickly realized that Ruth had an extra room in her house that needed furnishings. She called Ruth and asked, "Ruth, what do you think I should do with the furniture from Donna's room?"

Without hesitation, Ruth said, "Mom, I'll be glad to take it. It would be perfect for the empty bedroom here."

Pieces of the Tapestry

"You know, you are right. How will we take it out?" Mom asked.

"Don't worry. I'll get a neighbor who has a truck. We can take it all out this evening," Ruth said, unhesitatingly. Ruth's room had been unfurnished for a few months and she did not plan to purchase furniture. She wanted to keep her expenses down as she had recently been divorced.

"So I'll leave it up to you to take care," Mom said.

On the following day, Mom met Kenneth. He was tall, had a mustache, spoke with a Russian accent, but had a fair command of English in spite of his having lived in the coal mines of the Ukraine all his life. Kenneth was in his late thirties, was a student at a technological university, majoring in mechanical engineering and had a strong interest in computer science.

Knowing that Kenneth needed to move in over the weekend, Mom began to dismantle Donna's room. She took off those blue bedspreads, as she prepared the room for the movers. She folded the spreads, placing them inside the plastic bags. She had to ask someone to help her put away those heavy spreads, as Mom could not do as much work as she had once done.

"Could you kindly place these upstairs in the big closet?" she asked one of the movers. The blue spreads were put away temporarily.

On Monday Kenneth drove up the driveway and came up to the front door. He asked, "Is my room ready?"

Mom showed him inside the house, careful to open the door to Donna's room. She announced, "So, here is your room. Everything perfect. Nice big closet. Clean curtains, sunshine, everything. Perfect."

"Ziz O.K.," Kenneth said, as he strained his neck to see inside the closet. Even after he said this, he looked around the room, which had been painted white from the usual light pink to off-white.

He peered into the backyard and admired the expanse of land and trees there. Kenneth smiled and commented, "Dis is just vhat we had in Russia."

Mom asked, "Such a big yard you had there?"

"My fadher was in the Russian army. So, we moved to the countryside while he was away. It was plenty room der," Kenneth commented.

Just to be convinced that he would have ample space, Kenneth looked again inside the huge closet that had shelves and a light. He thought for a minute and added, "Oh, yes, I will be able to put all my running shoes on dis shelf."

Mom agreed there was plenty of space. So, she and Kenneth orally agreed that he would move in the following Sunday. She quietly left the room, as if she were recapitulating whether she had done the right thing or not.

♍︎♒︎♋︎■♑︎♏︎

Kenneth had been living in Mom's house for several months when I had to become an overnight guest there myself. On a stormy rainy night, when Kenneth was out of town on some personal business, Mom asked me to sleep over. I was hesitant as I preferred my own room and my own bed. From the look in her eyes, I could see that Mom was uneasy to remain alone, and so reluctantly, I said, "OK." But in my mind, I envisioned Kenneth's room was not Donna's old room. I thought about Kenneth's single bed. It did not look as comfortable as Donna's old bed. But I had promised Mom I would stay overnight.

As soon as bedtime arrived, I found myself in Kenneth's room with a huge picture of his father staring at me all night. Sure enough, as I entered the room, the glaring face of his father wearing the Russian army uniform almost jumped at me. Deciphering those medals, dangling from his chest, was tedious. I could not figure out if they represented bravery in action or bravery on a ski course. There he was holding back a smile, almost a grimace. Somehow, when I looked at his face sideways, the father reminded me of a Nazi general I had seen in a movie. "Do I have to look at that all night?" I asked myself.

I finally pulled the cover up over me, trying to snuggle under it to keep warm. After about twenty minutes, I realized a buzzing sound kept coming from somewhere in the room. Though I looked around, tapping on the walls, peering outside the window, I could hear nor see anything. I tried pulling the covers over my ears. I still heard this buzz, buzz sound. Then, I spotted a green light, small almost hidden. The green light indicated the buzzing sound came from the huge stereo set which Kenneth had left on. "Well," I thought, "that's no problem. I can cut that off." Little did I know that this machine represented a complete maze of controls and wires which were all connected somehow, trailing over the

Pieces of the Tapestry

room. If I cut one thing off, everything goes off. "Nuts. I cannot sleep here," I thought. "What can I do? Looking at Kenneth's Nazi general father and hearing this buzz all night is enough to drive me crazy," I decided.

Just then, the room became ice cold. I put my hand outside the cover and my fingers were frosty already. "What happened to the heat?" I wondered. "Did Kenneth cut that off too? I became very irritated and tossed and turned in the tiny bed, wishing I was back in my own bed at home. Then, I thought, "Well, it will be light soon. I'll get up, get dressed, and go home early."

The room was like an igloo. The green light reminded me of an interrogation room in a police station because the light focused only on me as if I had something to reveal. The constant buzz of the stereo set echoed a droning sound which never went away. "This is a wonderful way to spend the night," I thought to myself. "How refreshing!" I said sarcastically.

Trying to waste away some minutes before finding light coming through the window, I decided to look at Kenneth's books. I could not sleep anyway. "Computer books, Russian history, Tolstoy, Russian composers, more computer books, Aha! There is the computer. That looks sharp in the corner staring at me as if monitoring my every breath." With a quick wince of my eye I saw Kenneth's father, the general, staring back at me. "Oh, boy! I have got to get out of here," I mused.

I quickly stuck my legs into a pair of slacks and threw on my blouse without buttoning it. I grabbed my books and pocketbook, sneaked out of the house, digging in my bag to find the car keys. Quickly opening the car door, I took a deep breath and yelled, "You thought you had me, but general, I got away from you, you Russian KGB."

As I drove the ten miles to my house, I began to see images of Donna's old room. The blue bedspreads with the frilly flowers encircling the center were still in place. Even the mahogany furniture had its familiar shine from lemon oil polish. The pink walls emitted a pleasant feeling as the veil-like white curtains dipped from the soft breeze. Even Van Johnson, the movie star, smiled down from his picture frame. He was happy too, to be in Donna's room. I thought, "Finally, Donna's room will always be Donna's room."

)(

Pieces of the Tapestry

Sun, shine on flowers,
Kiss sweet earth and bless all trees;
Let spring grass grow green.

ι

-Elizabeth Bowers-

THE KISS
by
Eleanor Freemer

"Mr. Butler wants you in his office right away," Miss Pickett, my first grade teacher says, out loud so everyone in the room can hear. "You must go down to the principal's office, right now."

The kids giggle and make faces at me, saying behind their hands, "Ha, ha, Eleanor is in trouble," as I get up from my desk to drag my feet towards the door. Then quickly, I turn around, stick out my tongue, then skip out before Miss Pickett catches me. She sees and knows everything. She has eyes behind her head. I hate them all.

Mr. Butler tells me to sit down on a straight back chair, so high, only the scuffed round toes of my black Mary Janes pointing down, can reach the floor. I watch them swing back and forth. I keep my head down so he can't see my eyes get all teary and see my nose run. I don't have a handkerchief with me and am afraid to use my hand.

Oh, what is he saying? My mother had come to school, and told him about the two boys who were following me home every day. My mother had come to school! I want to die. I want to go to the bathroom.

"Eleanor," he asks gently, "tell me in your own words what happened?"

How can I tell him? I can hardly speak. I'm shaking so much that I'm scared I'll shake right off the chair. He waits. If I want to go back to my room, I'll have to tell him, but the words won't get past the thumping lump in my throat. I know I am going to throw up all over me, Mr. Butler and the floor.

He hands me a big white handkerchief from his pocket that smells like the summer fields outside our back yard.

I wipe my nose and eyes and look into his face that reminds me of my papa, so sad and so kind. "It's those two boys from the third grade. Jim and Reilly, that's all I know. They call each other those names, Jim and Reilly. Once I walked away from the school ..." I whisper. My words crackle like my Uncle Sam's radio. How can I get them out? How can I tell him, when I am running a fever? And why should I tell him when he knows? My momma has told him. Why should I tell him too? I shut my eyes real tight so I can't see him looking at me.

"One grabs me, and the other kisses me. Other boys from the third grade make a circle all around and hoot and laugh. Then, they beat me home and climb on the roof of our wood shed and call my name over and over again. I don't even know how they know my name." I crumble up his handkerchief and wipe my eyes and blow my nose and want to go to the bathroom so bad.

The door of his office slowly opens and there they stand, big and square, looking at me as hang dogged and scared as me. I nod my head yes, when Mr. Butler asks if they are the boys. I feel real bad cause I don't really want to get them in trouble.

Back in my room, Miss Picket doesn't say a word. I guess she knows. She sees and knows everything. The kids all look at me. Their eyes say, "What happened to you?" I just pick up my chin and sit down as if nothing had happened.

Something did happen to me, which I didn't understand when I was six years old. They had chased me. They had caught me. They had kissed me. It was a show, a form of release after being pent up in school all day, a game played out for the other kids to make them stop and look and laugh and hoot while I tried not to cry. It made them feel big, two big clowns ~ two big, brave third graders picking on some little kid. Now they would call it sexual harassment. But this happened a long time ago, before such actions had a name.

I think back wistfully, to that skinny girl with knobby knees and arms. Her auburn hair had been cut in a sever Buster Brown haircut and she had big blue eyes that stared innocently at the world. I still wonder, "Why me?"

)(

CANTALOUPE SKY
by
Elizabeth Bowers

Farewell, claustrophobic air, hot and stale;
Final resting place of bureaucratic warriors,
Slaughter house of clear blue dreams,
Haven of urgent appointments, deadlines and glutted lives.

A cloud thick with allegations of gray soapy water,
Rains dirty laundry upon cranberry pies,
Turning bulging lemons into cantaloupe skies,
Like bitter-sweet vulnerability lulled by plastic promises.

Four seasons call me to clutterless time
And empty social calendars mellowed
By crystalline pure nights of star studded skies
Far from wheezing sounds of bureaucratic battlefields.

Like a cloud thick with longing to breath easily
Of Stone Mountain scented with magnolia air,
I go where cold Pacific waters are only pine scented dreams
Of cantaloupe skies perfumed with odor of fresh peach pie.

⚭

Pieces of the Tapestry

Clouds, to earth's call come
Dancing forth as splashing waves
Upon sultry seas.

⋇

-Elizabeth Bowers-

DADDY'S PITCHFORK
by

Elizabeth Bowers

"No man knows the hour of the coming of the Lord," I heard Daddy say one Sunday morning after breakfast. "May he have mercy upon the babes born in the last day before the judgment cometh."

I knew I was one of those last day babes. Many of my uncles and cousins who served as cannon fodder for the American Army lay dead and dying on the Battle Fields of Cassino and Leyte Gulf, when I made my grand entrance into planet earth. I awoke to a season of war and bitter hatred. The world was drinking of the wrath of its own fornication. Hitler's mighty army had already laid waste to Dunkirk and God's chosen people had to flee for their lives or stand naked, inhaling death, in German gas chambers. The Pacific waters off the cost of Pearl Harbor bore the testimony of Japanese suicide fighter pilots, who called America to the battle when they painted its shores with its own blood. As war sirens raged, Daddy was in New Jersey sewing the seeds of the kingdom of God ~ far from the Devil's slaughtering armies.

"God shall stretch forth his mighty hand and snatch the elect out of the burning devastation of His fiery judgment. The Devil's minions shall be loosed to wreak havoc upon the four corners of the earth." Daddy's right hand was raised to heaven but his soulfully penetrating look, invoked the fear of God in me that Sunday morning.

Daddy must have been one of the elect. In the early morning hours of May 15, 1944, Allied forces crawled through snake-infested mud in the Philippines, bleeding and dying, and searching for the enemy. Not Daddy. He stood beaming at me, his third child, through the window of the

Pieces of the Tapestry

colored section of an American hospital waiting room. I wonder if he might have been thinking then, about how blessed he had been when God's saving right hand had caused a stack of tires to bury him beneath their back-breaking weight, just hours before the thunderous roar of the call to armageddon.

♍︎♒︎♋︎■♉︎♏︎

I worried about airplanes. If any flew over my head during the day, that night I would be afraid to go to sleep. Shadows that evoked images of airplanes with me in them crashing into the fiery furnace of hell, moved about on my bedroom wall. I was terrified that the devil would get me before God could save me, and I would cry. Daddy would always come and get me.

"He'll fix it for you. Just you believe," he would comfort me. Satan can do his worst, but God can do him one better," Daddy would tell me. "God knows all about it."

On those occasions, Daddy would put me into the big bed between Mommy and him and I would fall asleep while he told me stories about the everlasting life of angels in heaven. When I would wake up in the morning, I was always amazed to find myself back in the bedroom that I shared with my brother and sisters. I wondered if the angels had carried me there.

♍︎♒︎♋︎■♉︎♏︎🕯

"God is moving across the face of the earth. He is getting us ready for His great day which comes as a thief in the night," Daddy hurled forth from our kitchen, the day our plug-in ice box arrived.

"This is one of God's great miracles," he announced. "See. Look how it plugs in. We don't have to use ice any more." Daddy smiled and lifted me high into the air. "It's called a refrigerator," he said proudly.

I wondered if that meant that the ice-man would never come again. I wanted to lick the chunks of ice that fell off the block in the back of his wagon.

One Friday evening, I overheard Daddy say to Mommy, "Piers, boardwalks, and auction sales hold pleasures that ruin man." He moved the big, mahogany radio off the table that stood near the floor vent in the parlor, and set it on the hard wood floor. He left the room and returned, carrying a big boxy looking thing that had a window on it.

"I've never seen anything like that before. What is it Daddy?" I inquired.

"This is a television set."

"I never heard of a television set. Is that a new word?" Daddy was always teaching me new words. He said I'd need to know them when I started school.

"Yes. It is another one of God's miracles. A television is a radio that lets you see the people who are talking."

That night, Mommy popped corn and we all dangled our feet over the warmth of the vent, and stared in amazement at the black and white talking pictures.

♍︎ ♒︎ ♋︎ ■ ♑︎ ♏︎

The Word of God did battle with the beast all across planet earth during my growing up years. Through his Sunday morning sermons, Daddy kept me informed of prophecy fulfilling world events that were occurring almost on a daily basis. The H-bomb proved its effectiveness as an efficient killing machine, when it rained down fire upon Iwo Jima and Nagasaki, just about a month before my little sister arrived on planet earth. The discovery of the bomb gave humankind the mighty power of the atom. Earth was never the same. My sister's arrival took from me, my place in the family order as the youngest child. My life was never the same. World War II guns were heaped up in rusty silence but rumors of wars abounded as I struggled to figure out my own private world.

On my fourth birthday, Daddy literally jumped up and down, smiling and cuddling my second youngest sister who was born several months before Daddy preached about Hindu India being set free from British rule.

He held her up to heaven's window and said, "Praise be to God. The trumpet call to the mercy seat of God has been sounded. The ocean is a great, wide place, but God has it all in hand. The children of Israel have crossed the mighty ocean of tribulation and have come in from the wilderness. God will provide."

Pieces of the Tapestry

Earlier that day, my older brother and sister took me to the woods bordering our property and we picked a pail of blackberries. We took them home to Mommy and she churned them into blackberry ice cream. I got to help squeeze the lemons and stir the batter for the cake she was making for my birthday. My big brother got to lick the spoon. He always grabbed the spoon and licked it before anyone else had a chance to get it. Now, my cake was all decorated with white frosting and sitting in the center of the dinning room table. I wanted a piece of it, but Daddy was busy talking about the Gospel coming on strong now that the prophesy was fulfilled.

♍︎♒︎♋︎■♑︎♏︎

Absecon, my home town, is a very small city with a population of less than seven thousand. It had several churches.

"The churches here are for Methodists, Catholics and Presbyterians, not for the children of colored people. We are saved and sanctified by the Blood of the Holy Spirit," my Daddy told me one day when I wanted to visit the red brick church with the big, white steeple that you could see from the baseball diamond.

Daddy conducted church services for us in our living room every Sunday morning. Mommy would play the piano and Daddy would play his guitar while my brother, sisters and I sang *Peace in the Valley*, and *Jacob's Ladder*.

Then Daddy would lean his guitar down against the upright piano, clear his throat several times, and adjust his glasses. "A pitch fork is used for throwing hay. It never brings to you. It throws away." He would hurl his fist to heaven like he was throwing hay.

My brother and I sometimes got very tickled when he did this and we laughed out loud, accidentally.

Daddy would look at us sternly and say, "This may seem funny. Just you sit and take. Don't use the pitchfork, but the rake. You better listen to me. Don't condemn my words. When you poke fun at the Gospel, you are condemning the word of God. Be careful about that."

I didn't know what the Gospel really was. I'd never actually heard God talk, so I wasn't sure what his words were either. I was, however, very familiar with the sanctified look that came into Daddy's eyes when he talked about being careful about God. On those occasions, I'd force myself to stop laughing, though it took the power of all the angels in heaven to aid me, and put on the ecclesiastical look that I used to practice for hours in front of Mommy's big dresser mirror.

My brother was not so fortunate. The angels never seemed to come to his aid. He was usually banished from the room by the pointing finger of Mommy, when his laughter became louder than the Gospel. He never seemed to mind.

By the time Daddy began preaching about the communist recapturing Seoul Korea, I could read very well. Daddy always called upon me to read from the scriptures that he picked out to accompany the Sunday sermon. I particularly loved the one about "*In my father's house are many mansions.*" I memorized it because the words were very pretty to me. In those days, Daddy's Sunday sermons included stuff about, "God will provide, and though shalt not sit in the seat of the scornful."

To Daddy's great joy, Absecon had no movie theaters or discos. There was many a Sunday morning when he'd preach to us about the evils of listening to 'devil's music,' and dancing for any reason but the joy of God. Music that did not sing the praises of God or country belonged to Satan's communists and Daddy forbade it in our house.

Sometimes old people who called Daddy Reverend, and Mommy Sister, even though they were not kin to her, came to our home and sat around the piano with us as Daddy preached about how we should give our hearts to God so we can spend eternity with the Lord. Mommy usually played softly on the piano as Daddy told everyone what "Thus sayeth the Lord." Afterward, Everyone gathered around the long dinning room table and held hands while Daddy talked out loud to God.

He always started by saying, "I can't stop loving you, God. You mean all the world to me. You suffered many horrible things for us all, then they hanged you on that rugged tree."

Mommy would serve up big platters of fried chicken, boiled cabbage with carrots and ham cooked in, potato salad, all kinds of fresh baked pies and home-made peach ice-cream. Daddy always got served first. Then the company would choose their portions. My brother and sisters and I always went last. Mommy was too busy serving to eat. Daddy said that was the way of the Lord. I never mind being served last. I never really felt like eating after hearing the sad story about the Lord hanging from a tree.

Pieces of the Tapestry

After everyone had their fill of the gospel, fried chicken and peach ice cream, Daddy pulled out the bingo game and we all played. He was always the caller and Mommy was his not so silent partner. I liked winning, but it was often hard because I'm sure my brother cheated. He was banished from the sermons so often that I suspected the devil's hand-maidens had gotten to him and put deceit on his bingo card. He won most of the games and, therefore, got to stay up a half hour longer than my sisters and me.

Daddy often sermonized about the wicked ways of the world back then. In my heart, I didn't really know what he was talking about. Those were the days when even the walls of our home seemed to smile at me and the mulberry tree in my backyard stood in the joy of the Lord. I was still in the peaceful valley where the Lord has mercy upon the babes born in the terrible last days before the judgment comes.

⋇

Pieces of the Tapestry

Golden sun gives strength
To weeping willow hearts that
Pry for peace on earth.
ℋ
-Elizabeth Bowers-

THE HANUKAH GIFT
by
Helen Tulis

The radio talk show host was talking about aids awareness. The background music almost masked what he was saying so early in the morning. Margo listened intently, amazed at the statistics on deaths from aids. She felt drowsy though, and wanted to sleep a little longer, having suffered from a migraine the night before.

Peacefully, calmly, Margo found herself awakening from an ineffable experience. She heard herself crying out, "O God. O, God." Margo pulled the blanket up over her shoulders and neck, trying to assess what she had seen and heard in a dream, which muted her feelings, divorcing her from her emotions. Strong doubt entered her mind as she strained to recall the dream.

As Margo relived this vision, she found herself in a classroom with about twenty-five students. One student was at the front of the class, lecturing. He captivated the audience with his subject of individualism. His choice of words indicated he had fully matured and was quite academic. Never before was he able to speak in front of a group with such amazing clarity. Everyone was listening to him. Then suddenly, he faded away and Margo saw shadows on the windows behind him. She grabbed her two sons, who, in the dream, had regressed to ages eight and seven. She quickly left the classroom, following the shadows she had seen on the green tinted windows leading to the hallway.

Pieces of the Tapestry

Much to Margo's surprise, she saw her father who had been dead seven years that day. "Dad, what happened to you? What happened?" she shrieked, not believing he had come to visit them at school.

He had the gray stubble of a beard, wore an ivory and blue sweater, and answered quickly, "You give me too many lists of things you need."

Her two sons did not speak, but her father acknowledged them with a pat on their heads. Then Margo turned to him and asked, "How did you find this school? How did you find where I was?" Margo was astounded that he knew.

He looked at her without speaking a word. Margo stared at her father like those faithful ones who stare at the Virgin Mary as she is revealed in religious rites. Like those faithful congregants, Margo had her doubts. Yet, there is no word for doubt in the Biblical Hebrew. Doubt is an act in which the mind inspects its ideas. On the other hand, the Bible has many expressions of wonder.

When the dream faded, Margo longed to talk to her father, to touch his hand, to watch his facial expressions, to hear his voice. She was happy to have seen this vision of her father. It was truly a miracle, especially at this time of the year-Chanukah, a holiday of miracles.

♍︎ ♒︎ ♋︎ ■ ♑︎ ♏︎

On the following day, Margo remembered a parable that was told by her Hebrew teacher. It was about a prince who lived far away from his father with whom he was close. He became homesick for his father. He received a letter from the father, which he treasured, but it only increased his longing for home. He would sit and complain saying, "Oh, if I could only touch his hand. If he would extend his hand to me, I would kiss every finger in my great longing for my father."

While he was in the midst of this melancholia, a thought came to his mind. "Don't I have my father's letter, written in his own hand? Is not his handwriting comparable to his hand?" A great joy overcame him.

"When I look at the Heavens, the work of Thy fingers," (𝔓𝔰𝔞𝔩𝔪 8:4).

The visit from Margo's father in the dream fastened her mind on why she had this dream and what was the meaning of this dream. "Why did Dad refer to a list? What list?" Her sense of awe directed her to: *"In Thy light, we see light,"* (𝔓𝔰𝔞𝔩𝔪 36:9).

♓

Pieces of the Tapestry

Bluejay sings good day
To sleepy black-spored quillwort,
At Stone Mountain's gate.

-Elizabeth Bowers-

THE PINOCHLE PLAYER
by
Eleanor Freemer

Poppa put a nitroglycerine pill under his tongue, took a deep breath, then banged his broad hand in the area of his heart. From beneath the canopy of full silver eyebrows his bright blue eyes glared angrily. "Chaser. You always have to win?"

"Poppa!"

"Don't poppa me." He threw the cards down and walked slowly into the living room to watch a bit of television.

This was a routine we played out several times a week. I would bring my eighty-six year old father over to our house, where we enjoyed a few hands of knock rummy, followed by lunch. I danced on a tight wire. Whichever way I moved, I was heading for a fall. When I let him win too often, he said I played a sloppy game, and if I won more then two hands in a row, I was just a pig. Keeping my balance had been difficult, and doing so I had developed a deep dislike for playing cards.

Since I was five years old, Poppa and I have played cards. He taught me, Go Fish, War, finally graduating me to Casino and Knock Rummy. My sister Amanda often joined Mom and Dad in a friendly game of Pinochle, when we were all living at home. Poppa would always fuss with them. He hated when they laughed if somehow one or the other out maneuvered him. They were never allowed to let a little bit of gossip divert them from the game.

Pieces of the Tapestry

Watching from the side lines, he would wink at me, when he made a smart move of his own. "Did you see that?"

If I saw, I didn't understand, and swore I would never learn the intricacies of that game.

In his autumn years, he attempted giving lessons to the grandchildren. Our oldest daughter was the only one who enjoyed playing with her grandfather. She bragged to him that when she was enrolling in classes at Temple University, she could hold her own in a game being played out on the stairs, while waiting in line to register for classes.

Before my mother's health had deteriorated, they would play two-handed pinochle after their shoe store closed for the evening. It was only in their senior years that the game was a peaceful one. After my mother died, the games went on. Poppa kept score for both of them.

For some reason, I always thought Pinochle was a Jewish game, never knowing anyone else who played. When I was very young, Momma and Poppa, made a foursome with Mom's cousin Michael and his wife Virginia, who had a dry goods store on Orthodox street. Our family lived on that street the year I was born. My parent's shoe store was sandwiched between the Kessler's dry good store and Lewis's wall paper business.

When I was around four years old, under pressure from my mother, we made our first move, to Virginia. Poppa may have been a pretty good pinochle player, but as a business man, he was not a success. Perhaps part of the problem was his being tugged in several directions by Momma and her very forceful sisters. Momma was the youngest, and thought her siblings always knew what was best for us. After several moves, like jumps on a checker board, by 1936 we had come full circle. We were back in Philadelphia on Orthodox Street, with less then we had when we started out.

Except for the Jewish people who owned businesses and became wealthy along that strip, the neighborhood was predominately poor Irish, Polish, Italian, and Catholic. On Wilmot Street where we lived, most of the people were blue collar workers, who looked suspiciously at their only Jewish neighbors.

Outside of Christmas and Easter, I was more comfortable with the friends I made on our street and in school. The Kessler's daughter, Martha and the Lewis's daughter, Helen, who were my age, always made me feel gauche. Mr. Kessler, who was always a jokester, would pull out a picture of us three girls as babies on a blanket in someone's backyard. I, a rolly polly baby weighing in at ten pounds at birth, was the only one still on her back like a turtle, with legs waving in the air at seven months.

According to Carolyn, her child was destined to be a prima ballerina. Professional pictures of her were displayed all over the house. Unfortunately, they did not resemble the skinny girl whose nervous energy worked a switch on her tongue as well as her body. Her pinched features were modeled after her mother, and not her handsome father.

That shoe store opened and closed within a matter of months. During that bitter winter, Poppa went from saloon to saloon, trying to sell interest in dart board games.

Once we were back in the old neighborhood, my folks took to playing pinochle with the Kessler's on Saturday nights. I would have to tag along to play with Martha and Helen. The only good memories of those evenings were the fancy spread Carolyn would put out for us all, as a peace offering. I was made to feel insignificant by my peers, while a different kind of war was going on downstairs at the card table.

"Greenie, dummy," Michael would laugh at his wife.

She would curse him with a fury unrelated to the game. He always called her Greenie, because he had been born in the United State, but she had come here as a child. That she was more clever than her husband, did not take away the sting from his words. Soon all four would be enmeshed in an argument over cards, which would go on over coffee and cake.

"What a fun evening," I would think, listening to those tirades. "I will never play cards," I swore to myself. However, cards became my father's prime interest when he could not go out by himself. I could not deny him that pleasure.

After lunch, I would often drive over to a mall, where we would walk until he tired. Then I would leave him on a bench and do a little shopping. When I would come to pick him up, Poppa would be deep in conversation with whoever sat down beside him. Sometimes it would be young mothers with children, widowed women who would be happy to have someone to talk to, or elderly retirees like himself, who had the solution to most of the world's problems.

The best times were when I would go over to my sister's and Poppa and I would sit around the dinning table with the Jewish Forward spread out. He would read to me stories just as he did when I was a child. After

Pieces of the Tapestry

he read the *Bintel Brief*, we discussed the age old problems that could have been taken from *Dear Abby's* column. Then Poppa would repeat the stories told to him as they rested on the benches.

"Jewish, Gentile," Poppa would say. "It is hard being alone. Some of these people remarry and end up taking on another burden, a sick husband or a sick wife. What's the sense?" Poppa would brag to them how lucky he was with his children.

Once he opened up to tell me about a woman he met when he went to stay for a few weeks with his sister in Atlantic City. They began to talk while sitting on a bench listening to the concerts at Garden Pier. Sometimes in the evening, Poppa would get dressed up, suite pressed and shoes polished. He would put on a perky bow tie, and take her to the movies or out for dinner in a Jewish style restaurant on Pacific Avenue. The lady had a son who paid for her rooms during the summer, so she could get away from the city's heat. He and his wife and children never came to see her, all summer long, until it was time to go home. Her Bintel brief was that she had a hard first marriage, struggled with her husband in a grocery store. When he got sick, they had to give up the business and she took care of him until he died several years ago. She told Poppa that she doesn't need money, she doesn't need them to pay for her vacation, but if money is all they can give, she lets them. Her daughter-in-law and grandchildren don't like Atlantic City. Maybe she'll marry again.

"Not me," Poppa said. "Why don't her children come to visit? Did she do something wrong? I loved Momma, and did all I could when she was sick. I would never want to take care of another woman. I have good children, I tell all these woman," he smiled. "I'm never lonesome. I would never marry again. I'll give them a little company, but nothing else."

Poppa had nothing but contempt for his widower friends who carried on at their spouses' funerals, then before the year was up, got married. "Those women will kill them within a year," Poppa said, wisely. "I'm free to come and go as I please."

It astounded me that, after my mother died, strange women would call, widows who read other women's obituaries. Same first name basis, "Can I do anything for you? I could bring over a home cooked dinner, help clean up your house."

Poppa would get angry at first. Then he would laugh, "Never knew I was such a Beau Brummel."

Pieces of the Tapestry

Where we went, my father went. We took him on his first trip to Miami Beach. Several other trips followed. When my husband was transferred to Atlanta, my father came to stay from the High Holidays to around Passover with us. He learned to wear Bermuda shorts until almost the first snow. In his old age, he became a regular at Sabbath and Holiday Services with our family. He made friends with members of the Arberter Ring, old timers who still communicated in Yiddish. On his eighty-second birthday I made him the first birthday party he ever had. Twenty friends crowded into our house to pay homage to him.

In 1970, to my husband's joy, and my father's great disappointment, we were back living in Philadelphia.

My father was unhappy with my husband's transfer. "Where will I go next winter?" he complained.

Poppa was thrilled when, after three years, we talked about a new job in Atlanta. He was looking forward to that. He was also looking forward to our son's Bar Mitzvah in September. Papa confided that he had asked God to let him live to see his great-grandson Bar Mitzvahed.

So the days were spent playing cards, laughing, arguing and making plans for the next day. "What are we going to do tomorrow?" He would ask me.

"We'll see." I would tell him. "We'll do something."

He never stopped looking toward the future. However, man plans, and God does what God does. Poppa died after the first Sedar in 1973.

I only hope that if he is in heaven, he is enjoying his weekly pinochle game. How else could it be heaven for him?

א

WONDERMENT
by
Helen Tulis

Wonderment,
Today I watched
An old woman
Walking under her sunhat,
Trailing multi-colored ribbons
With her every step,
"I have everything I need," she says,
"Living only on social security."

Wonderment,
Conflict between two sisters
Agreeing to disagree with one another;
One smugly rich,
Not hearing the poorer one;
Imagine, they both liked strawberry ice cream
When they were young.

Wonderment,
A visit to a friend
Who is in and out of lucidity,
When he spoke with rationality;
He had sound judgment and clarity
Just yesterday.
Now mumble, jumble,
Hit or miss,
Covers all his claims.
Once he was an artist,

Pieces of the Tapestry

His brush strokes painted a horse, a ballet dancer,
A unicorn and Napoleon.
Now only the crematorium awaits
To diminish his tracks
With its walls of fire.

Wonderment,
At powerlessness of a dizzying brain,
Exhibiting a horrendous drain.
Wonderment,
Stretches like a veil
Separating "meaningful" from "meaningless."

)(

SHAKY PEACE
by
Elizabeth Bowers

"The cold war has ended, a shaky peace prevails,"
Sings the war-stained cormorant to the rising moon.
"Thoughts of nuclear holocaust no longer scare earth's children,
As the decade of the first global intent of freedom assails.

Sweet earth is alive with a new vibration that is fuel
To cormorants riding on backs of windblown whales,
And fire to agape love, binding nations together
In a war to end poverty, disease, and inhumanity's rule.

Out of the bowels of chaos, a new world order is the label,"
Sings the ceaseless cormorant to sweet rainbow of hope,
"Given to nations that strive together against an economy
That fails to provide wholesome bread for earth's table."

But on a sandy smoke scented beach somewhere around
The Persian Gulf, an oil soaked cormorant quietly
Swims in the hot oily waters of its dying ocean home,
Stopping once in a while to brush aside a turtle,
Floating upside down, making neither a ripple nor a sound.

While on western waters the cormorant's distant kin do
Enjoy the clear blue purity of a gently rolling sea,
Stopping now and then to fill up on toxin free guppies,
By a buoy near a floating sign, green with algae, that reads,
"I will work for food, my family and me, God bless you."

MARGE
by
Eleanor Freemer

At last, I would have known her anywhere;
Waltzing across the room, flooding me with images
Of my childhood friend whose face, like a painted
Keepsake, I still carry in the locket of my memory.

Through a distorted glass, she looked the same;
Her years brushed away as if by a feathered broom,
While I felt creased and wrinkled, as an unpressed
Dress, left carelessly to droop over a chair too long.

I waved my hand and called out her name, "Marge."
Did she recognize me? I still couldn't see,
As she traversed that distance between time and space,
moving swiftly like a dancer to a two step song.

While I crept slowly onward at a tortoise's pace
Til we hugged, clasped hands, and then I could see
That she too wore a spidery network marking each mile
Of her own journey through life, smile by smile.

)(

THE LESSON
1938
by
ELEANOR FREEMER

In deep guttural tones, she whispers,
"Listen, my little barbarians, to this music;
"The Moldou," which you have never heard
before because of your abysmal ignorance.
Drink in with your ears, your heart, your soul,
a nectar more potent than the wine
sipped by the gods on Mount Olympus.
Then, my little monsters, paint what you see."

Slowly she bows, turns the handle of the victrola,
signals us with a finger on her bright red lips for silence.
She pulls her lace shawl tightly across narrow rounded shoulders.
Her long jet black beaded earrings, swing against her high rouged cheeks
as gently she places the needle on the record. We sit on our hard yellow
oak chairs and giggle behind our hands,
"What is she doing now, this crazy art teacher,
whose reputation has proceeded us down the corridors of time through
laughter and myths from one sibling to the next?"
Our fingers play among the pots of paint,
lined up across stained scarred tables,
like colorful tin soldiers on parade.

Waiting, anticipating some familiar sounds;
what we hear is a blare of wood winds,
a rippling of strings, a flurry of water
spewing, exploding from the record player,
rolling into the room on a clash of timpani,
lapping against our feet: dancing upon the tables
and chairs, washing like thunder
against the black board, drowning us in its wake.

Pieces of the Tapestry

With damp nervous fingers, I clutch my brush.
Paint swirls onto my paper
in a medley of cool greens and blues;
hot reds and oranges of a sun shining down
from an azure sky where cirrus clouds float
like angels on a Sunday morning,
seeking their reflections in the turbulent water below.

Beneath the table my feet dance along with the
sprightly rhythm of a mazurka.
"Hurry, hurry", calls the cello as I
rush making clumsy impatient strokes;
trying to paint all I see and feel.
I draw a wedding party as it twirls down
a flower strewn path,
leading to a white spired church.

Bells in the tower chime in joy as the triangles sing out,
chased by violins and flutes gaily tossing
ribbons from the bridesmaid's caps,
high into the summer breeze.
And that river, the Moldou,
 joins the festivities, embracing the shore
as the orchestra soars into a crescendo.
Then flows back into silence.

The music stops.
A sigh quivers through the room.
My tongue laps the Mouldou's sweet water
as it washes down from my eyes into my mouth,
blending with the rain from that sudden storm
that falls like a blessing on the spirited wedding party.

The music stops,
and I remain in Smetena's small Bavarian village,
forever a thirteen year old, hearing his music
for that very first time.

Pieces of the Tapestry

Forever I see my teacher, her flowing shawl,
her jet earrings, her wild nest of orange hair
looming over our shoulders as she sadly moves
around the room peering with myopic eyes
at our stick like figures.

The music stops,
but she continues to pantomime,
conduct, play each instrument, humming softly to herself,
her silver bracelets tinkling out their own nostalgic song.
I see again and again, her blue lidded eyes
shutting us out, transporting herself
far from her rowdy class,
far away to her war torn country,
back to the Moldou.

⋊

MIRROR MIRROR ON THE WALL
by
Eleanor Freemer

I will not look at you if you force me to see
This Dorian Gray Portrait you've painted of me.
It's of an old woman wearing a necklace of wrinkles,
Whose watery, short-sighted eye no longer twinkles;
Whose hair is a dull gray, whose figure is squat,
And you say that it's me, well I say that it's not;

For when I close my eyes, what I see, is a dame,
Sparkling, scintillating, who looks the same
As she did let's say, at the mere age of fifty,
When her skin was clear and her figure still nifty;
A woman at her pinnacle, just reaching her prime,
Not as you have portrayed me, like a victim of time.

Oh mirror, you're warped to reflect a picture so stark
I swear, I'll only face you when I'm alone in the dark.

⚯

COLORBLIND
by
Eleanor Freemer

When I view the world without my glasses,
There are no races, there are no classes,
No color lines, no ethnic nose,
No slanting eyes, no funny clothes;
All is rosy until the time when
I put my spectacles on again.

⚯

Pieces of the Tapestry

KNOTS AND STITCHES
by
Eleanor Freemer

Two roads diverged in a yellow wood,
And sorry I could not travel both
And be one traveler......

begins Robert Frost's poem. Does he describe merely a fork in the road, or a time and place to make choices? When I was young, I took the route expected of me ~ the road well traveled.

I graduated from high school in 1943. America was recovering from the depression, but in the throes of the second World War. It was a time when the more daring young girls plunged into that mysterious unknown undergrowth, finding excitement and adventure. I, well aware of my family's financial straits, made my way down the well traveled path. Armed with newly acquired skills, I took an office job with the government earning more than I would have been able to earn at any time before.

Mundane, safe, I happily kept on that traditional road which lead to marriage, home and children. Furthering my education was never part of my plans. I was satisfied to read and learn with my husband who was earning his degree on the GI Bill after his discharge from the army.

"Momma, go back to school," our children pleaded when they were attending college, "other mothers do it."

"At my age?" I laughed. Why would I want to rack my brain with things I would never use or knowledge I felt too old to absorb? I devoured all types of books ~ fiction, biographies, history, poetry ~ never worrying about being tested on what I had read. If I was secretly envious of other women who were more heroic than myself, I did not let it shake me from the prosaic life I lived. I took care of my father who lived with us, worked in the school library as a volunteer and took over the heady leadership of our daughter's girl scout troop. I joined the socially acceptable charity organizations, raising moneys for good causes, never the initiator but always willing to do my share.

What kind of person was I who never marched in a protest, joined a sit-in, or even thought of joining the peace corps? Satisfied. My father, even when he was in his eighties, loved to share with me stories from the

Pieces of the Tapestry

Jewish Forward, slices of life, lives of Jewish heroes whose names never appeared in my school books. When he died in 1973, I felt lost. Cut off from the link with my past, I decided then that I must form myself into the vessel in which our family history would be carried. Haltingly, I began to retrace the steps I took as a child. That fork in the road I was afraid to traverse then, is the one I have begun to travel on now.

At this stage in my life I have found the time to go out to learn the poetry of language and the chronology of history. Clutching these shiny new words, like colored crayons, I draw a map for our children and their children to follow. I plot the road which led from our grandparents to where they are now.

The stories of our past must be put down like music. The children must see through my eyes, my father, sitting at the kitchen table with the paper spread out before us, wetting his finger to turn the pages. They must hear our laughter or sighs as we shared these human comedies, and my father's experiences he sometimes compared to those in the bintle brief. They must hear as I heard, my mother sing as she worked in the house and my father's rich baritone, as he sang me lullabies, and feel the fear and exaltation of the generation before us as they took the hazardous road to America.

I have struggled. Learning and remembering have become more difficult but I have written that down too. They will know their father and me as more than mere parents and grandparents. They will see us as young people whose decisions have made their lives stronger and richer.

I am their past, and I am their future. I am the listener and the troubadour. I am the teacher, and again, a child learning. I am a weaver with a million colored threads in my hands. As this tapestry takes shape, one thought, like a golden thread, slides another thought in place. I work between laughter and tears as sights and sounds and smells I thought I had long forgotten, fill in another corner of our lives.

Will the knowledge of our struggles, disappointments, and yes ~ many joys ~ help give them the courage to take a road less traveled? The recording of all these goes well, despite knots and missed and lost stitches. These memories will be recorded before I reach the end of my road. Unlike Robert Frost, I have traveled both roads. Now, I took the one less traveled by, And that has made all the difference.

ℵ

4 HOT COFFEE AND COLORFUL THREADS

*Tangled rainbows stuck
In rivers of mud,
Color me with life.*

♓

-Elizabeth Bowers-

Pieces of the Tapestry

IN THE COMPANY OF WOMEN
by
ELEANOR FREEMER

Laughter, sighs,
bubble like water in a stream;
and we are the pebbles
washed, scoured, shaped
by the ebb and flow of words.

We four, breaking bread together,
at a table sprinkled with words,
like crumbs for a flock of birds
waiting to join us.
And would the birds be more different
in this company of women than we are
to one another?

The coffee cups
stained brown like the Colombian
whose fingers plucked the beans
from a bush so far from where we sit,
its aroma ebbs and flows,
fills the room in tones
like our words, rich and deep
A Bach oratorio,
A Negro spiritual,
A cantorial niggen,
An Irish Laye.

For this is who we are,
slaves brought up from Egypt,

Pieces of the Tapestry

Africa or the Irish coast;
Tied to our past
to those bonds of slavery
that lock our hands together
as the words bind our minds.

Words shape us, cleanse us
like the pebbles in the stream,
and we see the need for one another
In the ebb and flow
of our words.

Our hearts hands and heads
meet and touch over the table;
our words are of yesterday
today and tomorrow,
of our sameness
of our differences.

There is anger here, hot as the slave's back;
laughter, cool as the stream we crossed.
We four will not change who we are
in the ebb and flow of words
but we will learn who the other is,
and the anger will not burn us,
nor will we drown in the
tears of the stream
as it ebbs and flows.

Why shouldn't we talk
of old hatreds, old fears
that stain the soul
like the black coffee
stains the white porcelain cups?

Why shouldn't we talk of
prejudices, that each carries

Pieces of the Tapestry

like crumbs to feed the vultures of hate?
In this ebb and flow
of words we learn.

Sing a slave song,
Go down Moses,
Lead me through the wilderness
with words chiseled in stone
That teach Thou shalt,
Thou shalt not.
Lead us through the waters
that cleanse us,
washing us like a pebble
with words that will free us.

For the words will sing
as we reach out to one another
with laughter and joy and tears,
for we are a company of women
who are different
but who are the same in our need
for each other
in the ebb and flow of words.

♓

Pieces of the Tapestry

Soft motion of spring's
Best rose, cannot visit light
On soaring snow birds.

❋

-Elizabeth Bowers-

TAKING A CHANCE
by
Elizabeth Bowers

    Artemisa Etienne felt uncomfortable as she walked into the Loyalist Room, where the weekly Blue Prelude Writer's Group meeting was already in progress. Her hands felt wet and clammy as she looked upon the stern white faces seated around the conference table. "What on God's green earth am I doing in this place?" she wondered. It seemed to her that no one in the room had bothered to acknowledge her entrance.
    Uncomfortably conscious of her single Black presence there, Artemisa smoothed out the back of her skirt, and took the vacant seat at the far end of the wide "I" shaped table. Artemisa rubbed her hands together in a futile effort to calm herself. It was her turn to read next. She felt unprepared.
    "These white people don't want to hear anything I have to say. I ought to get out of here before Dr. Hill calls on me." Artemisa took a deep breath of air lightly scented with jasmine perfume. She felt a light tapping on her shoulder.
    "Did Ruth call you this morning?" The women's green eyes squinted through rimmed glasses that were almost as dark brown in color as Artemisa's skin.
    Artemisa raised an arched eyebrow, her sable eyes slightly squinting. "Well Marge, if she did, it must have been while I was still on my morning walk around Stone Mountain Park. I don't usually get back home before 10:30." Her expression was sober. "What would she have been calling me about? I hardly know her."

Pieces of the Tapestry

Marge reached out a cream colored hand and placed it along side the lean rich chocolate that was Artemisa's bare arm. "Well, Lenora, Ruth and I, are going to start getting together at each other's houses so we can work on our writing and get to know each other better. All of us want you to be a part of our group," Marge said, engaging Artemisa with a questioning smile.

Artemisa looked over the assemblage. Lenora and Ruth were not present. "I don't ..." She was drawn into silence by the husky, southern draw of Dr. Hill.

"We gotta get on with it now. Artemisa, You're up." Dr. Hill stretched his long, slender neck forward. His narrow gray eyes peered at her through thick lenses.

Artemisa nervously shuffled the pages of her story. For a fleeting moment, she let her eyes dart about the waspish group. Her throat became dry and her hands would not be still. She could hear her stomach growling and hoped to heaven that no one else could hear its loud rumble.

"I have no idea what I'm doing on this planet," Artemisa read from her neatly typed papers. She was self conscious about sharing her work in public and wondered for a moment if her voice was too high or if it was clear enough. She wondered if anyone was paying her any mind. Her eyes remained glued to her printed words.

From far off in the distance, she heard the sound of her own alto tones. "A long time ago, people used to tell me that life is all about having kids and baking cakes for PTA fund drives. My friend May, who used to live across the street from me when I was in college, says we're all here to go to school so we can get out and work and make enough money to live the American dream. Jack, the homeless guy who lives behind the fast food restaurant on 5th and Main, told me once that life isn't even real. He said it's all just a figment of my imagination."

Artemisa shifted uncomfortably in her seat. "Who knows? Maybe Jack's right," she continued. "But, if this is all just a figment of my imagination, I have to do something to change the picture in my head. The way things are right now, I'm just hanging on to what ~ I do not know."

There was empty silence at the table after she finished her story. Embarrassed, Artemisa felt a hot blush engulf her face. She forced herself to search the eyes of the group for a clue as to their response to her story. No eyes returned her gaze.

When the meeting ended, Artemisa collected her papers and started to make a quick departure. She felt a warm gentle pressure upon her shoulder as she approached the open exit door. She turned her head to one side and met Marge's smiling face.

"Your story needs a bit of touching up. Maybe you can sort of center it around the old man. Make Jack a kind of sage or possibly an angel sent down from heaven to check on the ways of humankind."

Artemisa forced her lips into a smile. Now she felt better about having shared her story. Some white people can hear beyond skin color. Marge heard. Marge offered good critic. "Thanks Marge. I'll go home and play with the story. I like your suggestion about the old man. It could be that he is a wise sage," Artemisa said thoughtfully.

Marge's freckled face broke out into a spring smile. "I really enjoyed what you've done so far. As I tried to tell you earlier, Lenora, Ruth and I are forming a small critic group. We're going to take turns meeting at each other's homes. We really want you to join us."

"Well, thanks. Maybe I will sometime," Artemisa smiled nervously.

"Well how about next week?" Marge's eyes, level, held a look of sincerity.

Artemisa felt as though the others only tolerated her presence at the weekly writer's group meetings. Marge seemed different. Marge seemed not to even notice Artemisa's dark skin, as did the others, she was certain.

. "Come on. What do you say? Be in our group," Marge whispered softly so not to be overheard by the others. "We're going to meet next Tuesday afternoon at my house. I'll fix lunch. Twelve thirty."

Sensing the sincerity in Marge's voice, Artemisa felt okay to take the risk. "Sure. I'd love to come."

※

Pieces of the Tapestry

Star dust born on winds
Of changing seasons scatters
Over fields of sun.

)(

-Elizabeth Bowers-

A SECOND THOUGHT
by
Helen Tulis

Parasol spills across the sky,
Trumpet, billowing and multicolored,
The lofty pillow jousting with the wind and cloud,
A mere whisper from the winch boat,
"Take hold and fly three hundred fifty feet up,"
With boldness you are tugged
Leaping above the shimmering sands,
Hovering gently above the emerald ocean,
The guidelines tracking the beachcombers,
They look up
Testifying to your bravery
While they scan the multicolored pillow,
Under which the rider sails,
Only to see him as a dot,
Before his energizing, dry and safe
But reluctant to live the great adventure again.

)(

Pieces of the Tapestry

Rohdea, lost in shades
Of trembling lily leaves, gives
Shy smile to winter.

ℋ

-Elizabeth Bowers-

WHAT AM I DOING HERE?
by
Eleanor Freemer

The voice on the phone said, "Sure, we meet every Wednesday afternoon in room #213, building 'C.' Very informal. Please come."

The small ad under Arts in Dekalb was an obligatory open notice from a writer's group that met at the local College, for anyone interested in creative writing. She hadn't asked for my name so I was completely anonymous and had a week to syc myself up to go or not to go.

"I am a creative writer," I told myself. "I have had a few essays published, was even paid for one or two." My daughter says that makes me a professional, even if the pay wasn't much. So by Wednesday afternoon, when I walked into that classroom, I was feeling pretty confident. But when I took a look at the kids lounging bonelessly on the wooden chairs set in a semi circle, I was ready to take off. Young! Even the professors looked younger than my own children. Let's face it. When you're over sixty, everyone looks young, brash, and assured.

So I sat down near the door, put a false smile on my face, and waited to see what would happen. Before the meeting started, everyone introduced themselves ~ name, rank and what college degrees they had, or were working towards. I felt all this was done for my benefit.

"See who we are." They all seemed to know one another. I could feel an easy camaraderie among the ten or so that day.

Was I to be awed by the fact that even the one member who looked well past retirement age, was going for a degree?

Pieces of the Tapestry

They listened without comment as I recited my credentials. "Housewife, mother, grandmother and high school graduate in the year 1943."

They must have seen me as a strange specimen, surely. But I must have passed muster, or was being tested. They asked me to bring something to read the following week.

I drove home wrapped in a blanket of euphoria. The people I had met today were professionals. They were not meeting to pat one another on the back with a "My, that's great." Each offered whatever expertise they had gained to help improve what had been presented. In turn, each expected to be treated with the same respect. I liked that. Even though I felt like a dinosaur, I knew I could produce a paper as good as some I had heard that afternoon.

By listening, I learned. By next quarter, I really felt accepted, and took as well as I gave. We then became "FORUM," and moved into more comfortable quarters. Other people joined the group, some older, closer to my age. All were part of the college system or alumnus of other institutions of higher education. It was a constant changing tide of new and old friends, forming and reforming, drawn not by the moon, but by work and school schedules.

When Artemisa joined the Forum, she became the catalyst for our forming our own small off shoot group. She spoke of her face being slick from fear when she first read. I saw her face glowing like warm chiseled mahogany. So strong, so sure of herself, her voice like velvet, as she read parts of the fantasy she was writing. Her brown eyes softened as she spoke of her family, and we learned of an extraordinary person as she dipped into her huge journals to share with us her letters to God.

Did she feel the strands of love reaching out, weaving this tapestry between the four of us, as her spirit reached out to us? The woof and warp of Artemisa's strength pulled us from the various parts of the room and we gathered together after the session and decided we must meet one day every other week to talk, to write, to be friends.

I feel humble and inadequate in the light of their talent and ambition. Ruth, the professor with her Ph.D., becomes technical. Her dark head bobs up and down in approval as we read. Little exclamations emit from her lips. Quickly, she marks spots on our papers for our enlightenment. Ruth's sense of humor, enthusiasm and compassion glints through the stories of her father, which reveals so much of Ruth herself. She races to finish this saga as a gift to her mother.

Marge's pale face closes up as she retreats behind her shield, restive, wanting to go on. Marge is the romantic. Her pathos, her love stories and poems, stir us to silence. Her heart is laid open and so vulnerable. Her husky cigarette laugh, cheers us when she is up; and when she is down and rejects us, we tug and pull her back. If her thread is broken, the whole tapestry will unravel.

Artemisa reads and researches how we must go about presenting this opus. She writes everything down. Artemisa writes. How I envy her exuberance. Her experience in the years before we met has prepared her for our project. They each have their expertise. Fifty pages from each of us, Artemisa pronounces.

Oh Lord, what can I offer? What am I doing here?

)(

Pieces of the Tapestry
*Dreaming Woodlands hold
Secrets of true challenge, in
Season of great strength.*

✹

-Elizabeth Bowers-

FEAR

by
Elizabeth Bowers, Eleanor Freemer & Helen Tulis

Characters   (All women over forty)
Ruth   (Jewish)
Artemisa   (Black American)
Marge   (Irish Catholic)
Lenora   (Jewish)

Before Rise: Beethoven's Symphony No. 9 plays softly under the clash of a dish hitting a tiled floor and the shrill shriek of a cat.

Marge: (snapping) Damn cat! Get the hell off the counter.

Time: May 10, 1995 at around 12:30 noon.

Setting: A spacious dinning room.   A platter of bagels and a carved watermelon filled with fresh sliced fruit sit in the center of a table set with service for four. Obvious containers of low-fat cottage cheese and cream cheese flank the water-melon. The chairs and china closet are made of the same highly polished oak as is the table and the buffet.

At Rise: Ruth, Artemisa and Lenora are sitting around the table chatting. Marge walks in carrying a silver tray containing a matching coffee service, a black and white cat at her heals.

Pieces of the Tapestry

Marge (rushes in): Sorry about all that noise. My daughter is still in Ireland. She took the children to visit their great Aunt Anna. I'm baby-sitting their untrained cat. The darn thing keeps getting up on my kitchen counter. (She sets the coffee service on the table and proceeds to serve the other three.)

Ruth: (rummaging through a notebook): So whose turn is it to read today? I took up the whole session last week.

Lenora (nonchalantly reaching for the cream): I've got a thing I did on Fear. I'll read it while we eat desert. (She looks at Marge). Well, have you called her yet to check on things?

Marge (wistfully): Boy, you want to talk about fear! I live on a pension. I don't have any money. I don't call anyone long distance any more. Not since Mac died.

Ruth: (reassuring) But you see now how it is. They all call you.

Marge (sarcastically): Yes. When they need me to baby-sit.

Artemisa (interrupting): My big fear is worrying about my Jason. It's been hard for me since he finished graduate school and left home. I'm so used to being his mother, you know. Now he's on his own and I feel at loose ends. I call him long distance every day. I've got to stop it though. It makes him think I don't trust him. It's not good.

Ruth (supportively): You will stop.

Lenora (aghast): I certainly hope so!

Artemisa (matter-of-factly): My phone bill's going to be out of this world if I don't.
Ruth (sympathetically): You raised Jason right so you know if anything were to occur and he needs you, he'll call. You see, he may not need you right this minute. Next month ~ you'll cook this and this. He'll be home.

Pieces of the Tapestry

Artemisa (demure): You know, I found out he doesn't cook. The last time I went to visit him, I went into his kitchen. His freezer and cupboards were full of the exact same foods that I packed for him to take with him when he moved. The price tags were still on the pans. He hadn't used them. He eats restaurant food. That's not good.

Lenora (clinically): He will cook soon. Just give him time.

Marge (spreading cream cheese on a bagel): I don't know about that. My Scott has been on his own for almost ten years. He never cooks. I can't worry about it though. It's his body.

Artemisa (through sips of coffee): Well, a lot of its because he travels. He goes everywhere, all over the South. God, how I hate that! And so he doesn't ... When he's home, he says he's too tired to cook anything. He orders in.

Ruth (looks aside at Lenora and winks): You can't blame him.

Artemisa (to Ruth): Yes, but the restaurant food is loaded down with fat. I get afraid when he goes to those one stop Southern towns. Bigots, you know.

Marge (absentmindedly interrupting): Mac pays me alimony only when he feels like it. Nobody wants to hire someone my age. They want young and thin. I'm afraid of being poor.

Ruth (lecturing): Everybody's got fears. I get afraid sometimes when I look in the mirror and see this old woman with sagging cheeks and graying hair looking back at me. How about you Lenora?

Lenora (Matter-of-factly)   Well, this is what I wrote about. When I see a gang of kids at the mall, or on the street, jostling one another, their laughter loud and wild, I feel a shiver of fear.

Marge: (through sips of coffee): Are you afraid because they are Black boys? I mean, it seems a natural question these days.

Pieces of the Tapestry

Artemisa: (interrupting): Well that makes me darn mad. I can't even watch the six o'clock news anymore because it is so completely biased against Black Americans.

Lenora (with might and main): Did I say they were Blacks? Did I say they were boys?

Artemisa: (stiffly to herself): But that's what you meant.

Lenora (forcefully): No. All I said was that kids in a bunch frighten me. It is not the color. It's the number. It is their attitude that I, an elderly woman alone; am invading their territory. They sometimes walk shoulder to shoulder and defy me to walk between them, to break down their wall.

Ruth (to Lenora, analytically): Well, you know I used to love to work for hours alone in the library at my synagogue, arranging books and updating things. But I don't stay there alone anymore. Not since the fire bombing. I could have been killed. But what kind of fear makes people want to bomb a synagogue or cross the street because they see a group of youths? Let's try to shed light on where this fear comes from. Maybe we should do some research and write a book about it together.

Marge (through bits of food): That was terrible about the synagogue. I thought that kind of thing was all over.

Artemisa (a dry laugh): Don't we wish! I like the idea about us all writing a book together. We don't have to just limit it to fear though. Maybe we can fictionalize aspects of our own lives. You know, write about our parents, our child hoods, falling in love, our children. Our book can be about issues of living that we all have in common.

Ruth (aside to Lenora): That might be a good way to bring out the matter of where our fears come from. That way, maybe we only have to mention fear once or twice. People will get the message. What do you think Lenora? Maybe your paper on fear can be the first chapter. Where did this fear you described come from?

Pieces of the Tapestry

Lenora (thoughtfully): I don't know. Maybe from the time when I was in High School. We often stayed late for some school activity, especially in our senior year. And, the walk down Snyder Avenue through Philadelphia's Italian neighborhood was like going through a war zone. The boys threw bottles at us. We girls would run breathlessly down their street, our arms wrapped around our heads, giggling in fear.

Artemisa (matter-of-factly): But then, you were young girls running down the street. That's a whole lot different than being over 40 and walking through a mall crowded with high school kids.

Ruth (probing): Sometimes it is the unknown we fear. Maybe it is from some terror we lived through in our past. Remembering, reliving makes our hearts pump and the adrenaline push us beyond our strength.

Lenora (confidentially): When I was about four years old, I developed some type of bulge in my neck.

Marge (amazed): Oh my God! That sounds horrible.

Lenora (looks aside at Marge): The doctors could not diagnose it. They hadn't discovered the miracle drugs yet. Thinking it was my tonsils, the doctor put me in the hospital for what was, in those days, serious surgery.

Artemisa (sympathetically): You must have been terrified.

Lenora (nods her head affirmatively): My mother was not allowed to stay with me so I cried and cried, finding no peace. A nun in a long black robe, a white wimple, and a cross on her chest tried to comfort me.

Ruth (calmly): Well, did it help?

Lenora (aside to Ruth): No. All this kind creature did was frighten me, almost more than the sounds and smells of the hospital.
Ruth (probing): You were afraid of her uniform?
Marge (interrupting): Well I've been catholic all my life so the uniforms don't bother me. You're Jewish. I guess to a Jewish child, the long black robes trimmed in white would be terrifying.

Pieces of the Tapestry

Lenora (nods): The next morning my mother came as early as they would allow her in. She stayed until my tonsils and adenoids were removed. After a few hours, my mother's brother came to take me home.

Ruth (analytically): So how does that affect you know?

Lenora (aside to Ruth): For years the Nuns invaded my dreams. They chased me up and down dark alleys, past iron gates, where my little hands clung to the bars in fear that these black creatures would fly away with me.

Artemisa (nods, looks insulted): So the Nuns made you afraid of Blacks? I'm Black. You're not afraid of me.

Ruth (conciliatory): She's just trying to get to the root of her fears. That's what we all have to do.

Marge (matter-of-factly): Sometimes in explaining things, we say one thing and whoever is listening hears something entirely different. The words get twisted. Mutilated. Like now.

Lenora (defensively): I'm just trying to be honest. My fears are not irrational. Just look at the evening news or read the morning paper with your breakfast and you'll find yourself looking over your shoulder all day long. Watch ... is the working word! Watch where you park your car; watch who drives too close to you on the expressway; watch out for anyone who walks too close to you in the mall; and always watch out for the stranger.

Artemisa (matter-of-factly): I cannot have my mind messed up like that. That's why I stopped watching network TV news. I only get the weekend paper for the business summary and the coupons. You can't imagine how much it hurts to hear nothing but terrible things about your own people day in and day out. None of the good. Only the bad. If I watched, I'd be bitter.

Marge (nodding): Some times I think its all a plot to keep the races separate. But look at the four of us. Irish catholic, Jewish, and Black. We sip Irish coffee with our bagels, and we eat fresh fruit served in a water-melon rind.

Ruth (reflectively): I wonder, do the young, like little animals, smell our fears and find that exciting. Is this all part of the facade they present, a persona like we have never encountered in this life?

Artemisa (excitedly): That's it! That's what we'll call our book, "The Facade."

At Close: Marge begins to clear the lunch dishes from the table, as they all begin talking at once, excitedly about "The Facade." The cat races off stage.

)(

Pieces of the Tapestry
MAROONED
by
Eleanor Freemer

Mourn, mourn, for a friend lost,
swept away in a maelstrom
of tears, anger, accusations.
We three are survivors of a ship
tossed, broken against a rocky shore.
Our spirits strewn like sticks
across the desolate landscape.

Sitting helpless amid
the void she left behind,
we listen for her smoky laughter,
as she calls us precious.
Yes, we were precious to one another.
Only her empty chair reminds
us of what we once were.

Can we just forget her, our friend,
whose blue eyes mirrored her every mood,
dark with sorrow, light with joy;
heaven's child whose temperament
moved by the cycles of night and day,
of winter and summer, of spring and fall.

We worry, where has she gone?
Is she marooned on a lonely island
an empty beach, etching her thoughts
into the sand to be consumed each day
by the tides?
How far is she from our voices, our reach,
the love we still feel for her?
Our friend.

⚥

Pieces of the Tapestry

See the flower of
My heart, dressed in golden sun
And racing moonbeams.

✳

-Elizabeth Bowers-

RESEARCH
by
Eleanor Freemer

    We three sip ice tea sitting around a kitchen table that looks like a besieged island. Every inch is covered with books, papers, and computer discs. The conversation is lively, sometimes bombastic, often sentimental but never boring. We move from what we are writing, to what others have written. Inevitably, someone takes a U Turn and we are on a road marked, spirituality.
    My friends do the animated talking, on religion, and metaphysical matters, a science they take very seriously. They speak of forged chains linking their souls to their minds, to their bodies. Names of Great writers, philosophers, fly from one friend's lips to be caught in a nod of agreement by the other.
    I turn my head like a tennis spectator, listening, thinking, "They should be at peace with themselves, not fine combing through their beliefs." One woman converses with God and the other with a holy spirit, they both agree brings them peace. While they speak of harmony, my heart pounds from the turbulence they are generating. I close my eyes, not able to watch them searching out passages, highlighting sentences, like Monks holding up tapers that throw dancing shadows across catacomb-like walls. Are they finding answers in those scribbled hieroglyphics that waver and fade as the light goes out?

Pieces of the Tapestry

I envy them their accomplishments, their knowledge. I once admired their self assurance. Now I see they are like children afraid of the unknown, of the dark. With awe, they swallow the indigestible words of these sages; wind them around and around their arms like the straps from the Phylacteries, to follow as a lifeline, hoping to be led out into the sunshine.

I am with them, yet I feel alone. Leafing through each book, I pick out catch phrases and shake my head in bewilderment. Anger boils up like lava from a long dead volcano. Is it my ignorance, that makes me profess my denial?

Picking up a newly discovered book, I read aloud, stopping to look at my two dear friends and laugh. "Excuse me, but why should I care that crumbs from my brain swim down to connect all the parts of my body? Will that induce me to strip and stand in front of a mirror and study this sagging edifice? Can I command my crumbling brain to send signals to this aging body to straighten up and thin out?"

How can my intelligent friends live their lives by other people's credo's, other people's wisdom? Why don't they listen to their own souls? Why do they embrace philosophers, whose formulated catch phrases are telling them things they have known since the day they were born.

We all learn to cope with what life serves us, good or bad. We learn that by living. Those of us who are strong will survive merely because we are survivors. We can not travel well or fast while wearing someone else's mantle; it may either drag us down by its weight, or be too short for our stride. Why would we want to erase chapters from our biographies, then rewrite them to make them all more palatable? Won't the scars remain from the indigestible ink; the pains still throb? It is our past that gives us the strength, the experience, to weave our futures, and share with others our own undeniable wisdom.

Do I believe in God? Do I believe in a spirit who guides the universe? I have lived so long; seen so much tragedy, hate, chaos, yet miraculously I have survived. Is my life in someone's hands who has allowed me to finally run my race; who has given me this new found strength to believe in my own worth? Only now have I the courage to write what I feel, what I know, leaving a legacy for my children.

Pieces of the Tapestry

"I believe," I tell these worldly women, "that the good coming from reading these books is that they confirm ideas once thought to have originated with us."

I fan myself with the book in my hand, and proffer it across the table. "So, my dears, I believe, you are as smart as they are. These guys are making a lot of money by telling you truths you have always known." Myself, I long to scream "charlatan" and sweep everything onto the floor. Maybe it's because they make me feel small; or are too erudite for me to understand. Frankly, I find myself becoming too arthritic, to squat down at some Swami's feet.

Sitting at this table I have too much to say, while seeking guidance from my friends on how to say it well. We three meet to share our ideas, our experiences. They listen to me, when I tell them what I have learned about myself and my place in this gigantic universe. I suck up with a straw, their wisdom, like juice from an orange. I have too little time to waste in searching through these Atlas's finding pathways to my soul. I must hurry home and write.

♓

Pieces of the Tapestry

Sparrow digs for joy
In scattered dust of fallen
Mountain's rise to faith.

✶

-Elizabeth Bowers-

WITNESS
by
Elizabeth Bowers

The one who sees the trembling
Behind the facade
Of a struggling soul,
Grouping through rubbery shadows
In plastic meadows
And asphalt fields whipped by
Wind blown doubts
And fear, like clashing thunder in
The brightness of day,
Searching for God in the Hinterland
Of souls attached to miry clay;
Looks past nylon glances and fiberglass words
And beholds the unseeable mountain
Of forever, bright as the diamond of truth.

✶

5. Growing Out Of Pain

Season of Wisdom
Rides nightingale wings through clouds
Of breathing thunder.

♓

-Elizabeth Bowers-

ME
by
Eleanor Freemer

I can remember the me
that used to be
when passion coated my skin
like cream, and I could
feel your presence,
like the scent of balsam wood,
sweet and pungent wherever
I was and you walked by.

I was warm but you were cool,
You the jester and I a fool
for loving you, a star
that glided through the night,
uncaring, hard but bright
and far beyond my reach.

Now I comb the sunny sands
for star fish, like floating cans,
washed up on the summer beach,
their empty husks remind me of you
so I throw them back into the sea.

♓

Pieces of the Tapestry

Lilies sleep in time
Of shadows and ice, as snow
Dove flies through window.

✷

Elizabeth Bowers

I HEAR YOU MAYA
by
Elizabeth Bowers

I Hear you Maya, 'on the pulse
Of this good morning' as you tell about
The long departed parade of species,
'Hosted by a Rock, a River, a Tree,'
Formed from the dust of all that
Walk the sands of creation,
On the occasion of the inauguration of change,
Which sounds the curtain call to unity and service.

Maya, my torn soul trembles as the Rock
That houses the material atoms
Of all that I am calls me to account saying,
"Dance no more in a nightmare of bloody dreams;
Wake up, for the time of sleeping is past."

Terrified, that I can no longer hide
In the shadows of past glories,
Nor find a safe port in my own aloneness,
I rush forward to the Tree,
Hoping to bury myself deep within its roots
So I will not have to walk new paths.
But the Tree will give me no rest;
It turns me around to face
A dying city filled with sadness and disease.

Pieces of the Tapestry

I cry as I walk into the city
Of fat rats crawling over children, clad in rags,
Huddling in alleys, eating scraps of garbage.

There is no time to return to the River
That you spoke of Maya, no, not now,
Though its song of rest is alluring;
For the Tree has shown me my work.
My only hope of a haven now
Lies somewhere in the dying city,
As I look to the Rock for strength
To do what I can to
Mend its broken, tattered frame.
And the Tree says to me, "Embrace the city,
Sculpt it into the shape of inclusion,
As you gently hold it with your heart,
And a way will be made out of no way for
The healing of its wounds
So that prosperity and vigor
Will be the reward
Of the body of the city
As every talent is put into service."
Then peace and order will be my haven.

Even as I awaken to a new reality,
My soul still yearns to
Answer the song of the River,
But the cry of the Tree touches my heart;
And I am folded in change,
As I hear the Tree say, "Walk into the wind
Holding the hands of all the children."

Now, I hear the Tree say, "Lean on the Rock
But also be the vessel for the River
And go forward, though the wind be strong."

Pieces of the Tapestry

Maya, far too long, I struggled in the darkness,
Separated from the wisdom of the Rock.
But I have no weapons to use against
Drugs, homelessness, and unemployment.
Bigotry and disassociation are my attendants.
And Maya, as you know only too well,
When I thought I had the answers,
I had no answers at all and I fell,
Because I was separated from the Rock.
For a long time, I could not hear the Rock
As it said, "Come to me here by the River."
I did not understand what it meant as
It said, "Plant yourself by the River."
For a short while, I did rest
With the Rock but then I strayed,
And fear drove me back into my own shadow,
And my feet began to bleed and I fled,
Leaving only my bloody footsteps behind.
And in a stolen moment of time,
I arrived on a nightmare and lost my soul
To burning tears and sad songs,
As I relived a terrible history full of lost hopes.

But in my terror,
I heard the Rock say,
"Step into the shadow of the tree,
And turn away from the nightmare."

And so, in the shadow of the Tree
I walk with my face to the wind,
Doing battle with fear, doubt and disunity,
Holding the hands of all the children,
Their blood and the blood of all the ages,
Flowing through my veins, nourishing
Every atom, every cell, and organ,
Of my body, giving material being to my soul.

Pieces of the Tapestry

My eyes are wide open and I am aware
That I hold the seeds of my new beginning
In the palms of my hands.

Dreams of a bright day of morning
Filled with inclusion for all
Spring forth from the River and flow
Forward into my reality,
For the Rock has paid my passage,
And I have accepted the ride
Into changes for the better
For me and the whole human race.

And dear Maya, on the pulse
Of this fine morning,
I am aware of my oneness with
The Rock, the River and the Tree,
As I look up into the faces of
My husband, my children, my friends
And even strangers
And, in faith, wish them all a good morning.

)(

Pieces of the Tapestry

Weak branch draws life from
True vine as winter rains turn
Fallen leaves to mulch.

){

-Elizabeth Bowers-

KOSHER IS KOSHER?
by
Eleanor Freemer

"Momma, I forgot to tell you, when you asked us over for dinner tonight, we're only eating GLATT KOSHER meat from now on."

"*Glatt Kosher*" I repeated like a parrot, "I'm marinating Martin's favorite steak for dinner, can't *Glatt Kosher* wait till tomorrow?"

"No Momma," our youngest daughter declared firmly. "It's something we decided we must do *now*."

Fine, I thought. For your father and me kosher is kosher, so we will eat steak, and you and your family will eat ground turkey burgers.

Kosher was good enough for them for fifteen years. Now only Glatt Kosher is pure. I resented this new restriction that thrust me farther into some no man's land, where again I was found wanting. The silence between the two phone lines throbbed with emotion.

"If it's a hardship we won't come."

"It's not a hardship, but this new directive could have come before I went to the butcher."

"Sorry."

She didn't sound sorry at all. Gently I replaced the receiver, wondering, what's next.

"What's next?" This has become our family motto since our daughter adopted an orthodox life style. When she started college in Atlanta, she joined Hillel. A very persuasive young Rabbi guided his young disciples like converts into a new intense experience. Our home was turned upside down. Labels appeared on sinks, dish shelves, cutlery drawers and pantries, MILK ~ MEAT, as if I didn't know which was which.

After candle lighting on Shabbath, we were careful to ascend the stairs to our bedroom before the timers on the living room lamps plunged the house into darkness. She lectured me on my old system of Kashruth, inherited from my mother of blessed memory. I didn't read labels on products I bought as carefully as I should. K was out, and I was given a list to study on what I could and could not use.

To tell the truth she was getting me on my nerves. Our daughter seemed to have lost her sense of humor as she wrapped herself in the mantel of righteousness. When she said she was leaving for Israel after graduation, though never a Zionist, I sighed; "Oh Pioneer you're what Israel needs." Our friends and relatives wondered where we had gone wrong.

My husband and I exchanged war stories with other parents in the community whose children became Orthodox. One friend, told me tearfully that after her son graduated from college he moved out of the home she ritually koshered for his sake. He moved into an apartment with a shiksa. She laughed bitterly, saying she not only lost a son but gained three sets of everything from towels to pots and pans. Was she trying to console me that my child would one day leave this stringent path?

Our daughter married a young American she met in Israel, who is as religious as she is. Eventually they moved back to Atlanta. We saw more restrictions in their lives, and in turn ours. New mitzvahs were adopted, but some, like the Glatt Kosher, I refused to give in to.

One Saturday night we were invited to a Malave Malka (a term which was unfamiliar to us) at our daughter's new home. We felt as if we had wandered into a country far from Atlanta. Women greeted each other wearing long dresses, with sleeves down to their wrists, and scarves covering their heads. The men all bearded and in black hats, milled around in a room separate from their wives. We looked for our daughter, but we were among complete strangers. Then, a young girl with long blonde hair turned around, and smiled, "Hi Mom." This was the first time we had seen her in a shatel. It carried me back to my old bubah, who wore an unflattering red wig low down on her forehead. Her clumsy head covering, in my mind, had more religious meaning then the finely styled one my daughter sported. For some reason, this angered me. As a symbol, it seemed hypocritical.

My sister in law, who fortunately lives in Philadelphia, does not allow distance to keep her from telling us, in no nonsense terms, how deprived her brother and I are. We can not know the pleasure she and her husband share in taking their grandchild to Big Beef's for a hamburger on a Saturday afternoon after shopping at the mall.

I tell her sincerely that we have other spheres of pleasure with our grandchildren, like attending ceremonies as they receive their first Sedars, at school: listening to our two oldest granddaughters giving their dvar torahs at Bat Mitzvots, at age twelve: having our two daughters and their families together around her Sedar table: hearing the grandchildren read from the Haggadah, their lively discussions; and watching them grow up in their unquestioning beliefs in HaShem and Judaism.

We have been blessed with baby namings for our granddaughters and brit milahs for grandsons. All go to religious day schools, and each aspect of their lives is prefaced by a blessing and prayer, which we respect.

On our refrigerator we keep a book opened to a list of blessings that must be recited before washing and eating various foods. We check it before the youngest eats anything here. The three year old says a prayer, to be safe, each time he washes his hands, even after using the potty.

This year we had a special celebration; our little red headed grandson was having an "upshearing" his ritual hair cut. He spoke about this event for months before the affair, just like others spoke of the Super Bowl that occurred on the same day. There were as many people crowding into her house for this event as were for his brit.

Sometimes we wonder where our very bright grandsons will find their futures. Will our granddaughters always follow the ways of their mothers? Will they ever be comfortable in a secular society, or will they remain isolated in this soft cocoon, the only world they know?

⚘

Pieces of the Tapestry
RESTLESS
by
Eleanor Freemer

It's time for me to move on, free
and light like the leaves
sailing off from the dogwood trees
that now stand naked in the autumn breeze,
vulnerable to the first frost and snow.

I too must now blow
along the winter cluttered lane
fragile, brittle, rolling in pain
like a stone scuffed by the wind, washed by rain,
always on the go.

Do you see me, a ghost, a bone,
crouched in an oysters' deserted shell to hide
from nature's roiling furies outside,
wrapped in my own private hell inside,
washed by the changing tides alone?

Hear me come, an old jalopy
squealing with every twist and turn
of the road, a wheel stiff from summer's burn
and winter's ice, my heart a broken churn,
finding no resting place for me.

Pile up the vines that cling
to broken walls and summer grass.
Rake them up for a bonfire so I can pass
in light, through winter's silver and autumn's brass
into one more spring.

⚭

Pieces of the Tapestry

Lamb of shinning peace
Lays down upon prickly thorns
In season of rage.

⚹

-Elizabeth Bowers-

MORDA
by
Elizabeth Bowers

She ignored the sensation of queasiness twisting her stomach and reached for the phone, now on its sixth ring. "Morda Ruffin. Can I help you." Her accentless voice, crisp, held no hint of the apprehension she felt as the office walls swayed in rhythmic response to the earth tremor now in progress.

"This is Austin Tilman here. I've been trying to reach you all day but you never returned ... Whoa! Are you feeling that? My whole office is shaking. Tremors are coming in hot and heavy these days. Think maybe the Big One's on its way?" Austin's voice, a deep baritone, held a hint of strained humor.

"I sure hope not." Morda gripped the blue princess phone tightly between her neck and shoulders, hands pressed hard against the arms of the rectangular oak desk for support, as the earth tremor continued its roll, causing the floral drapes to ripple like wind waves in a lake filled with eastern sun. "Maybe this rolling is just the spirits talking to us. They're probably telling us to get home to our families who, no doubt, are feeling neglected by now," she laughed.

"You're probably right," replied Austin.

"But Austin, you didn't call me at this hour of the night to talk about any earthquake. What's up?" She half rose out of her seat and leaned across the neatly appointed oak desk, reaching in vain for the jade paperweight, Evan had given her for their fifteenth wedding anniversary, now rolling on to the plush burgundy carpet.

"Blanden. The Surfer gang leader. The DA wants you to personally prosecute the case. He wants a conviction this time and he feels you're the only one who can get it for him. Will you do it?" His tone was serious.

Morda put a hand to her free ear to block out the rattling sound of glass banging against metal hinges. "So I've heard. I've already reviewed the evidence file and frankly, there is a lot to consider here. I'm swimming in pending case files. Besides, taking on Blanden means taking on the whole lot of that White supremacist gang. The Surfers are not just a gathering of deprived kids, you know. They're very well connected in this county and quite dangerous."

"Sure. They're powerful but I've seen you in action before." He smiled recalling her court stance last week. She moved with an ageless air of fragile power; so self-contained. Her features, exotically African, unmarked by years of struggle to climb to the top of the legal field, held no trace of defeat. Her form, slender, average height, belied her cunning ability when pressed hard by a tough situation. "I've never met a woman quite like you. I'll tell you this, I'd never want to be on opposite sides in the court room with you. I'd say, you're up to the battle Morda." Austin's tone held a hint of challenge.

Morda sighed. "It's going to be a pretty rough ride dealing with them." Her fingers, slender and brown like fresh honey, hurriedly flipped through pages contained within the manila folder. Surfer insignia, a Nazi swastika held up on the head of a four eyed cobra, was on the outside cover.

A noise, like that of a full grown donkey trotting down a dirt road, thick with dry mulch, startled her. She looked toward the open office door, surprised to see her secretary, Susan Carpenter standing just inside the opening, as though measuring the various capacities of the room with searching eyes. Susan was an abundantly endowed woman in her middle forties, and a little dumpy and saggy in an oversized polyester suit, pea-green like her eyes. A half smile spread over Morda's face as she caught Susan's eye and waved her in, motioning her to sit in the blue swivel chair, like her own, facing the desk.

"Mrs. Ruffin, I was driving by and saw your car parked out front. When you get through ..." Susan whispered. She hurriedly stripped off her jacket, and hung it over the back of the chair before squeezing her bulk into the seat. Her massive thighs spread over the edges of the cushion as she leaned to the side and placed her purse on the floor.

She glanced aside at Susan. "Thanks. I'll be with you in a second." Morda rolled her tongue around in her cheek as she scanned the Surfer file. Her ebony eyes formed into narrow half moons as she strained to get a better look at the small print.

Morda pressed the telephone receiver to her ear. "Well, to tell you the truth Austin, it doesn't seem like we have a lot to go on. Your witness list is pretty shabby. They are either dead, dying or afraid to testify. I'll have to start from scratch and that's going to take a miracle considering the money you guys are offering."

"Come on Morda." Austin's voice held a persuasive urgency. "You know our hands are tied on the money. Come on. Help us get that scum off the streets before someone else gets hurt."

Morda seethed with agitation, although she doubted Austin could detect it. "Look. I'll tell you what," she snapped. "Even though I'd be the one facing him in court, it still involves my law partners. I'll need their agreement before I can go ahead with this." Lines of worry spread from the corners of her eyes.

Austin agreed with her argument but pressed on with his own agenda. "Hey. That could take up a lot of time. The DA wants to get started immediately," he coaxed.

Morda raised an arched eyebrow, exchanging a quick glance with Susan, who was listening intently. "Hey. They have a right to decide. If you recall, the last time his case went to trial, the prosecuting attorney's whole suite of offices went up in flames about a week into litigation. It effects us all."

"All right Morda. But do what you can to persuade the others. The DA has made it quite clear that he wants you in charge of prosecuting this case." Austin's tone was tense. "He said he doesn't think anyone else has the talent and endurance to stay the course to conviction and I agree with him."

"Save the flattery Austin, it's late. I'll get back with you after I have talked with my partners." Drained, Morda bit her lip as she hung up the phone.

Pieces of the Tapestry

Morda's hands, clenched tightly together, lay heavy on top of her head. Her thoughts whirled in confusion. She barely heard the rattle of windows as another earth tremor rolled in beneath her feet like an easterly wind through a willow tree. She found her own emotions and tensions running down. Now she only wanted to go home, kiss her children good night, soak in a hot bath for about an hour, then curl up next to Evan and sleep in peace for a week without having to worry or think about anything. Her mouth was a tight line as she stared at the case file in front of the desk blotter.

Susan pursed her lips. Her dimpled fingers played with the folds of the polyester skirt she wore. In a recess of her mind, there grew a sense of urgency crying out against the injustice of having been reduced to a mere gofer for a Black woman who carried herself with an uncharacteristic air of aristocratic haughtiness. It annoyed her that Morda obviously had no idea where her place was in the world. Susan looked sideways at her, eyes glaring. "Look, Mrs. Ruffin, I know it's late but tomorrow the Labor Day weekend begins, and I ..." She cleared her throat, her voice softly persuasive.

Morda's features lay exposed. Her high check bones, seemed to sag and her small nose, slightly rounded at the tip, twitched like an impatient rabbit. Her lips generous, and touched with a brush of autumn ember, were drawn.

Susan held her emotions in check as she waited for Morda's attention. "The office won't be open again until Monday and that'll be too late."

Morda drained the last drop of coffee, cold and stale, from her cup. "Susan, I'm really tired, but since you're here, I'll listen to what you have to say. But first, I've got to take a few minutes to recharge my batteries. My mind doesn't work when I'm in a fog like this. Can you run to the cafeteria and get me another cup of coffee please? Black." Morda ran a hand through the tangle of off-black curls that fell to her shoulders and sighed deeply.

Susan pursed her lips in injured silence. "Certainly," she snapped. "I'll go make us a fresh pot. But I ... ," She glanced aside at Morda. "I need to tell you what's been on my mind for quite some time." She leaned toward Morda. Her narrow eyes searched Morda's drawn face for a clue to her mood. "You are happy with my work, aren't you Mrs. Ruffin?" She held her gaze steady.

Morda stiffened her back, instinctively folding her hands on the desk as she tilted her head forward to meet Susan's gaze. "I don't have any problems with your work." It seemed to Morda for a moment that Susan's features had taken on a disquieting look as thick creases in her neck stretched up like stairs to meet her dimpled chin.

"Well then perhaps you might see your way clear to giving me a raise and an extra week's vacation." Susan's voice was frigid with dislike for the menial role she was playing.

Morda forced a smile to hide her aggravation. "Susan please. I'm drained. I've got to have a few minutes to center myself before we talk." Morda folded her arms on the desk and cradled her head on them.

In a huff, Susan reached out a short, chubby arm, and turned off the oval desk lamp. The hinges squeaked loudly as she stormed out of the room slamming the door shut with the force of a full grown elephant.

♍︎♒︎♋︎■♑︎♏︎

Now only the dim light of the quarter moon filtering through the open blinds in a window half hidden by burgundy draperies, gave light to the room. Morda felt weighted down by indecision. She raised her head and pushed slightly away from the rectangular desk. She swiveled around in her chair, and fixed her gaze out the window. "God help me to know if I am up to the battle, as Austin puts it. The Surfers. God!" She trembled at the thought of having to go up against them again. Dear God, what should I do? And Susan? Please give me a sign?" she whispered.

Like a butterfly on the last breeze of summer, Morda rose from her chair. Her hands clenched together behind her back as she glided softly to the large corner window, taking long, deep breathes all the way. She wet her lips with her tongue and drew in a deep breath. She set her own thoughts aside, as she stood like a bronze Buddha on a burgundy pedestal, caught in the experience of supreme exhalation. Slowly, she counted from ten to one, holding her breath and patiently coaxing her body into a state of deep relaxation.

"I am balance. Upon the waters of calm joy, have I set my sail wholeheartedly," Morda chanted as her eyes followed the outline of a pickup truck, headlights off, moving slowly through the side parking lot. As one standing on the edge of a dream, she watched until it moved out of sight leaving only dark night in its place. Caught up in the power of her chant, she drank deeply of the air, artificially sweetened with the scent of fresh apples, cleared her mind and let herself escape deeper into the silence of her soul.

♍︎ ♒︎ ♋︎ ■ ♑︎ ♏︎

A slight breeze tickled the center of her back as a loud creaking of hinges in need of oiling abruptly shattered the silence. Her reverie broken, Morda returned to her desk with the saintly air of a Buddhist Monk just purified by the sound of a thousand gongs. She sat impassively with her eyes fixed straight ahead, hands resting on the arms of her chair.

Susan smothered irritation at being ignored, drew in a deep breath, then cleared her throat. "Shall I turn the lamp back on, Mrs. Ruffin?" she said, eyeing Morda's silhouetted form. Without waiting for an answer, Susan placed the silver on white china coffee service on the blotter, reached across the desk and turned the lamp on to full bright. She stood with her head cocked to one side, waiting.

There was a brief moment of silence before Morda shifted her chair around to face Susan's eyes, bloodshot and surrounded with darkening shadows that showed the lateness of the hour. "That's not going to be enough light. Better turn on the over heads," Morda said a little louder than she intended. "We've had a few earth tremors tonight and I need to see well to make sure everything's in order before we go." Morda managed a smiled, pulled herself erect and reached for her cup of coffee. "It's going to be a long weekend."

Susan struggled to keep hidden, her intense dislike for Morda's arrogant airs, as obediently, she did as she was told. Tonight, she was not going to give Morda any reason to bite off her head. She felt the roughness of the fabric as she gave her skirt a quick sweep with the palms of her hands before flicking the light switch. In calculated silence, she settled into the chair.

Morda studied Susan's oval face, framed with flaming red curls cropped short, that sat perfectly atop a meaty stump of a neck. She could not help wondering at Susan's motivation as she looked upon her nearly chalk-white complexion, the kind of unhealthy paler that comes from years of hard living. Between sips of hot coffee; bitter as though reheated from a much earlier brew, she said, "What's going on with you Susan? You know as well as I, that after hours is hardly the time to negotiate pay raises and vacation schedules. So what's really up?" Her eyes, dark with the brilliance of a beam of coffee in the midnight hour, stared down at Susan, measuring, waiting.

Susan lifted her balk out of the chair, strode to the window and silently watched the dance of the night, then turned to Morda. "I was at the police station earlier this evening and I heard some rather disturbing news. It seems that Hank and Danny, those two Surfers you put away a few years ago broke out of jail late this afternoon. I thought you'd want to know because the word is that they're after revenge." She went very still, avoiding Morda's gaze.

Feeling the tightness of her muscles clamoring for attention, Morda arched her back and stretched her neck. Out of the corner of her eye, she caught a glimpse of the heart- shaped clock on the wall above the mauve chesterfield sofa. Her mouth flew open when she realized that it was already half past eleven. Most reasonable folks were already in bed by now, she thought. She picked up the Surfer case file and waved it in Susan's direction. "Look, I appreciate your taking the time to let me know about this but in all honesty, I couldn't stay in this business if I let these kinds of things get to me." Morda's tone was conciliatory. "Listen, It's very late. I need to get home. I've got a lot of stuff I have to take care of there. Let's get out of here."

"Yes, Mrs. Ruffin." Susan knew well the lateness of the hour but made no comment about it. Unlike herself, she knew Morda always loved working until all hours of the day and night. But tonight, she would enjoy her work too. "But you really ought to take those guys more seriously. I wouldn't take this new case if I were you. Blanden is ..." The sound of the telephone startled her into silence.

Susan glanced aside at Morda's face, satin smooth and nut-brown in the glare of the overhead light. "Shall I get that Mrs. Ruffin?"

In answer to Susan's question, Morda reached for the phone and lifted it off the base, cradling the receiver close to her ear as she rummaged through the case folder. "Hello." Her tone was soft, like spun sugar. "Oh! Hi Honey." There was a brief pause.

Pieces of the Tapestry

Evan's voice had an angry edge to it. "What time do you think you'll be getting out of there?" he asked. "Did you forget about our trip tomorrow?"

Morda found her emotions and tensions running down as guilt engulfed her. For years she had grappled with the best of them in the legal and political arena, and prided herself on never forgetting a name or an appointment. Somehow, when it came to her personal life, things were forgotten all too often. She squeezed her eyes shut tightly and slapped her free hand upside her head in exasperation. In just a few minutes it would be the eve of their long awaited cruise up the coast. How could she have let work get in the way of an event that important to her husband and children, she wondered. Embarrassed, she said, "I'll shut it down now and be on my way home real soon."

"Yes. I've heard that stuff before." I hope you really mean it this time." There was a loud click as Evan's voice faded.

Morda felt her stomach tighten as she hung up the phone. She found herself in the grip of an odd feeling of disquiet and fell silent, her eyes staring vacantly at the white walls.

"Sorry about this," Morda said, turning to face Susan. "That was Evan. We're leaving in the morning and I haven't even packed yet." Morda ran a hand over the stacks of folders piled high on the corner of her desk. "There's so much stuff to be done around here but, I've got to do this or Evan and the children will never speak to me again." There was a tense urgency in Morda's voice.

Susan pushed herself up from her seat, stretching. With a sigh, she strode back to the window and watched the advance of a truck as it made its way through the side gate. "I think you need to go with me on this one Mrs. Ruffin. Don't tangle with the Surfers again. Let the DA get somebody else to prosecute the case." She turned and faced Morda.

Morda remembered her first encounter with the Surfers, the terror and revulsion she'd experienced then was still fresh in her mind but so was the taste of victory when she won the case against two of them. "That one's still up for debate. I'll give it some thought this weekend." Morda thought she saw a glint of mirth in Susan's eyes but dismissed it. "Take care of these files on Tuesday, will you?"

Susan kept a smile hidden as an after-shock moved through the office like a rolling sea. The office door flew open and the pictures on the wall rattled in its wake. Luck and a swift retreat by the fearless Black warrior bent on accommodating everybody, bought Susan to the point where she needed to be right now. Susan nodded. "Yes Mrs. Ruffin. I'll see to them." Her tone was one of forced respect. "Oh, by the way, I dismissed the guard out front because he said he was really nervous about all the tremors and needed to get home. He already secured the front so we'll have to leave by the rear exit. I'm parked in the back so I'll drive you around front to your car."

"Okay. No problem." Satisfied that everything was in order, Morda got up to leave. She slipped her arms into her jacket, then felt the softness of gray cashmere against her palms as she smoothed a day's worth of wrinkles from her skirt. The muscles in her back groaned as she bent forward and picked up her brief case. Her tension eased as she stepped through the opened door and into the well-lighted hallway leading to the rear exit where Susan stood, back resting against the door jam, looking very much like an over-stuffed rag doll.

♍︎ ♒︎ ♋︎ ■ ♑︎ ♏︎

The moon had long sense retreated behind a thick patch of midnight clouds. An ominous chill filled the night air. Darkness hung like a thick blanket, unbroken by running lights of planes or stars. Morda felt her stomach tighten as she made her way through the maze of parking stalls beside Susan, a light rain falling. "I guess somebody forgot to turn the flood lights on," she said, turning to Susan, voice shaking slightly.

Susan's breathing was uneven. "They must have been damaged by all those tremors because I made sure they were on when I went to make your coffee," she hissed between clenched teeth.

Morda's grip tightened on her briefcase as something cold and mushy like mashed potatoes that have sat too long on the plate, hit her on the side of her face. Recoiling, she reached a hand up and grabbed it from flight. A chill ran through her as she realized what it was. "My God," she groaned, "an over-ripe banana peel. Where in all the world did this come from?" She looked at Susan. Her eyes wide open like round jewels, held a glint of fear. "Come on Susan, something's not right. We'd better get out of here fast."

Pieces of the Tapestry

Susan nodded affirmatively. "I think you're right. Banana peels don't fly in light wind. Besides, I've got an awful feeling in the pit of my stomach."

There was a breathless silence between them as they walked quickly toward the staff parking spaces. As they approached Susan's blue station wagon, Morda was sickened by a rancid smell like that of a lubricant used to ease the tension of metal jams. She turned her head around and winced at the sudden introduction of a pair of head-lights turned on full bright, coming from the back of the parking lot near the chain link fence. She nearly tripped over her own feet as she looked upon the leering faces of two men walking toward them.

"Susan, we're in trouble. Let's get out of here fast." There was soft urgency in her tone.

Susan was amazingly calm as she inserted the key into the car door lock. She eased her bulk into the front seat and locked the door. "I just had my car oiled so it should start easy." She adjusted her mirror, then turned on the ignition.

Morda turned toward the men, surveying the distance between where they stood and Susan's car. Quickly, she dashed to the passenger side of the blue station wagon. She could almost feel the power of the men as they advanced toward her, slowly, deliberately.

More angry than scared, Morda grabbed the car door handle. "My soul! Susan it's locked. Please unlock the door. We've got to get out of here." Morda caught a glimpse of intense rigidity on Susan's face and decided that her assistant was too overcome with fear to respond to her pleading. All of Susan's attention seemed to be focused on her own need to get her car started and get away to safety fast.

Susan hesitated for a second, then turned to Morda as though to speak, an unmistakable look of malice in her eyes and an ominous expression on her face. "I have ..."

Morda could tell by the sound of their footsteps that they were gaining ground. Her throat constricted with an unimaginable spasm of fear that lasted for just a second. Determined to save herself, she grabbed hold of Susan's car door and tried to pry it open with her bare hands. "Open this confounded door!" There was vinegar and bitter lemon in Morda's tone. "For mercy's sake, let me in."

Susan's face broke out into a crooked smile as she gunned her engine and skidded forward like a shot, down the long expanse of the one-way ramp leading to the exit gate. The smell of burning rubber mixed with exhaust fumes hung in her wake.

Morda stood, legs astride and mouth open wide, in disbelief at what had just transpired. She felt a wash of terrible outrage well up in the pit of her stomach as she watched Susan's car disappear from view.

In that instance, a sick feeling of being caught in a web of her own spinning, came over her and she deeply regretted making the life choices that had brought her to this moment. With all her being, she wished she had left work at five o'clock, along with everyone else in the building. Tears welled up in her eyes at the thought of never seeing Evan and the children again. If she lived through this night, she would do things a lot differently, she vowed.

The sound of water, dripping slowly but steadily in a tinkling rhythm like freezing rain bouncing off a metal roof, brought her back to the business at hand. Too angry to be terrified, she pulled out the shoulder strap of her briefcase and slung it over her neck as a shield. Determined to survive, she stepped out of her high heel shoes and fitted them for war, one in each hand.

A powerful heat weld up within her face and neck, driving away the last remnants of ordinary thought as like a soldier in full battle gear, she turned, ready for the dance of war. "Angry clouds wage war with determined blue sky on rainbow laced with gold," she chanted in earnest, speaking the words of her faith chant under her breath, centering herself. Now it was as though she were being consumed by some other force. Powerful.

The headlights flashing from the battered pickup truck gave her a clear view of her attackers. One was a little over six feet tall, and gangly like a gray hound. In the glare of the lights, his skin looked to be the color of wet Kenyan beach sand. It clashed terribly with the orange short sleeve shirt rolled tight above his upper muscles. Morda braced herself for danger when the light flashed on the tattoo of a Nazi swastika held up by a four eyed cobra on the outer portion of his upper arm. His long, stringy hair, off-brown like his eyes, was oily and in great need of washing.

It was the short fat one that held Morda's attention. His eyes held the glint of a wild cat teasing his cornered pray. His blond hair was long and stringy like a horse hair rope pulled loose by a forward moving tractor in an oil field. Through his dingy-white T-shirt, soaking wet with rain and perspiration, she could see Surfer insignia. The zipper in the front of his blue jeans was wide open exposing a stubby appendage that he grabbed, then started waving about as though it were a weapon. Disgusted at the sight of it, Morda gagged as she struggled hard to keep from throwing up the meager contents of her stomach.

"I got somethin' for you black berry," said the short fellow, moisture pouring down the side of his face in rivulets. "Come on here and git it Sheba." His nose, pointed at the tip and wide at the base, seemed to twitch like that of a jack-rabbit trying to decide its next move.

Morda waved her high heel shoes at him in response, then turned and ran like a cheetah chased by a big game hunter in the thick of an African jungle. She felt the grit of the cold, wet asphalt against the soles of her stocking feet as she raced toward the building. Somehow, she had to make it to her car. It was her only hope. But the truck! How could she escape it? Someone had to be in it because the headlights were flashing on and off in a controlled manner. How could she slip by them and ease her way to the front of the building, she wondered. Once there, would other Surfers be waiting for her? If she could just make it back to the side door, she could slip back into the building, call for help, she thought.

In the shadow of the building, she risked a look over her shoulder to see if they were gaining on her, but saw nothing. She took several steps backward, still scanning for movement, then stifled a scream as her right foot met with the sharp edge of a piece of glass. "Oh, my soul, that hurts." Dizzy with pain, Morda rested her back against the darkened flood light pole, and quickly examined her injured foot as best she could in the dark. With a steady hand, she removed the large, jagged piece of broken flood light that was lodged deep in the sole of her foot.

Morda heard the sound of rushing water splashing hard against concrete but did not spare mental energy to speculate about it. She knew the men were still somewhere in the parking lot laying in wait for her. Getting to a telephone inside the building was her only hope. For an instant, doubt crept into her mind, doubt born of the logical probability that her attackers would most likely catch her before she could make it to a phone. With the mental control of a shaman, Morda let that thought go by focusing all of her energy upon the task of getting steady on her feet. Though the pain was excruciating, she forced herself to ignore it and darted in and out of walled parking stalls. As she made her way toward the building, she occasionally looked over her shoulder. She had to be sure no one was near.

Lightning flashed through the glittering blackness of the night, making the rear door to the building visible for a second. The tall man was leaning up against the side door, a drawn switch blade in his hand. Shaken, Morda ducked into a nearby utility shed. She shivered as a steady stream of cold water fell from the metal roof in buckets, hitting hard against her body. A breath of musty air sent a shiver through her as she realized that she would have to quickly come up with another plan of escape or die.

Over the chattering of her teeth, Morda heard the loud hissing of a heavy breather and realized that one of her attackers was close. She could not give in to fear though, or she would surely fall to defeat. No. She had to keep her wits about her. It was the only way to survive. Soon there would be another flash of lightening and she would use it as a lamp to point out his whereabouts.

The water stopped falling on her and Morda felt something pressed up against the small of her back like a hot coal. The foul scent of onions and garlic mixed with stale tobacco and cheap bourbon, made her gag.

Morda summoned courage. "Lamb of shinning peace, lays down upon prickly thorn in season of rage," she chanted to herself, breathing deeply. Then, in a single motion, she turned around and faced her attacker. Her voice rose, reflecting the strength that suddenly jumped in her eyes. "What are you people after" she demanded.

"Listen jungle bunny, we hear you're going after our main man. Well, you ain't gonna be prosecution' none of us no more. But first, chocolate cakes, me and my boys, we got somethin for you," he leered, pinning her back to the wall as he pressed his body hard up against her suggestively.

Morda ignored the disgust she felt and instead, summoned up sufficient strength to push him off of her. Quickly, she raised her left knee and pressed it hard into his groin, then struck him sharply about the eyes with the pointed heels of her shoes. He let out with an agonizing scream and grabbed his crouch with one hand and his eyes with the other.

Pieces of the Tapestry

"You don't have anything I want," she yelled, then turned and limped toward the ramp leading to the exit gate. When she felt that she was far enough away, she looked back just as the two men were climbing into the front seat of the pickup truck. The driver gunned the engine hard, slicing the air with the noise.

Over the awful coughing of the truck's engine, Morda heard a loud roar like a freight train rumbling through the parking lot, and the ramp started shaking as though it were a small motor boat rocked by the wake of a sea-going tanker. Water began shooting up high into the air like a gushing oil well. Alarmed, she dropped her shoes and crouched down on the ramp just as the parking lot began to rise in the middle then split, as though it were a loaf of bread cut in half by a dull knife. Conveniently for her, the fissure separated the ramp and the building from the red pickup truck.

Another flash of lightning came just as she paused to catch her breath. She watched in horror as truck and passengers were swallowed up by the open fissure. She heard a terrible popping sound and watched in stunned amazement as flames came up from where the truck went down. Tears welled up in her eyes as blessed darkness fell upon her like a curtain, screening out the pain.

♍ ♒ ♋ ■ ♑ ♏

Evan was kneeling over her, a somber smile on his light brown face, when she awakened. His eyes, soft and dark like Brazil nuts, held a look of relief as she smiled back at him. She reached up a hand and gently ran her fingers through his hair, thick like the wool of a black sheep forgotten at shearing time. She looked about her, memory foggy, and was surprised that she was in her own bed. "Evan what happened to me? How did I get here?"

He placed an arm under Morda's head and lifted her slightly, pressing his lips against hers. "There was an earthquake. A pretty big one. It caused quite a bit of damage."

A pulse throbbed at her neck as she remembered the explosion. "My building. Was there any damage to my building?" she cried.

Evan looked at Morda hesitating. "Some. Not too much to the structure but the back parking lot is a mess and the main water pipe busted and ..." he explained in a tense whisper. "If you would have made it to your car, and started it, you probably would have had a bad accident. A lubricant was spilled all in your break-lining and steering mechanism."

Morda stiffened, remembering the smell of lubricant around Susan's car. "Was anybody besides me hurt?" She felt a tension racing through her like a rolling wave on an evening sea and fought it with her mind.

Evan studied her face for a moment to see if it was safe to tell her what happened. It held a look like none he had seen on her before. "Four people died but everybody else is okay. A fissure opened up in the back parking lot about twenty five feet away from the exit ramp where I found you bleeding and unconscious." A look of cautious concern filled his eyes as he paused to catch his breath. "I'm so sorry to tell you this." He held her face in his big, strong hands, a look of concern in his eyes. "They found your secretary. Susan's remains were with the charred bodies of three men inside the cab of a large red pickup truck. It was buried in the rubble." He reached a hand into the back pocket of his trousers and pulled out a jade paperweight. "I believe this is yours. It was the only thing in the truck that wasn't burned."

Realization hit her like a sledge hammer. "Tongue of anguished sea lashes out at exploding heart of volcano," She chanted, loud enough to cause a minor earth tremor. "Evan, I need you to do me a favor." She pulled the covers away from her chest to free her hand and reached for her address book on the nearby night stand.

"Anything."

"Get Austin on the phone for me. Tell him that I am up for the battle." She handed him the book. "I'll take on Blanden."

"Looks like a higher power took over. Blanden was one of the guys in the red truck. Hank and Danny were the others." He managed a weak smile. "You're exhausted. Doc Blankinship says you have to rest for at least a week before he'll release you to go back to work. Besides, Not much will be happening around here. The freeways are down and the major highways won't be passable for about a month."

Morda closed her eyes as she felt the heat of Evan's sweet breath against the softness of her partially opened mouth and the moistness of tears of relief upon her cheeks.

)(

Pieces of the Tapestry

FIREFLIES AND RAIN
by
Eleanor Freemer

There was no moon that night,
yet the garden was a ghostly gray,
as if clinging to wisps of the passing day.
Through the black trees, one light
flickered, then another iridescent glow
of garnets and topaz began to grow.

Tiny flames outshining the stars,
held in silver strands of rain,
like candlesticks wrought in ancient Spain.

We followed them over that rain glazed lawn.
On naked feet, we danced across an empty stage,
crushing the emerald mint and purple sage,

whose perfume marked where we had gone
to rest beneath the dripping trees,
to gaze up through the shinning leaves

and watch through ragged limbs, like iron bars,
the cathrine wheels drop spangled flares
that bathed your eyes and bathed your hair.

Oh the silence of that summer night
When down pillow s rested under their head
Like the moment when true lovers are wed.

Today she murmurs a strange request,
"Come sing to me the songs we sung,
the old fashioned ones
from when we were young.
Come lets dance the fox trot;
put your hand on my hip,
like Rogers and Astair;
we'll swoop and we'll dip,
we'll show the world we're still such a pair.

⚭

Pieces of the Tapestry

RACHEL
by
Eleanor Freemer

"Rachel!" From the moment he tossed her name into the house, like a gauntlet, he knew she was gone. His words, his footsteps echoed in an unfamiliar silence. He raced up the stairs, two at a time, calling her name, hoping to find her there but knew the room would be empty. The bed they had shared for the past two years, was neatly made; the coverlet pulled smoothly across the wide expanse. Its hem brushed the hard wood floor, shinning like the highly polished dresser and night tables.

Jacob pushed open the door of the bathroom. "Rachel?" He ached to see her slim small figure rise from the bubbly water, but the only trace of Rachel was in the scent of her favorite apple soap that still clung to a light film of steam on the flowered walls. Fresh towels hung evenly on the rack near the sink and the tub lay pristine and modest behind the shower curtain.

"Rachel, where are you?" It was a cry that would find no answer in this deserted room. He caught his reflection in the mirror on her closet door, and saw a young man whose clean cut, blonde hair looked raked and ravaged by his fingers. His striped conservative tie loosened from its Windsor knot, and the cool, efficient lawyer who had left his office at noon was now the insecure and frightened husband whose shoulders sagged as he retraced his steps down into the den.

This, her favorite room also looked naked to him. No books tumbled across the desk, no week's supply of local and out of town papers fought for proprietary space on the coffee table. Only sunshine, spilling through the open curtains, left a stain on the smooth white carpet. A shiver ran down his spine as he felt the eyes of his mother staring down from a picture that Rachel must have hung over the fireplace that morning. His mother seemed to be surveying the room with a genteel smile of approval. Yes, his mother would approve of this neatness, this order.

"Oh God," he groaned. Did he really want Rachel to be like his mother, and his home like the one he hated when he was growing up? Always, it had been ready for unexpected company, a showplace, not comfortable like this one was. Rachel had brought a new dimension to his arid life. She had given him unquestioning love and joy, and what had he given her? A hard time.

"Rachel." He remembered first seeing her three years ago when friends had dragged him to a poetry reading at the Lullwater Tavern, saying he lacked culture. Even a lawyer, they tried to convince him, needed to know more than torts and legal phrases. He sat and listened. Half of what was read made no sense to him. If that was poetry, it was not to his taste, but Rachel was. She sat next to him, hip to hip, in a crowded booth; her warm, husky voice teasing him, as his eyebrows rose higher and higher over each satirical phrase. The laughter in her brown eyes captivated him. He discovered real poetry and music in her every word, and great artistry in the graceful movement of her slender hands.

After graduation, and joining his father's law firm, they were married. Jacob felt this meant that Rachel would change a little. At least, she would try to become more like the wives of his young colleagues, conform to his hard gained stature in the city. Last night, Rachel had not filled that crucial role.

He had called in the afternoon to say he was bringing an important out of town client home for dinner. He had not been able to reach her until five o'clock.

"Oh Jake, I'm sorry. I was in the studio putting the finishes on the poster for the Spring Fling Ball. I was so engrossed, I didn't hear the phone." She gave a nervous giggle, "I guess I had the bell turned off. You know what a deadline does to me."

His voice was stiff and cold. "I hope you can meet a deadline for me. I've invited Michael Ash for dinner tonight. You know how he hates eating out. Do you think you can take a break from your arts and crafts to hustle something up by seven?"

"Aye, aye Captain," she laughed. "I'll even find time to make some strong frozen daiquiris so he won't notice if the food isn't up to New York standards. Don't worry, everything will be fine. Even me."

She was fine. Michael's eyes lit up when she walked into the den, looking like a Gypsy in a peasant dress and a pair of dangling earrings that Jacob had bought her in Madrid. Michael didn't seem to notice the books and papers all over. Some were spread out on the sofa like bed sheets. He casually pushed a pair of her shoes under the chair when he sat down. He didn't even mind that the steak was over-done and the potatoes not quite done. The conversation and the salad however, were to his liking, and the drinks, as she predicted, were potent. Michael Ash, since his first visit to their house, had been enchanted with her.

After dinner, Michael had teetered back and forth on his heels before the flower filled fireplace, looking up to admire the oil painting Rachel had painted of the cobblestone plaza in front of the hotel where she and Jacob had spent the first night of their honeymoon in a small village in Spain. It was all mauve and silver, the moon casting a spell over the fountain that seemed to reach up its arms to their room.

♍︎♒︎♋︎■♌︎♏︎

The picture and Rachel, were now both gone. With a heavy heart, Jacob walked into the kitchen that had lost its very soul. No empty cups or sauce pans filled the sink. Any aroma of fresh baked bread was covered by the antiseptic smell of pine soap, and the after-taste from the argument he had started after taking Michael back to his hotel last night. Had it been jealousy or stupidity that made him carry on so?

He towered over her, a menacing figure, as she leaned down ready to put the last platter into the dishwasher. He took it from her hand and slammed it against the table. The heavy pottery plate rang out as if in protest, but remained undamaged. His anger fed on itself like a roaring flame, consuming everything in its path. That was the moment, and here was the place where he threw at her the classical remark on the way his mother did things. "She would never use such plates for company when she had beautiful wedding china and crystal." Was Rachel afraid of making a good impression. Clients judged him by his home, his wife, and a look of prosperity. Maybe it was a fallacy, but they thought if you did well for yourself, you would do well for them.

She sat leaning against the cabinet, listening with a stunned look on her flushed face. "Michael is not like that Jacob. You know he is a client and a friend. Why are you so angry?"

"Michael might not mind, but I do. This is my house too Rachel and I don't ever want to bring a client here and be embarrassed."

He stormed out of the room and up to bed, leaving her there on the floor nodding her head in agreement like one of those little toy birds that

Pieces of the Tapestry

bob up and down in a glass of water. Yes, if that was what Jacob wanted, that is what he would have.

Breakfast was a silent meal. He left early for the office. Finishing his business with Michael, he drove him to the airport. Michael's conversation floated around Jacob's head but it seemed that the reason he stayed with Jacob's law firm was that he enjoyed his visits with them. The warmth and unpretentiousness of their life style gave him the feeling that they would always do the right thing for his company. In New York, lawyers were a dime a dozen but they were all too hard pressure for a guy whose roots would always be down South.

♏︎♒︎♋︎■♑︎♏︎

He had driven home right from the airport, wanting to make amends but she had vanished, leaving behind a place he knew he didn't really want. Would she ever forgive him? He had no idea where she would be at this time of the day. Feeling like a fool, he picked up the phone and called her friends. The answers varied. She could be at the art gallery on Highland, reviewing a new exhibit or maybe at the bookstore on Peachtree. She loved the musical afternoons there. Did he know if today was her day volunteering at the children's hospital? Their warm laughter said Rachel could be anyplace. How little he knew her anymore.

His eyes searched beyond the deck as he stepped outside and was shocked to see the plants she treated so tenderly in the house, drooping like sad weeds out here in the sun. He could hear himself complaining to Rachel that her damn pots were always in his way no matter where she had put them. "God, what a fool I've been." Then, he saw them. Her shoes, one or another of them could always be found under the sofa or lying like a booby trap on the steps, now marched like footprints across the lawn. Breathlessly, he followed them to where they stopped at the edge of the creek in back of the yard.

"Rachel," he cried out across this desolate wilderness where all he could see was a smug looking green frog staring at him with unblinking eyes from a fallen tree limb.

"Rachel, Rachel, where are you?" The frog's body swelled up like a giant bubble. Then it seemed to wink at Jacob before belching out with a loud, insolent, "Hurumph."

♓︎

Pieces of the Tapestry

*Sunshine keeps its sweet
Song hidden in the blink of
Gray cloud's solemn eye.*

ι

-Elizabeth Bowers-

MOM
by
Helen Tulis

When I dial my mother's phone number, I usually hear, "Ring, ring." Then I wait. I wait, until mother can navigate the room, to reach the phone. This requires much patience. Sometimes many minutes slip by as I look at the clock, and listen as the phone continues to ring. My emotions and thoughts fly in all directions. "Ring, ring." No answer.

I know my Mom is 92 years old, and I should not expect her to quickly run to the phone the minute she hears it ring, but I cannot accept her aging. I want her to be perky and quick like she used to be. I want my mom to still be agile and perceptive like the woman she was when I was young. Unrealistic you say? Of course.

I do not want my mother to withdraw from her body when its limitations are set. It is difficult for me to accept my mother's use of the cane when only two years ago she could walk up and down flights of stairs several times a day. Now she considers her cane a part of her body, as she holds it to steady her gait. But of course I am unrealistic. Mother once said, "Just like little babies get stronger each day, so I get weaker and weaker. Do you understand?"

I do understand, but do not want to accept my mother's fragility. The indignity of frailty is insoluble. It combines both injury and destruction in its meaning. My mother is frail like delicate crystal, and she cannot see center vision. Just the other day she began to hold onto me tighter, as she walked. Even small levels like the curbs are difficult for her to judge. She holds onto her cane more deliberately. Getting out of the

Pieces of the Tapestry

car is not an easy task for her, as she lacks cartilage in her knee, preventing her from bending them to get up. Then, Mom's body is an object. She sighs. "It is not so easy to get in and out of a car lately." She places her cane down first before she steps out.

Nothing is easy for my mother at this stage of her life. Always independent, she lives in her own home with a young man as a boarder, so she will not be alone at night. These days, getting her own breakfast of juice, oatmeal, toast and coffee, has become a real chore for her. It hurts to remember the enormous breakfast Mom made for all of us when we were young.

In her younger days Mom squeezed fresh oranges every morning, to make juice. She got up, earlier then the rest of the family, to cook cereal, make French toast, rolls; or homemade waffle batter for bran waffles. Dishes were cleared and washed while we were all dressing for school. Then Mom made our lunches, wrapping sandwiches, and bags of vegetables and fruits. We left home with full stomachs and anticipating "what's for lunch?"

Now Mom talks about food with little enthusiasm. She complains about food she has cooked herself. "I have no appetite." Then she puts the cooked food back into the refrigerator. "I'll eat these leftovers tomorrow."

Tomorrows come and go and Mom still insists that she is not hungry. She either throws away the leftovers or gives it to the birds. The birds are getting fatter and fatter, while Mom seems as if she is fading away. I long to hug her tight and ask "Mom, do you know how my mouth still waters for your delicious homemade waffles, and how I long for another chance to eat even just one more." But that would be too emotional for both of us.

"You don't know how I struggle to eat what your sister brings me." Mom complains.

I know my sister is a good cook, I am happy she brings some over to Mom, until Mom goes on about it.

"I never liked someone else's cooking. I like my own better," Mom goes on.

My Mom was once a wonderful cook. Preparing meals for 20 to 30 people, was always a pleasure for her. Every party or celebration became a banquet. Mom's gelatin molds with layers of various fruits molded into a design was a real specialty. Even though I often watched her make it, I can never duplicate them. Layer cakes were an easy task for her too. The three-layer chocolate cake with pineapple filling was everyone's favorite. I used to sneak three or four pieces after the company was gone to eat later. Gefilte fish made from scratch, including grinding the fresh fish, was a delicacy during Passover, that Mom made too. It is inevitable that Mom would not like someone else's cooking because it makes her feel as though she is incompetent.

Again I call Mom. The phone rings, "Ring, Ring" I wait minutes, that seem like hours. Finally I peer at the clock, "Why doesn't she answer?" I begin to worry. "Maybe she didn't hear it ring, maybe she's sick and can't get to the phone. Maybe I better drive over and check in on her?"

Then she answers, thinking I am one of my sisters. She talks to me about things she would never say to me.

"Mom, this is me." I break in.

"Oh, I thought I was talking to your sister," she excuses herself.

Often, my mother and I eat out together, so I can be sure she won't become undernourished. Lately, she has been enjoying Chinese food. She always orders her favorite soup, and egg rolls, though she tells me, "Don't order egg rolls, it's too filling." I smile when I look in her plate and notice she has devoured one egg roll and finished her soup. Mom loves vegetables, so we order a Chinese dish with plenty of vegetables and rice. Mom always leaves some vegetables, which the waiter packs up for her to take home. The surprise comes when we get our fortune cookies. Just the other night Mom opened her fortune cookie to find this; "You will have many years of good health." We looked at each other and both of us smiled at such a good fortune.

Recently, one morning, I called Mom, and she answered the phone almost immediately. "Mom, you OK?"

"Sure, I'm eating my breakfast now. Call me back later," she answered in a voice filled with vim and vigor.

If spirit is essence and is indestructible, then my Mom can live forever.

⋇

Nightingale, sing your song
Of empty shadows in
Field of broken dreams.

♓

-Elizabeth Bowers-

JUDGMENT
by
Elizabeth Bowers

Judgment weaves a tapestry of pain
Upon strained hearts, like needles tearing into flesh,
Untouched by patterns of formal skies
Blooming with true apologies.
In the tightness of the weave,
It is a cutting thing, needing expanse,
Wanting the amenity of knotted threads
And missed stitches, like trickling icy waters;
Weaving patterns of sorrow between waves in a rising sea.

♓

Pieces of the Tapestry
Diamond lights midnight
Garden on silken threads, like
Golden rays on thorns.

-Elizabeth Bowers-

OUR SON
by
Eleanor Freemer

This was one of the few times in his life that he arrived when expected; August 16, 1960, at 8 PM. His birth was induced, so he really had no choice but to hang around, until he was ready. The doctor did not want to take any chances with the third child of an RH negative mother. He sent me to the hospital across the street from his office, right after my last scheduled visit.

A BOY, after two girls, had my husband ecstatic. He came the next day hidden behind a huge bouquet of flowers and a big grin. Daniel Yoessel, would be his name, in memory of my mother, who had passed away in 1958, and a brother of his father, who most likely died somewhere in Europe.

Daniel Yoessel, 7.2 pounds, with a white cap of hair, blue eyes, a mouth like his father's, long slim perfect fingers and toes, but one foot turned in from the way he lay curled inside me. Our pediatrician said he was perfect, and I agreed. My father walked over to see me everyday, from where he lived with my sister. He would look in the nursery at his only grandson, who slept peacefully in his swaddling blanket, then come back to my room where we would talk about Momma, who kept nudging me about having another child ~ three children she had ~ I should do the same. This one was for her.

The foot straightened out, he walked, and talked and was toilet trained, but was never a social child. It seemed he was never a baby, but a little man, his mind always trying to unknot some vast problem that he faced each day. When the girls were growing up, a mere six and eight years before, this was a brand new neighborhood with a brand new crop

Pieces of the Tapestry

of babies. They always had someone to play with. But by the time Daniel came along, there seemed to be no one for him. He scorned to play with someone just his age. They were babies. Feeling he needed interaction with girls and boys his age, at three I enrolled him at the synagogue day school program. He hated it. He did not like the orchestrated activities; the regimentation of midmorning naps. After one session, he dropped out. I entertained him myself at home.

Physically he was thin, delicate looking. My sister-in-law called him chicken bone. Even at that age, did I secretly fear his appearance was fey, effeminate? His imagination baffled and frightened me. He loved to draw, and he often covered all the walls of the upstairs bedrooms and hallway. I bought him rolls of "butcher paper" as an alternative, for him to draw his purple mountains, green valleys and blue rivers and streams, which he would describe to me. With this gift he promised not to crayon on the walls again. He once drew a picture of how it looked and felt before he was born, and I looked silently at this three year old and wondered what was next. Then he insisted he was born in Japan, and cried over a trip, that we had never taken, to Canada and left him home alone.

We finally had new neighbors move in and they had a little girl who was a few months older then Daniel, and they became friends. He seemed to feel more comfortable playing with girls. We thought it was because they were non combative, and even at age four he looked like a good wind would blow him over. Did I feel more protective of him then I did with our daughters. Bossy Miriam could always take care of herself. She would never let anyone intimidate her. Dorothy moved in a wake of tears or smiles. One way or another she got what she wanted.

My husband was suddenly transferred to Atlanta. We had to put the house up for sale, get a mover, and arrange for the two girls to fly down to Atlanta, after we reached our destination, an apartment Martin had rented for us when he went to start on his job.

Martin said we needed a rug for the floor of the apartment as it was on the second floor and some kind of covering would be needed to smother the noise for the downstairs neighbor, when a family of five moved over them. Daniel wanted to go with us to the store for this purchase, but when Martin was ready to go he was not around, so we left without him. When we returned home with the roll of carpeting, my heart pumped up with anger, as I followed a trail of red crayon from the

Pieces of the Tapestry

basement up to the second floor. Daniel faced me in front of a bright mural in the dining room, his face set, waiting for me.

"You promised you wouldn't crayon on the walls again," I screamed, thinking of the job to clean them off before prospective customers came to look at this, my beloved home.

His little chin came out. His fists rested on his none existing hips, and calmly answered. "You promised to take me to the store with you. You are a promise breaker, so I am a promise breaker too." I hugged him and apologized, to this four year old who looked up at me defiantly. "Yes, a promise is a promise. Whoever makes it, then breaks it is wrong."

When we moved to Atlanta in 1964, again he revolted at the idea of going to any kind of preschool. I was happy when he finally started first grade, and he would be with lots of children his age, and perhaps among thirty or so he could make at least one friend. He made competitors, anyone who did better then himself; they had to be challenged; anyone whose parents offered them an opportunity to learn of a new undertaking, he must try it also. One boy told how his father had bought him stocks in the then budding Atlanta Braves. Daniel had to have stocks in some other enterprise and sat down with his father looking over perspectives; then choose a copper mine in Tanzania, something different, but never successful.

He confronted his first and second grade teachers on their teaching methods — hated audibly, when they repeated a lesson. He Sat shaking his blonde head, "No," when he did not agree with what they were saying. He soon was nicknamed Dennis the Menace, and spent much of second grade thrown out of the classroom, wandering the halls. When I confronted the teacher, she shook her shoulders, and said he wasn't missing anything in class. This angered me. Daniel needed a challenge which she wasn't willing or able to offer him.

I loved him, worried about him. He had no boyfriends in elementary school, ignoring any boy who even made an effort to be friends with him. He hung around his sisters and their friends, feeling more comfortable with the then teenagers. He did play with the girls in the neighborhood. I sent him to day camp in the summer, again a loner, but he did learn to swim and play base ball. One summer, we were really daring, and sent him to an overnight camp in the Smokies. His cards came home full of longing to leave. The counselor sent us a note that Daniel at eight was soiling himself, and I took this as a loud cry for help.

Our pediatrician, said it was only a phase he was going through, and not to worry. However we did worry, and felt something had to be done NOW. Thus started our trips to Child Psychologists, first at Emory, then when we moved back to Philadelphia for three years, to a private doctor. Were we doing this for Daniel, or for ourselves? We saw no improvement in his anti social behavior. In the higher grades he was teased by the boys in his class. Daniel was different and they saw it. Children are cruel. I didn't know what to do.

After three years we returned to Atlanta, and again I started with the psychologist, until Daniel refused to go any longer. Painfully, I accepted this lovable child for what he was.

♍︎ ♒︎ ♋︎ ■ ♑︎ ♏︎

The girls in high school were very attracted to Daniel. He was very good looking, clever, and had a great sense of humor. He would complain to me, "How can I tell them not to bother me, not to call me?"
He confessed later, that he had experimented with sex with one girl, who would never take no for an answer. I tried to tell him that because he was not successful with one girl it did not mean he could not have a satisfactory relationship with someone else. "No."

Daniel understood my bewilderment, his father's hurt; our son, not really a son. We tried. He told us, we had to back off, and accept him for what he is.

At sixteen he learned to drive. Once he had wheels, he could not be contained. His friends were night people; and even then he would come driving home at 3 o'clock in the morning. We would lecture, explaining that it was not that we didn't trust him, but we worried about him driving home at that time. We talked, took the car away from him, but this never changed his life style until this day.

It is always the same story, "We were talking, and didn't realize the time."

"Can't you call?" we countered.

"Time? I realized what time it was, I thought it was too late to call." Daniel was always logical.

Pieces of the Tapestry

♍ ♒ ♋ ■ ♑ ♏

Daniel is still a loner. He had a relationship with a young man for over five years, but it seems that even that kind of relationship is not what he wants. With the aids epidemic, we have worried and prayed, but he says we shouldn't worry about him. Could we, his father and I have done anything different? Is it something in our genes, passed down from one generation to another? There have been others in our family who have been gay ~ though never acknowledged.

Daniel has his music, and friends who have the same interest as he has. He holds down a good job, where he is respected and liked. Why do we worry that he is still vulnerable? Our hearts ache for his aloneness. Why do we still want to protect him from a cruel world? Is it just because we love him very much? He is such an important part of our family. His sisters, his nieces and nephews, feel that a family affair is not really a family affair without Uncle Daniel.

♓

Pieces of the Tapestry

Soul of morning star
Holds dread secrete of cruel night's
Dance with angry clouds.

)(

-Elizabeth Bowers-

ALONENESS
by
Elizabeth Bowers

Aloneness weaves a tapestry of nightingale's
Secrete dreams, clad in moon-bows hidden in starless skies,
Devoid of sweet melody of evening sparrow,
When angry clouds rage against
Love bird's first hour of budtime jubilation.
Threads of joy, degraded in loose weave,
Cannot form tight pattern of sparrow
Swimming in glory pond at mountain's feet.

)(

Pieces of the Tapestry

Heavenly waters
Sigh, in morning's fragile light
Heavy with longing.

ι

-Elizabeth Bowers-

Great Wide Ocean
by
Elizabeth Bowers

"The ocean is a great wide place and so is the world of sin," Daddy told me that night at dinner when I described my first day of school.

That was the year he preached about the Russians learning how to make atomic bombs and I learned how to make mud pies and stew from mulberry leaves, and wild thyme mixed with wet soil. I got a new pair of shinny black shoes with straps that buckled and five new dresses. My big brother and sister were already going to school. Now it was my turn, and I could hardly wait.

"Maryjane Foster and some of the other kids in my class stuck their tongues out at me while we were lined up at the water fountain. They said I was a coddy." I didn't know what a coddy was, but I knew it had to be something bad by the way they said it.

When it happened, I tried hard not to let the tears out that had welled up in my eyes. I fought them off valiantly. I'd promised Mommy and Daddy that I wouldn't cry when it was my turn to go to school.

"God doesn't like little children to break their promises," Daddy had told me many times.

♍ ♒ ♋ ■ ♑ ♏

Just as I was bending down to get a drink of water, I felt rough hands pulling hard on the back of my upper arm. My feet were in the air and my arms hurt.

Pieces of the Tapestry

Mrs. Cross's face was red and snarling. Her dull blue eyes flashed anger as she dangled my limp body before her. "How dare you stick your tongue at Maryjane Foster. Just who do you think you are?" She dropped me to the floor.

"She stuck her tongue at me." My stomach felt funny, like it was rolling fast. "I didn't stick my tongue at her," I whispered. "Only the children of the Devil do things like that. Daddy says that I'm a child of God."

I watched in horror as Mrs. Cross's right hand went high into the air, then landed, stingingly, across the side of my face.

"Liar! Now get back in the classroom and put your head down on the desk. I do not want to see your black face again until the bell rings for dismissal." Mrs. Cross drug me back to my seat in her kindergarten classroom and forced me into my chair.

I started to talk but she pushed my head down onto the desk with enough force to make me forget what I was about to say.

♍︎♒︎♋︎■♑︎♏︎

"I didn't get to learn anything today," I told Daddy. "The other kids did though." I told Daddy about what Mrs. Cross did to me.

Daddy looked at Mommy, then back at me. "What did the other kids learn about?" he inquired.

"They got to hear a story. But it wasn't about God. It was about a little baby deer named Bambi."

"Oh, I know that story," said my big brother. "Its mother got burned up in a big fire." My brother always knew everything, I discovered.

"They got to dance too. It wasn't to the songs of the Lord though, I don't think." I had heard the other children singing a song about circling to the left around a red wagon, while stomping their feet and clapping their hands to the music.

"Billowing waves roar loud but it is the wise drop of ocean that listens to the saving message in the wind. What else did your teacher teach the other children?" Daddy jabbed at his fork as though he were pitching hay.

"Lot's of it was the same stuff Mommy already told me about. The teacher told them about numbers and letters. All the colors too. She doesn't really know her colors though because she called me black." I

Pieces of the Tapestry

stretched out my arm in front of me and pointed to it with my free hand. "See. Look, I'm brown, not black," I insisted. "All the other kids are pink, like Mrs. Cross."

Daddy stopped eating and looked side-ways at Mommy, who had also stopped eating. "I want us all to stand for a moment of prayer," Daddy commanded.

His voice shook as he talked to God. "Dear Heavenly Father," he said, "Bless my little ones. Give them the strength to deal mightily with the slings and arrows of the evil one." Daddy raised his hands up to heaven.

I wondered if the gospel was about to come on strong like it did the time my big sister came home from the hospital. It did. Daddy waved his arms and preached like it was Sunday Morning and the living room was filled with us and visitors. He talked about the evil ways of the poor lost sheep and me, his blessed Hope.

"Open up the mind and heart of my blessed Hope to your goodness and your love. Give her the strength to overcome the wickedness of this world." After Daddy said amen, he sat down and picked up his fork.

That was our cue to sit down and finish our dinner, which by now, was luke-warm.

Daddy looked down the table at me. "With all thy getting, get ye first understanding. God wants you to learn, no matter what. Pray for those who despitefully use you, and get on with the business of God."

That night, I didn't think God would mind if I cried just a little bit. I'd been holding the tears back all day. I had to give them up to the great wide ocean. It's hard to pray when your stomach hurts. I had to pray for Mrs. Cross and for Maryjane Foster.

)(

Pieces of the Tapestry

Rain upon the rue
Hides autumn from the moonlight
Of my thorn filled soul.

♓

-Elizabeth Bowers-

PAIN
by
Elizabeth Bowers

Rashness weaves a tapestry of pain
Upon my heart like burning timber,
Untouched by threads of loving kindness;
In the tightness of the weave,
It is a choked thing, wanting expanse,
Needing the amenity of gentle silence
Trickling with life, like a cooling spring rain
Weaving rainbows between clouds.

♓

6. DREAM OF THE FUTURE

On wind blown sand stands
Cosmic flower, waiting for
Light of golden joy.

♓

-Elizabeth Bowers-

THE JACKS PLAYERS

by
Eleanor Freemer

Two pigtailed girls with summer knees
bruised like fallen apples from a tree,
sit crossed legged on a shaded porch,
tossing a moon shaped ball high
up into the summer sky;
while nimble fingers quickly pluck
star shaped jacks
into their summer warmed hands.

Where are they now that summer's gone?
Have they fled indoors
with Barbie Dolls in fancy dresses
and fancy names,
to play a different kind of game
made up of dreams and make believe,
searching for the grown ups
they soon will be?

Before next summer comes along,
they will be gone from the shaded porch,
and the jacks will wait
for other younger nimbler sun
kissed hands to toss and pluck
between their out stretched legs,
the age old game
of Jacks.

Pieces of the Tapestry

Season of Change sneaks
Up on peaceful fields of fall
With slothful vengeance.

※

-Elizabeth Bowers-

CHANGE OF SEASONS
by
Helen Tulis

The small house, situated near the beach, looked just like its advertisements. It set right in the middle of the luscious grassy space, allowing passers-by to see the porch. A few green palms spaced methodically, gave shady areas to the sidewalk.

Janet had always wanted to live in Northern Florida, not far from the beach. The metaphor in her meditation exercises was the word, "Beach." For a few years she had used the image of the beach to calm her down, to soothe her senses, and to dream of the future. Here, she was living in the very area around which she had created the beach image.

Today, she couldn't go to the beach. She was planning a two month trip to visit her children up North and had to swap her usual summer clothes for winter weather clothes. "After all, there is snow and blustery wind up North during the winter holiday season," Janet thought.

Her married sons had begged Janet to come for a visit. Ryan said, "Mom, it'll be cold. Pack some warm suits. You probably don't remember just how cold it gets here. You have been living in Florida long enough to forget."

"Oh, I haven't forgotten. I'll bring my wool scarf and some gloves. Don't worry," Janet assured him over the telephone.

As soon as Janet hung up, she went to the cedar closet and began pulling out scarves. The strong scent of moth balls stung her throat,

Pieces of the Tapestry

penetrating her nostrils. She began putting away seasonal clothes and pulling out sweaters. The aroma of cedar and moth balls pinged her nostrils and soared through her brain. Her mind became clouded, and fit only to recall some early childhood memories of cedar closet surprises.

♍︎♒︎♋︎■♑︎♏︎

Janet thought about a time when her sisters were five and one year old. She had been almost nine then. Her mother used to carry out a seasonal ritual.

As soon as the weather cooled down, and summer sun crept into hiding, her mother would say, "Come girls, it is time to put away all the summer clothes."

Janet never looked forward to this ritual because there were many sunsuits and shorts to fold and pack away. "How come we have to fold everything in half, then in half again?" she would whine.

"Because it is time to change for new season," her mother would answer.

Her sister, Emily, used to try on every piece of clothing before putting it into the pile to be folded. "Isn't this pretty? I like that. I can wear this sun-suit again next summer," Emily would say to the annoyance of her mother.

There was a huge cedar closet in the long hall off the master bedroom. The closet held all kinds of surprises for Janet. Clothes from her cousin Sharon, which were hand-me-downs, and sweaters from cousins in New York whom she had never met, hung in neat rows. Soft woolly blankets, and the floral bed spreads she helped her mother make last winter, were piled high on shelves. The only bothersome thing about this activity was the sharp odor of mothballs, stinging her nostrils and making her cough. Janet wondered why her mother never packed away winter clothes without stuffing the pockets and linings with mothballs. She doubted whether the moths could even find most of the clothes because they were folded and hidden inside the huge cedar closet.

Evening came and Janet was still helping her mother straighten out layers of summer shorts and cotton play-suits. She was annoyed with her sister Emily. "Those things are too small for you. Give them here so I can put them away. You are holding up everything," Janet snapped.

"I don't have to. This is mine. It fits me," cried Emily, struggling to fasten the snap on the side of a pair of blue shorts.

Janet pulled a pink sweater from a low shelf in the big cedar closet. "Why don't you try this on Emily," she said.

The sweater was at least three sizes too small for Emily. Still, she modeled it in front of the mirror and insisted upon having it. "Oh, pretty. This is mine. It fits nice," Emily smiled at her reflection in the mirror. "See Mom. See Janet. This is my pretty pink sweater."

Janet recognized the sweater from years ago. "That sweater belongs to me but you can have it. It is very pretty," said Janet deciding to keep the peace.

Emily was satisfied with her new acquisition and began to work harder to finish folding clothes. Their mother came behind them and threw mothballs all over the garments. Then, she quickly shut the door of the closet, letting the mothballs do their work.

Janet was glad she had finally finished her dreaded task. She could hardly wait to get to her bedroom and shut the door. Her joy quickly changed to dread.

Her mother tossed another handful of mothballs into the closet. Then she faced her daughters and said, "Now, let's see what's doing with those fall and winter clothes."

The thought of more work horrified Janet. She did not want to invade boxes filled with mothball soaked winter clothes. Her nostrils cringed as her mother opened those boxes. The clothes were generously sprinkled with mothball flakes.

"You take the boxes and carefully lay out all the sweaters," she said to Janet. "You may have to try on the clothes so I can decide which ones to give away. Some will be too small on you this year."

Janet tried on at least twelve skirts and sweaters before protesting. "I don't want these hand-me-downs. I want to give them all away," she said.

"Somebody will be glad to have these. Look at this lovely lavender dress. It's hand-knitted. Beautiful," said her mother.

"Well I think it's ugly. I don't care if it is hand-knitted. Besides, it looks awful on me," Janet protested. She was sure that if she wore it to

Pieces of the Tapestry

school, the other kids would poke fun at her. "It'll look good on Emily though. It may be a little big for her now, but she will grow into it."

Before her mother could comment, Emily grabbed the dress from Janet and was slipping it on over her sun-suit. "I'm going to look pretty in this," she said.

After they had looked over all the items, picking and choosing what would fit and what would be given away, Janet's thoughts turned to food. "Come on Mom. Can we take a break? I'm hungry for some delicious hot chocolate and that soft, springy sponge-cake that you made this morning."

They sat at the kitchen table nibbling on large chunks of sponge-cake and listening to their mother talk about the work still left to be done. Emily's eye lids fell shut on more than one occasion then. Her head hung limp as she half sipped her hot chocolate. By the time Janet had finished eating her cake, Emily was fast asleep, her head resting on the table. Janet wasn't at all tired. She just needed a rest from the boring routine of trying on mothball scented clothes.

♍︎♒︎♋︎■♑︎♏︎

With the familiar smell of mothballs emanating from the wool scarf hanging around her neck, Janet realized that she had been standing at her closet day-dreaming for nearly a half hour. "Today, taking out clothes for next season is not so much fun. I've already given away clothes that don't fit. Nothing accumulates. I wish I had a great big cedar closet like Mom's. I wish I had some live-in help to carry out the chores."

Janet looked at her reflection in the full-length mirror on the bedroom door. "Whew! My middle aged body," she cried and tucked up her sagging breast with her hands. "I used to have Japanese breasts. They pointed in different directions like east and west. What the hell happened to my waist line? I used to have a nice one. It seems this season, I just stepped right out of my body. Even my damn knees are fat." She held a black knit suit in front of her. "Oh well, this body will just have to endure until the next one comes. I sure wish I could preserve my body with moth balls like I do the clothes."

♓︎

Pieces of the Tapestry

THE BELL OF ST. NIKOS
by
Eleanor Freemer

    Clang-Clang-Clang,
iron against iron, strident demanding,
the bell of St. Nikos rings out.
    It is a mournful dirge
that tolls up and down the city streets
plowing through alleys,
rattling beer cans piled against the trees
where cats sleep with lost souls
who could not find their way home
after a night of revelry.
    Cover your ears if you dare
to stop the voice shouting out
from heaven, the great bell of St. Nikos,
as it shatters the early Sunday morning calm,
shaking the dreams from the moistened eyes
of those who still lie in their darkened bedrooms,
still sleeping the sleep of the innocent.
    No lilting carillon songs for the old Patriarch
who stands at his pulpit, arms outstretched;
a Christ on his rood, his golden robe trembling
from the power of his words that boom out
iron against iron, harsh clamorous,
shaking awake the souls of his penitents,
echoing the mighty bell of St. Nikos.
    Iron against iron,
louder and Louder and LOUDER,
until the great Cathedral's doors burst open,
the chapel swells with the yawning supplicants
whose mouths open wide feigning song,
as they fall upon their knees and bow their heads,
and their prayers like smoke, spirals up to heaven
past the now silent bell.

)(

Pieces of the Tapestry
Skylark, in great day
Of morning-glory rides tail
Of faithful lightning.

※

-Elizabeth Bowers-

READY FOR THAT GREAT DAY
by
Elizabeth Bowers

"The great day of the Lord comes as a thief in the night," Daddy said the day he came to pick my sister and I up at the place where they give ice cream and peanut-butter sandwiches to lost children.

Earlier that day, my big brother had eaten the last of the large cinnamon cookies. We got them when Daddy took us to Grandmother's house that Sunday afternoon when he preached about President Truman ordering American troops to South Korea.

I really wanted another of those cookies. All I had to do was go straight down the White Horse Pike and turn right, a little way past the bridge where people stand to catch crabs. Then I'd be at Grandmother's house.

My sister Brenda was a year younger than me. She wanted one of those cookies just as much as I did. Together, we searched all the lower cupboards and the plug-in ice-box. There were no cookies to be found.

"Come on Brenda. Let's go get some more cookies from Grandmother. She has lots of them," I coaxed.

I held my little sister's hand as we walked to the right of the line separating the shoulder of the road from the advancing traffic. It seemed as though we had walked for hours. The bridge was nowhere in sight. We were determined to get cookies, so we pressed on.

After a while, a blue car pulled over next to us. Inside was a woman with hair like spun gold. I wondered if she might be the princess in the story about Briar Rose.

"What are you two little colored girls doing way out here all by yourselves?" she asked us.

"We're going to our Grandmother's house. She just lives around the corner on the other side of the draw bridge," I informed her.

"The draw bridge is a good ways from here. Come on. Get in. I'll take you to your Grandmother's house." The pretty lady reached over and opened her car door. Her long fingernails were painted red like the candied cherries in my Grandmother's cookies.

I thought about those wonderful big cookies again. They were real sweet and filled with nuts and green, red and orange fruits. I wanted one so bad I could almost taste it, and so I climbed into the car, pulling my sister in with me.

When the woman stopped her car, we were not at Grandmother's house. She grabbed each of us by the hand and escorted us into a place where the people asked us where we lived and fed us ice cream and peanut-butter sandwiches.

Later that day, Daddy and Mommy came rushing into the room. They fell all over us hugging us and pasting wet kisses on our cheeks. Mommy cried and Daddy praised the Lord.

That fall, Daddy talked to God before suppers about the evils of segregation and communism and I started first grade. I learned about tobacco going sour just like someone called Eisenhower who took showers underneath towers. On Sundays, Daddy preached about the devil's great weapon of communism before the great day of the Lord.

♍︎♒︎♋︎■♑︎♏︎

"Then shall His elect be lifted out of the pit of miry clay and set high upon the rock of faith," I heard Daddy preach the summer he praised God for the Korean War armistice being signed.

Daddy took us on a trip down South ~ a family reunion ~ he called it. I had to go to the bathroom at the same time the car needed gas. Daddy pulled up into a gas station next to a sign that read, "Wilson, North Carolina; 15 miles," and got out of the car.

A burly man with grease smudges all over his other-wise red face, strolled up to Daddy, a metal pipe in hand. "Listen here boy, we don't serve no colored folks here. Y'all gone have ta go on up ta road a piece."

Pieces of the Tapestry

I didn't understand. My brother was a boy. Daddy was a grown man. I decided that the man must have been a poor, half-blind sinner. My stomach was cramping up. I had to go to the bathroom really bad.

"The wicked ways of the evil one will be stopped on the day the Lord stretches out his mighty hand," Daddy said as he eased the car onto the main road.

Daddy cut-off on to a dirt road bordered by thick woods. The air there was thick with the scent of cow manure and rain soaked soil.

Mommy handed me a salad dressing jar. "Here. In the South, it's different. You'll have to go to the bathroom in this."

"Don't dump it," Daddy said. "I'm going to need it to make gas for the car."

Later that night, as I made my way to the outdoor toilet at my aunt Hattie's house, I heard Mommy and Daddy talking.

"That man could have killed us all with that big pipe, and no one on earth would have cared or done anything about it," Mommy said.

"But he didn't," said Daddy. "God surely was with us, or else we would not be here now talking about it."

♍ ♒ ♋ ■ ♑ ♏

"Thank the Lord. The great Supreme Court of the United States of America has taken on the mantle of justice and ruled against segregation in the *Brown vs. the Board of Education* case. Glory be to God," Daddy said during his Sunday sermon.

The next day, my fourth grade music teacher, Mrs. Benson, taught us songs about happy slaves who picked berries for their masters in a place called Dixie.

I remember that her mouth was open wider than the Grand Canyon, as she sang out, "*Old Black Joe.*" Her hands never left the keyboard as her blue eyes smiled her pleasure "Now class, I'll give you a cord and you will sing the line exactly as I did."

I wondered to myself how slaves forced to pick berries that were to be made into pies for other people to eat, could possibly be happy. "I hear their gentle voices calling ..." I didn't sing the last line.

By the end of the session, Danny Baxter and Timothy Anderson were laughing so hard, it was almost impossible to hear anything else. I

Pieces of the Tapestry

couldn't imagine why they kept looking at me and pointing. Surely I had remembered to comb my hair after taking out the four braids my mother had so painfully put in before sending me off to school.

After lunch, I saw some of the girls in my class clustered around Sharon Morgan. They were on the New Jersey Avenue side of the playground, which was across the street from Morgan's Candy Store. I stepped over to see what they were doing.

Sharon had a brown paper bag filled to overflowing with penny candy and was passing pieces of it out to the girls. "Now who will play double Dutch with me?" She untied the red jump rope that hung from her waist.

All the girls clustered around including me, raised their hands and shouted, "Me."

"One, two three four, five, six, seven," Sharon counted, tagging each girl on the shoulder, assigning them a number. "Oh Hope, I'm so sorry. You can't play," she told me. "I only have enough candy for seven people besides myself. It wouldn't be polite for us to eat in front of you."

"I'll be a turner," Connie Mitchell said, pushing past me, and grabbing an end of the rope.

"I will too," said Patty Harper. She took the other end of the rope and began to turn it.

I could feel my stomach rolling. My eyes were very scratchy. "I'm not allowed to eat candy," I lied. "I don't care if you eat in front of me. I just want to play. My sisters and I play double Dutch all the time. I'm a good jumper."

"No," yelled Connie. "On account of we don't want you here."

"Okay for you guys." Fighting tears, I ran off and stood with my back pressed up against the cold red-bricks of the elementary school. I shivered in the cold as I watched all the pink-faced girls with hair straight like my dog Dale's, take turns skipping rope. I wished God's great day would hurry up and come.

♍︎ ♒︎ ♋︎ ■ ♑︎ ♏︎

I walked along the railroad tracks on my way home from school that day so I wouldn't have to go past Morgan's Candy Store. When I got in front of the Lumber Company on New Road, the guard dog ran at me

Pieces of the Tapestry

and started barking. I got scared and walked on the shoulder of the roadway, away from the chain-link fence.

A man as white as the shirt he wore, pulled up along side me in a shiny black car. "I like pretty little Black girls," he told me. "Come on. Get in my car. I've got something real nice for you." The whites of his hazel eyes were speckled with red lines. He was bald except for a ring of straight dark brown hair that grew from ear to ear.

I could feel heaviness settling in all over my body. I knew instinctively that I had met the devil. I opened my mouth to scream but no sound came out.

The words of my father's sermon that past Sunday rushed to the forefront of my mind. Daddy always paraphrased the words of the holy scriptures ~ his word for the Bible ~ to make whatever point he thought needed to be made.

"King David wrote in the Psalms that even if a thousand people standing next to you, meet the devil, you will not be moved if you have the faith of God. With Almighty God at your side, you can overcome anything." The good Lord gave wings to my feet that afternoon. I turned away from the devil leering at me in the shiny car, and ran faster than I ever thought I could run, into the thick of the woods that border Ohio Avenue. I was completely numb all over. I sat by the stream where my brother and I caught the beautiful diamond-back snake that had frightened Mommy last fall. When the feeling came back into my mouth, I prayed the Lord's prayer with all my might. Then I cut through the woods to the baseball field and ran the rest of the way home.

"Hope, what did you learn today?" Daddy asked after he finished talking to God about the elect being lifted out of the fog of doubt and fear and on to the billowing cloud of faith.

"Nothing Daddy. I was too busy getting ready for the great day of the Lord," I answered. I couldn't tell Daddy that I had slipped into the fog of doubt and ran headlong into shame. "I hope it gets here soon."

♍︎♒︎♋︎■♑︎♏︎

"No. Daddy, don't let go of my hands," My brother shrieked.

In the strong afternoon sun, Daddy's skin was proud wet bark of Georgia Pine standing tall after a summer rain. I watched him toss my big brother into the green waters of Brigantine Beach. As I waited my turn to be dunked, I wondered if I would ever be as tall as Daddy. Then maybe the nasty green-headed flies wouldn't be able to zizz in my ears. I'd be up too high for that.

Soon my brother was splashing about on his own like he belonged in the water with the fishes. I wondered if he had been touched by the angel of the Lord.

I batted away a million large, sticky flies before it was finally my turn. I was afraid of Atlantic waters. They were full of crabs and dead flies. "I don't want to learn to swim today Daddy," I said. "You can teach me some other time. Besides, my hair might get wet. Aunt Trudie just pressed it the other day."

"Hope, your hair is fine wool of the lamb of God, blackened with the touch of midnight beauty. The pure waters of God's ocean will restore it to its natural condition," Daddy assured me.

"Okay Daddy." It was useless to argue.

My stomach started to roll as he scooped me up in his arms and carried me into the warm green Atlantic waters. "Don't put me down yet Daddy," I said through clenched teeth. "I'll fall under the water and drown. A fish might get me."

"Don't be afraid Hope. The water will hold you if you just tilt your head back and relax. Don't fight it. Water is the life blood of the earth. Just flow with it and it will carry you." He laid me down on top of the water, then let go.

At school that year, I learned that the cold war was really heating up. Communists were hiding behind the bushes and even under beds. I didn't care though because I could swim. Besides, I knew the great day of the Lord was coming. The evidence of changing times was all around me.

)(

Pieces of the Tapestry

Dark root stores promise
Of rose scented future in
Shadow dreams of faith.

ι
-Elizabeth Bowers-

QUESTIONS
by
Elizabeth Bowers

In my search for truth and heaven's sweet peace,
My thoughts are calm breezes, honesty still,
Eyes fixed upon a falling willow leaf,
Dancing as if by act of my own will;
It covers sleeping baby's tears below
Sweet clover's wide blanket of yearning life,
As clashing winds of changing seasons blow
Raven's shrill call to time upon a fife,
Through the mulch pile, stirring dry leaves ahead,
Like Spring's first seeds bursting through heaven's gate;
It rides great breezes to a change of face,
Drifting onward through the vastness of space.
Will it fly forever through morning sky,
Or drift through ivy and clover, then die?

Willow leaf, far beyond thoughts of today,
Changes like winter wind up from its rest,
Finding new thunder in clouds far away;
Riding the wings of storms, it thinks of best,
And worst seasons passed over in its flight,
That touched a small part of a willow tree;
And looks upon reflections in the light
Bouncing off rainbows, until it can see
Itself becoming a new creation;

Pieces of the Tapestry

An ocean, world, or cold winter season,
It divides into a peaceful nation.
Until gale force gives it a new reason
To ponder if winds change by acts of will,
As I search wild fields of honesty, still.

In search of truth, I watch in heaven's space,
Sweet after life of fallen willow tree,
Dancing in sun's day, then lost without trace;
Until in moon's vast velvet night I see
Its reflection drifting as a dark lake;
A periwinkle forever changing, or
A ship of lost souls caught in a wake
Created somewhere off heaven's great shore.
Winds rise and push it onward toward new fate
Conceived in night of rest before the dream
Of a full-grown willow tree with a mate;
A mulberry tree of children who scheme,
To catch a butterfly like orange sun,
While I sit quietly watching their fun.

)(

Pieces of the Tapestry

Winter hides fallen
Majesty of withering
Rose, beneath fresh snow.

ι

-Elizabeth Bowers-

OLD MEN ~ OLD WOMEN
by
Eleanor Freemer

  I preceded my husband into the plane to the tune of, "*Going home, going home, I am going home.*" It kept repeating itself crazily in my brain, like a needle stuck in the grove of an old 45 record. After a very long week in Philadelphia among family and friends, we were finally going home to Atlanta.

  These yearly excursions had become a guilt trip, leaving me nervous and depressed. Guilt was piled on top of guilt for we were the only members of either family who had left the old home town. Graphic pictures over the phone of what we were to expect prefaced each visit. Our siblings were getting older, and those we did not see today would not be around for our next visit. It was made clear that we were duty bound to make these pilgrimages, as we two were the youngest, and they no longer had the stamina to visit with us.

  A tab was kept by our kin folks on those they believed we visited the most; on where we went during the week, whom we ate with and where we slept. Angry words, and recriminating tears, put a strain on my feeling of affection and camaraderie. After three days, I cried to my husband, "I want to go home."

  My head pounded as we moved slowly through the plane. Now, all I wanted to do was hide my face behind my book and avoid any rehashing with my husband on what I said; what he said, and they said.

  When we reached our assigned row, I groaned. I saw there was no hope of my getting a widow seat on this crowded flight. Frustrated, I just stood there running my fingers through my short salt and pepper hair, while my husband firmly edged me into the middle seat next to an elderly gentleman.

Pieces of the Tapestry

Sitting down, my eyes quickly explored his granite like face, shadowed by a snap brimmed hat that he wore like a helmet during the entire flight. Streamers of gray curly hair flowed down to his checkered shirt, adding to my impression of a rough country man. His wrinkled brown hand clutched a wooden piece of gnarled hardwood. Though it was June, he was wearing a brown tweed jacket that gave off a faint aroma of moth balls and more than a few southern fried meals.

After one quick look at us, he kept his brown eyes, almost the same multi-color as his jacket, toward the window watching the luggage being stowed, checking to make sure his was going to make the trip. A dry cough erupted shaking his body like a small earthquake. He tapped his stick on the floor impatiently, waiting for the journey to end, although the plan still rested on the tarmac like a throbbing bird digesting the passengers as they slowly filed in.

Once everyone was settled, the crew announced we were ready for take off. Only then did we exchange a nod of greeting. After my husband released our three snack plates from their prison of plastic with his pocket knife, the old man offered me a friendly tid bit of information. He said he would be changing planes when we reached Atlanta. It was foolish, but that was how the airline ran its business. From there, he would head back to South Carolina where he was going to be met by his eldest grandson. From his breast pocket, he took out a finely creased piece of paper, with instructions to follow if for any unexplained reason, he missed his grandson at the airport in Columbus. He read them silently for reassurance, then tucked them back into his pocket.

Over coffee, he relaxed and smiled as he eased from a brown crumpled bill fold, some pictures that he handed me like a gift to admire, and I sincerely did.

"This here's my oldest boy," he proudly announced.

The oldest boy was a prosperous looking middle aged man with a remarkable resemblance to his father. He, and the one pointed out as his wife, sat posed stiffly in going to church clothes, surrounded by blonde smiling, blue eyed children, grandchildren and one great grand child. The old man pointed to a young woman and two teenagers who were his daughter-in-law's from a previous marriage. The two oldest children and great-grandchild were from his son's first marriage. The tightening of his

Pieces of the Tapestry

mouth spoke more than words of much disapproval on his kind of life style.

"This here is my youngest." A wiry thin soldier, dressed in battle gear, laughed into the camera. "He's in an army hospital in Virginia. He's no longer like this. Was made real sick by Agent Orange in Vietnam." His bent finger caressed the picture of this younger boy. "The older one was spared going into the army. Married and such nonsense."

He brushed the pictures, one by one, against his heart, before stowing them away again.

As the stewardess came to take our trays away, he turned his face toward the window. I imagined his old man eyes trying to penetrate the clouds, looking for familiar landmarks along the way. As he remained wrapped in his own thoughts, I went back to my book.

When she was gone, he sighed. "I told my wife, you get yourself up there and go see him."

Reluctantly, I closed my book and looked up into his sorrowful face. "You have a wife? Do you have her picture?"

"Yeah, I do have a wife, and no, I don't have a picture. Why would I?" His voice dripped with disgust. "Had a stroke two years ago. Needed someone to look after me. My wife, she wouldn't take care of me. You can believe it. We've been married sixty three years and all she does is nag and ask for money. Wants me to give her every cent I got. I moved myself into the old soldier's home in Yankee land. Only place I could get in." He gave me a sly look, "You sound like a Yankee."

"Guilty," I acknowledged with a smile.

"That's okay. They take pretty good care of us up there. Get my meals, and have a little spending money. What else do I need?"

"Where does your wife live?" Against my better judgment, I was intrigued.

I turned to look at my husband, who disapproved of what he called my yentening. His silvery head was bent over the airline magazine, engrossed in the crossword puzzle. Since he was oblivious to my conversation, I felt free to go on with my gentle quiz.

"She lives in Florida in a retirement home." He started another wheeze, "I think maybe she got herself a boy friend there. The old fool."

"Well, well," I thought. "Maybe life begins at eighty."

Pieces of the Tapestry

He stomped his cane again, as if trying to get back to his story, despite my interruptions. "My big boy said ... Momma's too old to go traipsing up from Florida to Virginia."

"No she ain't, ... I tell him. If she can go gadding up to South Carolina to take in some fishing with the grandkids, she can sure go see her boy. I called her and said ... you get yourself up there and spend some time with that poor boy. He needs his Momma."

"Will she be in South Caroline now? If she is, will you go fishing with them?"

He glowered at me, again tapping the floor with his cane. "No siree. I up and left her three years ago. I don't see her. I still love her, you know. But I just can't live with her. You know, I had a dream one night when we was still together. I dreamed I got real riled at her and ..." His breath wheezed out. "I punched her in the nose. The blood ran all over. I thought, my God, I better leave before she gets me in a snit and I hurt her for real, or worse, kill her. So I just up and left. I still talk to her on the phone near every week. I still love her you know." He shook his head as if he really didn't believe it. "But I just can't live with her anymore." He let out a little dribble of a chuckle. "Now ain't that the truth."

I nodded my head, understanding the truth of what he said. It all comes down to family obligations. I was feeling very sensitive to those emotions myself right then. More than once during our stay amidst our family, I felt the keen desire to murder off one or two, but I knew that within a week I would be home free.

I offered him a sympathetic smile as I mulled over his situation. Despite his proclamation of love for his errant wife, and his stroke, how much was actually a dream. He looked like a pretty strong man for his age.

When the plane landed, he waited for the stewardess who would help him make his connection.

"Have a good visit," I wished him.

"Thanks. Sure will. Sure enjoyed talking to you."

"Me too."

I followed my husband of forty-three years down the aisle, and took his arm as we headed for the terminal.

"You sure had a lot to say to that old man," he grumbled, a troubled scowl flickering across his handsome face. "You've gotten to be a real talker in your old age. What did the two of you have to talk about?"

My answer was a shrug of my shoulders and a shake of my head. Giving his arm a squeeze, I wondered, "Oh God, what will we be like in another twenty years. Will he tell some stranger, I love her, but can't live with her?"

He hurried me along. I grinned, thinking to myself, "Then again, we may not have to worry about that either. Hmm. Now ain't that the truth."

⋇

A FRONT PORCH
by
Eleanor Freemer

Some day I'd like to have a house
with a porch facing the street
where neighbors meet and stop to talk.

A wide porch, comfortable like a parlor,
with three rush bottomed chairs
whose rockers whisper and gossip
with the wooden floor, and the rain,
when it slithers down from the roof
onto the porch rail pegs that are
shaped like ladies' oversized legs.

I'd want an old fashioned swing
covered with soft cretonne cushions,
whose flowers look so real that

the birds and bees will come to perch on
its two heavy chains, hung from the ceiling.

A porch where children play
with dolls and jacks and cars and trains,
Turning ordinary chairs into magical caves,
that cup the sunshine and keep out the rain.

A porch trailing pink petunias
from a green planter, whose perfume colors the air
as I rock back and forth, cuddling and
crooning to some sleepy baby by the light
of a sweet cream colored moon.

Pieces of the Tapestry

Come winter I'll bundle up and stand
beneath my roof as the falling snow
dresses the bushes in a silvery wrap
And on long summer afternoons the sun
will seek me out to lie,
like a sleepy kitten, across my lap.

It must be a front porch,
not one hidden in the back
secluded, isolated, alone,
as if frightened by the sight
of joggers, walkers, bikers,
young mothers pushing baby carriages,
cars whose boom boxes blare out
with the latest music craze.

A porch, where the world becomes
my movie screen, in loving color;
my imagination, posing people
as tragic, happy, contented, angry;
anyway I choose to paint them
as they pass my front porch.

How could I have lived so many years
without a front porch?
When I tell my children "That's what y'all need."
they laugh "Mother we're too busy.
we have no time to sit and rock,"

No time, no time; for they are the joggers
the walkers the player of boom boxes.
With no interest in people
who pass their front doors.
Their shades are drawn against the sun
they say, but it's fear that
someone may see the barren souls that live
beyond the closed windows.

Pieces of the Tapestry

How I pity them, my children.
I tell them, "Just you wait.
Wait until you grow old,
as old as I am now
then you too will long for a front porch
big enough to hold a wooden swing and
three rush bottomed rockers."

)(

Pieces of the Tapestry

Transforming currents
Push fertile seed on through sea
Of flowering thyme.

♓

-Elizabeth Bowers-

MULTICOLORED PLAYGROUND
by
Helen Tulis

Pink paint purged the early evening sky,
Tingeing muted gray stripes of clouds,
Lounging in the background.
Purple and pink layers
Became children's crayolas,
Colors lying side by side.
Meanwhile, the moon deposited higher in the sky,
Sprouted a glowing light through
Its three quarter shape,
As if it were wrapped in a shroud.
The sky still warming a mood of distant blue,
Held shredded mauve pieces of cotton clouds,
Dancing as if their strings were being pulled
By the Divine Maker,
Who had scrawled His Word
Across the multicolored playground.

♓

GOOD TIMING
by
Helen Tulis

The crumbling of the old year,
Leaves gossamer threads of time
Looping over spilled negatives,
Creating a collage of memories.

Resolve no more repressed pictures,
Squeeze out a new montage of life,
Wait for no more peak experiences
To falter after their birth.

No more begging for seconds
That charge one another
Into predicted tinseled energy
From neurons filled of yesterdays.

Prance forward to the music,
Eat the apple; drink the wine;
Take pleasure unrestrained,
Capture creativity.

Adhere to resilience,
Tamper with new delights,
Unhinge electrifying discovery;
Add to life's review
Without closing the lens of the camera
And shutting out the glimmer of light.

⟊

Pieces of the Tapestry

*River of sunny
Thoughts is life to sweet vine of
My peaceful valley*

♓

-Elizabeth Bowers-

WOMAN HEED THE CALL
by
Elizabeth Bowers

Woman heed the call for harmony now,
Precious peace flower approaches full term,
And awaits your word in the birth canal;
Contractions like waves of rhythm so firm,
Urge tender spirit flower to inflate.
Your word , "Peace," bestrode by deep emotion,
A healing hand, draws heaven's gold through gate,
Beyond striving in social disorder,
To where you rise in blessedness of sun.

Woman stand up to war hawks of the world,
For your boy, your girl; do not let them be,
Marched off to a foreign shore to unfurl
Blood soaked banners; lost in a raging sea
Of sugar coated lies and injustice,
Fathers of eternal separation;
Or Spirit will birth a lesser peace with
People and nations waging war no more,
But sweet blessings of fellowship not won.

Pieces of the Tapestry

Woman shout your word, "Peace," let it be heard,
"Balance! the order of all creation,"
Let all join the vibration of your word.
Aid spirit flower; let great peace be won
In sweet calm, not war and devastation.
Mighty midwife of spirit, stand up to
Disharmony for your daughter and son;
For peace has entered the birth canal and
Awaits your word in faith to ease it through.

Woman heed the call, direct collective,
Mind toward peace and unification of
All nations, for by your word peace will live.
Let your voice be heard, "Let my word of love
Guide collective mind true, far from a thought
That would unleash disharmony and war;"
Mighty midwife shout "Peace," and let be wrought,
A calming breeze that makes light the journey
Of the souls of all life through a new door.

⚹

Pieces of the Tapestry
TOWARD THE CITY OF LIGHT
by
Elizabeth Bowers

Who is to blame for the pain
And murderous acts that bring shame
To the whole of creation?
Precious bodies of dead children
Lay slain in shallow graves;
Piles of naked hopelessness and waves,
As in a violent stormy sea, did turn
Into a bloodless death of dreams,
Victims of a holocaust, out of sight,
Miles from the city of light.

Who is to blame for the pain,
And the silent tears and shame?
Dreams of a bright tomorrow dashed apart
For a runaway child who gives birth
To a helpless baby one stormy night,
In shadows of gloomy aloneness and fright,
On a bare mattress, filthy and full of wholes
In an old abandoned tunnel
Full of rats and lost human souls,
Miles from the city of light.

Who is to blame for the pain,
And unprotected roads that lead to shame?
Where hope, unborn, lies dead in the path of
Disconnected souls that take their flight
Into fantasies shaped by cocaine at night;
And a young mother strung out on crack cocaine,
Gives birth to an infant shaking and writhing,
Half dead from the strain of being born
Into a faithless world where children morn,
Miles from the city of light.

Pieces of the Tapestry

Who is to blame for the pain,
And the homeless child's shame?
Faith gone, fathers disappear into hopelessness,
While mothers struggle but fail to pay rent;
Holding back silent tears and muffled sobs,
Walk with their children through countless mobs
Of slaughtered souls no longer fired by
The sight of the golden gleam of the morning star;
Frightened and hungry, they travel far,
Miles from the city of light.

Who is to blame for the pain,
And the hopelessness and shame
Of poisoned liberty and faithlessness
Born out of a failure to keep the sacred trust,
That so often attacks the human heart,
Keeping nations and people far apart?
Precious souls drifting in a sea of lies;
Bright stars cut off from the light of truth,
Traveling cold and alone in the night,
Miles from the city of light.

Who is to blame for the pain?
Answers float about in waking dreams,
That dance in the quiet of the streams
Of thoughts about the coming of a new age,
That does not include poverty or dissension;
But a new race of human kind, not inclined
Toward thoughts that do not forever bind
All of the people together as one world,
Governed by the light of truth shinning bright,
In the heart of the city of light.

)(

7. DEATH AND SURVIVAL

Shadow of death hides
In still silence of lost
Song bird's hopes and dreams.

♓

-Elizabeth Bowers-

Pieces of the Tapestry

JANUARY
by
Eleanor Freemer

January, a hoary specter, leans
its wet cheek against my window pane
to watch me grieve for summer's loss.
Cold ashes crumble on a cold grate;
all that remains of a dead love
whose image weighs heavy upon my heart
like molten dross.

Winter, she gaily paints the scenery
a bleak gray monochrome, a wash of gloom
that bleaches the color from the sun and sky.
I hear her mad icy laughter as she wrestles
the last stubborn wrinkled leaves
from the quaking toothless trees;

while I huddle deep within my rocking chair,
wrapped in the old sweater he left behind.
It bears his earthy smell, summer's
fresh mowed grass, spring's purple lilacs.
They seep out of each fiber like
from an uncapped vial, to fill
this winter room with memories.

I rock and weep and weep and rock.
My heart plummets to fathomless depths
in this ocean made of my tears
where I drown in wave after wave of sorrow.
Oh God, I cannot believe in another spring,
for how can the earth hold in its bowels
such pain and live?
How can I hope today for another tomorrow?

)(

Pieces of the Tapestry
Angry wind roars loud
As it moves through trees and brush,
Chasing rainbow's soul

☩

-Elizabeth Bowers-

THE BIG ONE
by
Helen Tulis

On a sunny, but very windy day in February I stood knee deep in memories in the garden of the funeral home. I stared at the variety of shrubs, still green with life, but carefully tried not to compare them to those I remembered in Maurice's front yard. I shivered, and pulled my scarf closer around my neck to ward off the vicious winds.

I arrived early for Maurice's memorial service and as I walked around the geometrically shaped gardens, I thought to myself, "This is a fitting way to recall a segment of Maurice's life, the time when I was his special friend." I glanced down at the petunias. Though they were deep yellow and purple, the colors appeared dirty looking. The flowers were curled up together fearing the cold winds. I recalled Maurice grew similar shrubs and flowers in his garden, of which he was so proud. I would tease him saying he thought he was another Claude Monet, an artist and a gardener.

He would insist that I take acuba that he had cut. "Take these home and plant them in your yard," he would urge.

"No, you know I don't really like to garden," I would reply.

As I circled the plot of greenery, prior to the memorial service, I suddenly realized, "Maurice has been cremated. I won't ever see him again." Tears streamed from my eyes. I wiped them away with the corner of my scarf. I sighed, feeling my lose, and continued my lonely journey

Pieces of the Tapestry

through the spacious grassy area. Near a wall surrounding the garden I came upon a statue of a lady. She was kneeling down, as if protecting her own little plot from cold winds. I stopped crying as I walked closer to the Madonna, longing to whisper to her, to tell her of my sadness, because Maurice was gone. But I didn't.

Pulling my scarf tighter around my neck, I thought, "Spring is very far from here, but is God close by?" A cross shaped from the wintry grass, a contrast to the greens, made this sculptured area most distinct. "My, how clever. This is so religious and meaningful for those who attend services here."

Religious. That word brought my thoughts back to today's services in honor of my friend, Maurice.

"They'll say something special; something from the Christian Science book, though Maurice had not been a true Christian Scientist." I shook my head, "No, if Maurice had gotten some help from a practitioner in Christian Science, he would have been directed to see a doctor. Too late, too late." The tears started their wet passage down my face again.

What disturbed me most was that Maurice had been cremated. I envisioned a huge vase would be needed to hold his slender but strong six-feet-two body. "There will be horses," I mused, "beautiful horses drawn on the vase. They will be galloping slowly as they appear near the greenery and delicately shaped blue flowers. A huge tree with branches heavily laden with leaves, will complete the piece of artwork on the huge slender vase." I saw it all. I could even hear the sound of horses' hooves on the cold frozen ground.

As I looked around, I saw people beginning to enter the funeral home. I checked my watch, and realized I had been day-dreaming. It was time for the memorial service to begin. Looking at the garden I glimpsed at the statue of the Lady. She seemed to be praying now.

♍ ♒ ♋ ■ ♑ ♏

I felt I had entered a mausoleum when I stepped inside the spacious building. The floors, stained and cleaned, seemed to have been a part of this building for centuries. The furniture, classic pieces, seemed as if no one had ever used them. The chairs were all backed up against the wall; they did not need to wear a sign warning, "Don't sit on me. I am reserved." The ivory decor blended in with the furniture. The feeling of frost permeated the entire room, as if the space were part of a cryogenic research lab. Even the people standing around the room were frozen into silence. No one spoke. A gentle hush prevailed. February had slipped in past the massive doors.

Tears welled up again. "Only Maurice will escape this cold," I thought.

From where I stood, I saw the members of the Scottish Hope, with whom Maurice had spent his leisure time. The lawyer gentleman announced freely to me, as I shook his hand, "Oh I knew the pretty lady would come." After chatting a few words, I nodded to another friend of Maurice's, the secretary-treasure of Scottish Hope. He, in turn, did the noble thing saying, "We are having a resolution drawn up in the name of Maurice at the Hope Lodge. I'll send you a copy."

Though I liked the slender genteel man who represented the Scottish Hope, his words could not be translated at that moment. I simply looked at him and said, "That's nice." I immediately walked away making my way toward Maurice's tall niece Kate, who was standing near her husband in a corner. Kate and I had met only once about ten years ago, but I was impressed with her intelligence. Maurice often spoke of her, though they had not seen one another recently.

Kate spoke quietly when I approached her. "My mother, you know, was Maurice's sister. She's been sick but is feeling a little better now. She even gets out to play bridge. But she wasn't able to travel so far yet." I suppose Kate was covering for her mother who had not written or contacted Maurice very much recently.

"Well, I am glad your Mom is better," I said coolly, "and how is your husband?" I inquired as I stared at Kate's mate as he stood guarding her.

"I was just telling Kate how much I like your city. If we weren't so entrenched in Boston, we would want to move here. We'd even move our horticulture business here," the broad shouldered gentleman said.

I glanced aside at him and smiled. Then, like a restless spirit, I moved downstairs to the sitting area. There I felt someone staring at me. I could not tell who it was, but the heat from a pair of eyes seared the back of my neck. Just then, I twisted around, and saw the two green eyes of the lady known as "Bird Dog." Norma, Maurice's sister in law, had given this lady that nickname. It had been Bird Dog who had sniffed out Maurice, knowing he was childless and alone. Maurice had become Bird Dog's prey as she swindled him out of his life and his money.

Bird Dog seemed to be sniffing me out as if she were checking my whereabouts. Her gray hair furnished some softness to her glinting eyes, creating the appearance of a matured dress-up doll. She clutched her pocketbook close to her bosom as if someone might steal it. Her beige coat and matching dress gave Bird Dog a demure look as thought she was an upstanding woman of the community. This was a decoy. I looked at her from far away. I saw her milling around Norma. Then, Bird Dog broke away, still staring at me. She spurted, "Don't you know who I am?"

I did not answer immediately. Bird Dog began to look agitated because I never answered her. Then she walked over and shook my arm. I felt rather uncomfortable, because I reflected on the role she had played in Maurice's demise. Yet, I stepped aside as she asked again, "Don't you know me?" She held the same piercing look I remembered at our meeting at the nursing home where Maurice had resided. I turned and walked away.

I began to cough. My throat was dry. I held my hand over my mouth, but realized a cold must be coming on, sending out a frightening sound. As I tip-toed into the vestibule before the memorial services, I was accosted by Bird Dog's daughter, the "Big One." Norma had given her this nickname too. The name fit her. She was huge, mammoth, not even embarrassed showing off her corpulent body as she strutted down the aisle.

The Big One asked, "Can I catch that from you? Your cold?"

I answered, "Oh don't worry. You will never get it. It only sticks to nice people like me." I shuddered as I walked off sizing her up as a replica of "Man Mountain Dean" as she passed through the aisle. I heard the floor creak as the Big One waddled, giving everyone a side view of her huge behind.

♍︎ ♒︎ ♋︎ ■ ♑︎ ♏︎

I pushed myself into an available pew in the middle of the room, then sat down hurriedly. The services were about to begin. Suddenly I heard a hushed voice from behind me. I did not have to turn around, as I recognized Kirk, Maurice's male nurse from the nursing home. He was talking to some people sitting next to him.

"I worked for my endowment. Maurice never needed anything that I didn't get for him. Whew! You know I worked hard." He seemed to wait to hear confirmation of his loyalty from his cohort, Sidney, the camouflaged redheaded sitter whom Maurice liked.

Her slightly English accented voice, murmured in response, like a member of a Greek chorus, "I thought I would get more money than I did. After all, I stayed on every evening, waiting on Maurice. Oh well, I shall miss the old gentleman."

The pew squeaked as the two of them moved and turned to one another making more remarks about Maurice, whose ashes were twisting inside that vase. Kirk never really liked Sidney, because she used to curl up in his tiny room and read her book, never paying attention to Maurice. When it was early evening, she merely helped him put on his pajamas. Norma always said that Maurice was mesmerized by Sidney. "Did you ever notice how close her breasts were to him once she put the blankets around him? I think she did it on purpose," Norma laughed. "I bet she did."

I overheard Sidney ramble on, "Poor thing, Maurice was not in his right mind for a while." Then she talked even softer when she referred to Maurice's close bout with septicemia. "Maurice was asleep most of the time I cared for him, but I got through to him anyway."

I wondered what she meant by that last statement as I peered towards the front of the room. There, a distinguished looking man walked up onto the podium. He wore glasses, was young, and well dressed. "I know you," I said to myself. "You're the reader. You used to talk to Maurice at the Christian Science church." He bowed his head and said, "Let us pray the Lord's Prayer." The memorial services had begun.

I looked between the two heads of those seated in front of me trying to check the vase containing Maurice's ashes. I smiled sadly, never thinking a grown man, like a Genie, could fit into such a small container. However, after being Maurice's friend for over fourteen years, I should not have been surprised by anything he did.

He kept a house key hidden up on the rafters of his wooden garage. One night he needed that extra key in a hurry. I was positive that, even with his great height, he could never reach it. After looking around and not finding a chair or a ladder, he jumped as high as a basketball player. I laughed and laughed watching him effortlessly stretch up and take down that old tin can where he kept the key.

I wanted somebody to say nice things about Maurice at the funeral. I waited for someone to speak about his being a fine artist, having studied art both in Boston and New York. Perhaps he did not share the magnificent collection of his own work with the people who were in this room. He never sold a picture, nor gave any away. They all had hung in his house, taking up all the wall space. My favorite, "The Artist and Model," remains encased in my mind because it was one I had wanted for myself, but Maurice never saw fit to part with it. I envisioned how lonely the artist and model might be without his presence. All the pictures were of his children who at this moment, had lost their father.

♍ ♒ ♋ ■ ♑ ♏

About a year before Maurice died, he was told by his friend, a judge, "Maurice, you can't drive anymore. You can't get your license renewed. It's just too dangerous for you to be out on the streets in your car."

Maurice just shook his head, refusing to believe that he was a menace on the street, even though he had been involved in four accidents within two months.

I told him, "Maurice, you have no need to drive. I'll take you to the doctor. I'll take you wherever you have to go. It's not a good idea to drive anymore, for your own sake."

Maurice never got over this. One of the greatest joys in his life was to drive that fifteen-year-old white Sedan which he constantly had repaired. I thought to myself, "Well, you haven't properly designated your estate. You won't eat right and you didn't go to the doctor. To hell with you. When you don't take care of your own affairs, somebody else steps in to check on your check book."

The little vase sitting up on the table seemed to vibrate, as the Christian Science reader said, "Let us pray."

A cascade of tears fell down my cheeks. I did not see pictures of shrubs or trees, or even one galloping horse on the vase. Only two years ago, after Maurice had seen a picture of horses hanging on my living room wall, he asked, "Why don't you give me that picture so I can outline the

Pieces of the Tapestry

white horses and you can see them better?" Maurice never worked on that picture. He stopped painting soon after that summer. He neglected his art and his garden. The acubas shriveled up. The tomatoes rotted in the backyard, and the roses disappeared. Finally, when he no longer drove the white Sedan, I realized his mission on earth had ended.

Unable to find a new purpose in life, Maurice began suffering from anxiety. His appetite waned. He no longer walked the four blocks to buy a newspaper and he refused to go to the doctor.

The fellow who owned the gas station down the block remarked, "Your friend doesn't even want me to come up there to cut his grass."

One day Maurice had fallen in his back yard. Before his neighbor could call for help, the Big One appeared like the harbinger of Maurice's demise.

"Oh, I'm here to help you. I'm going to take care of you. That's why I'm here. If we have to take you to the hospital, I'll get all your pictures down and bring them into your room. You don't need to worry. That's why I'm here."

The nursing home was his grave, and the Big One became his grave robber. All that was left was the fire, after the ice.

I strained my eyes for one last look at the vase. The last painting that Maurice completed was a canvass of white horses. In my mind's eye, I could see Maurice ~ six feet, two inches tall, strong, slender and powerful. He rose out of the vase, towering over the congregation, taking a deep breath. Jumping on to a galloping horse on the canvass, he held in his hands the reins, tugging and pulling for the horses to follow his directions.

I yelled, "Maurice, where are you going? Where are you going?"

Maurice urged the horses on. Using his whip, he made them go faster and faster. He looked back at me with a big grin on his face, "Why, I'm going after the BIG ONE. I'm going to go get my money back."

)(

SPRING BIRDS IN A SEASON OF RAGE
by
Elizabeth Bowers

At first light through springtime's window,
Comes clothed in lingering winter snow,
Red Robin, in pending motherhood at dawn;
Struggling to make the worm to
Rise up early into the shadow of clouds;
But, beak pecking hard into frozen clay,
Serves only to drive her prey away.

Slurred whistle of sweet season of birth,
Doused by the crippling fury of clashing
Elements competing in a hurricane of snow,
Gives no solace to Red Bird searching in vain,
For weed seeds buried far out of reach;
But has no potency to make the mercy seat to
Come from behind the backdrop of hidden blue.

Tops of trees, overburdened with winter's anger,
Kiss white meadows that lay in wait
For falling Bobolinks returning too soon,
To deliver ecstatic bubbling songs of praise
To a new born season of buds and seedlings;
But, humbly bow to winter's hunger for glory,
Giving up broken boughs to its stormy fury.

Dear God, quiet the rage of a dying season,
Furiously struggling to hold on to dominion
Over elements that color woodland thickets
In tangled weeds of frigid icy bitterness,
With your blessing of the shadow of the sun;
But, to the season of rose scented breezes and,
New born Blue Jays, give command of the land. Amen.

Pieces of the Tapestry

❦

Grisly death rides crest
Of muddy red torrent when
Dams breach and swamps cry.

❦

-Elizabeth Bowers-

CAUGHT IN A WEDGE
by
Elizabeth Bowers

    Maisha Taylor leaned against the old wooden dock rail, and breathed deeply of the fresh river air, as she somberly studied the horizon. The sun was high and surrounded by swaths of royal blue, but puffy gray clouds were spinning up from the West and zipping rapidly across the skyscape. A scattering of splintered lumber, thick and long like bridge trusses, drifted with the brisk current and she worried if the wind might create problems on the boat trip. She moved her shoulders uneasily and dabbed at the spray assaulting her face like a late winter rain.
    Above the gurgle of outboard engines and the lapping of water against the side of the dock, Maisha could hear the gentle creaking of timbers. She turned around to face a little girl and a slightly bigger boy coming toward her. Their blue shirts embossed with monarch butterflies in full flight, like the one she was wearing to hide the blue swimsuit that clung tightly to her slightly oversized hips, hung to the middle of their thighs. The girl stood about the size of a year old collie standing on all fours, but the boy was a full two inches taller. Her mood was lighter as she watched them skip down the old rigidity, weather beaten ramp and on to the gray, wooden walkway.
    "Come on Lealy and Derrick. Let's get going before the wind gets too strong. Daddy is already on the boat," called Maisha, a feigned sternness in her tone. During the few seconds it took for Lealy and Derrick to catch up, she buckled the front straps of the blue backpack full of first aid supplies, without taking her eyes off the children.

Pieces of the Tapestry

"Look Mommy," cried Lealy, black braids bobbing against the sides of her orange life-vest to below her shoulders. "I bought Pigala with me." Her round face, brown like oak leaves in winter, broke out into a broad smile revealing two very deep dimples. She reached a short, chubby arm into the red cloth bag strapped to her waist and pulled out an inflatable blue pig. "Derrick and I are going to play with Pigala when we get to our camping place." She hugged Pigala to her life-vest.

"That's nice Lealy, but put Pigala away for now. We have lots of work to do." Maisha watched nervously, a hand over her eyes shielding against the sun's glare, as Derrick and Lealy scampered up the walnut ladder and boarded their double deck houseboat like seasoned sailors. They were both good swimmers but knowing this was no comfort to Maisha when their little spindly legs had to stretched so far between rungs.

♍ ♒ ♋ ■ ♑ ♏

As the sun began its westward journey, strong breezes sent wind waves dancing upon the waters. Scattered markings of civilization's clutter pushed by wind surf, rolled chaotically at first, then with the current. Maisha turned and searched the waters to the sides and stern. Nothing was close save the shimmering ripples of the boat's wake in the bright July sun.

Maisha placed a slender arm around the muscular shoulders of the ruggedly handsome man sitting next to her on the red leather Captain's bench in the main cabin. She turned and looked up at his smiling honey colored face. "The waters seem rather deserted here, Jason. How long do you suppose it will be before we get to the upper reaches of the river?" She brushed back a cluster of sable curls, damp to the touch, that had fallen across her face.

Jason looked aside at her and winked, nudging her bare thigh with his own. "Let's see." He looked at the wide-face watch held fast to his wrist, thick with burnt auburn hairs, by a black leather band. "It is now 3:44 p.m. My guess is, we should be idling through the mouth of the outer harbor, well before dark. From there, we're talking about another hour or so to civilization," he said, scanning the wind-whipped waters ahead. "We'll still have plenty of daylight left to drop anchor and set up camp." He reached across her lap to the control panel and turned the

Pieces of the Tapestry

radio on to easy listening music.

"Good. I hate fooling around in the dark with ropes and pins. But this, I love. Even with all the constant watchfulness that comes with boating, there's no more peaceful place than here." Maisha sighed, scooting in close to Jason, surrendering to the sensuous tingling in the pit of her stomach. She rested her palm on the warmth of his thigh and closed her eyes.

♍ ♒ ♋ ■ ♑ ♏

After a while, the mood was shattered by a sound like wooden shoes clopping across a hardwood floor. "Holy bridges!" shouted Jason. He rose to his full 6'5," both hands firmly gripping the wheel, and looked to the surrounding water. "Looks like the inside of a freight yard on the starboard side."

The music on the radio was interrupted by an apologetic voice like thick syrup. "Ladies and gentlemen, we interrupt this broadcast to bring you this late braking story. A bridge collapsed just as a large freight, out of Los Angeles; bound for Atlanta; loaded down with shipping containers and open cargo, attempted to cross. So far, there are no reports of casualties. We do not have all the details yet but when we do, we'll bring you up to date. Stay Tuned."

A whistle sounded as two gallant tugs raced in the distance at flank speed. Startled, Maisha looked to port. To her horror, shipping containers made of heavy steal floated like menacing icebergs and wooden trusses drifted with the tide. "I'd better check on the kids. Make sure everything's all right in ..."

Maisha was interrupted by Lealy's shrill cry. "Pigala! Pigala! He fell over! Stop the boat!"

Maisha heard a loud splash, as though a fair sized steel crate, had hit the side of the boat. She rushed to the stern to investigate. Pigala, now fully inflated, was floating in the swirling water just off the stern. Sun bouncing off well-oiled, black hair, caught her eye. She put a hand to her mouth, stifling the scream in her throat, and looked in horror at Derrick and Lealy standing on tiptoes, bending over the swim step. Little fingers, brown like hickory shells, lowered a fishing net into the water to snare Pigala. Helplessly, she watched as a large wooden bench floated into the net, pulling the children forward into the churning waters.

Pieces of the Tapestry

Maisha pushed back a feeling of terror as she watched her children struggle against a current, made unpredictable by the wakes of rushing tug boats, toward the blue pig floating in waters made unsafe by civilization's clutter. "Lealy. Derrick. Don't try to swim," she yelled, fearing the power of the churning water. "Just hold on to the bench. I'll get you out in a second." Her eyes were on Lealy and Derrick as she called out in even tones, "I'm going in after them Jason. Kill the engine."

Without waiting to see if he had heard her, she seized a coiled nylon rope from the stern stowage box, climbed over the stainless steal rail and lowered herself to the swim step. "Catch this," Maisha called, holding the rope in the middle and tossing the ends to Lealy and Derrick. "I'll pull you in."

"Wait, I gotta get Pigala." One hand on the floating bench, Lealy reached around behind her and grabbed Pigala, then the rope. "Pigala is safe. I got Pigala," she cried, smiling and clutching pig and rope tightly to the bench.

"Okay Mommy. We're ready. Pull us in," called Derrick, paddling the foaming waters hard as he clutched his end of the rope.

As Maisha looked into the smiling faces of her children, she could see that they were having the time of their lives riding the ruffled waters like geese on a pond. She was glad that they were not afraid of their predicament as she tugged against a strong current to pull them back to the swim step. Lealy and Derrick kicked hard with their feet, occasionally letting go of one end of the bench to pat the water and submerge their faces. Patiently, Maisha guided them around scattered trusses and floating patio furniture, then lifted them over the stern rail and safely on to the boat.

♍︎ ♒︎ ♋︎ ■ ♑︎ ♏︎

A telephone pole grazed the side of the hull and a fair sized wake rolled under causing it to rock wildly just as Maisha raised her left leg to climb back into the boat. The boat began rocking wildly. Maisha lost her balance and dropped the rope as she went spinning into the depths of the water among the aluminum pontoons and humanity's sinking essentials.

Through blurred eyes, she saw remnants of a sofa covered in white fabric caught up in the churning propeller, but could do nothing to brake her fall as she hurtled toward it. Sharp pain tore into Maisha as she hit the open frame of the couch hard on the left side of her body. She tried to move but could not pry her swim suit away from the metal frame.

"Can't panic. Oh God help me please. I've gotta calm down. Everything's going to be all right," she told herself as she struggled against the flood of nauseating blackness attempting to engulf her.

Frantically, Maisha wiped out her legs in strong scissors kicks, struggling to free herself from the frame that now was her jailor. As she listened to the hum of engines fading, she felt her strength ebbing. The heaviness of the water upon her chest pulled her into near unconsciousness.

♍︎♒︎♋︎■♑︎♍︎

"The water's all bloody. Mommy's hair! Mommy's hair."

Derrick's cry was a deafening thunder crashing against her ears, bringing her to alertness. Through the clouded water, and the tangle of her own hair swirling wildly like a blood soaked string mop, Maisha saw Derrick bending over the edge of the boat pointing in her direction. Out of the corner of her eye, she saw the rope dangling off the swim step and reached for it, missing it by inches. She felt fire in her lungs and chose not to give up air to struggle with the rope. Breath was precious now. In her agony, she could hear Jason shouting orders to the children.

"Derrick, take your sister to the forward cabin and the two of you guard the helm while I go get Mommy." Jason's voice boomed over the waters.

Maisha felt a surge in the water as Jason dove off the stern in a twisting dive. The look of determination in his dark brown eyes, wide open, was her hope for another breath. The weight of the water on her chest eased as Jason cradled her in his arms and pressed his mouth against hers giving her his air slowly. She turned her head aside when she had enough and felt his hands slip off her back as he tugged at her swimsuit, pulling it free of the frame. She felt the power of his comforting hands supporting her back and legs as together, they shot up against the stalwart current to the surface.

"God help me please," Maisha heard Jason's frantic prayer as her back met the warm vinyl flooring of the deck.

Pieces of the Tapestry

For a moment, she lay unable to move, unable to breathe, yet very much aware of Lealy and Derrick bending over her. They were tending her wounds like navy nurses on the field of battle, with dressings from the blue backpack. She felt Jason's hand under her chin as he tilted her head back and brought his parted lips to hers. Acting on instinct, she opened her lips and received his gift of sweet breath.

After a while, Maisha felt her body sputter, then she began breathing on her own, labored at first, then smooth. She forced her eyelids open. Through blurred vision, she saw smiling down at her, the three sets of dark brown eyes that she loved most in the world.

)(

Pieces of the Tapestry

Summer's spider weaves
Tapestry of swallow's flight
Through winter's window.

-Elizabeth Bowers-

THE LAST JOURNEY

by

Eleanor Freemer

My mother had a pride of bearing that made her seem taller then her five feet four inches. She faced poverty, war, sibling rivalry, illness, and what she considered an unhappy marriage, with her head held high. Even the tears she shed took on the aura of an operatic aria.

Demonstrative affection embarrassed her; so she held us at arm's length. Though we loved her, there was no way of breaking down her barriers. Momma cringed when she had to face our father's large family who kissed and hugged; in a happy, noisy, affectionate way; each time they met. When they parted company it was as if it would be the last time.

My father loved her and was proud just to be seen with her. Momma was a handsome, full breasted woman, always dressed neatly from the moment she stepped out of bed. Her wry sense of humor was reigned in like a wild colt, as if it would run away out of control, taking with it her pride and self respect. Sometimes despite herself it broke loose and; like her keen intelligence; glinted out of her dark brown eyes, surprising us with her merry laughter. At those infrequent times, her dark face brightened with such an inner light, that we joined in her delight whether we understood the reason or not.

Mother made up stories for us when we were little, fairy tales with pictures she drew of little people. She sang as she worked around the house, songs she remembered from when she was a young girl and had first come to America.

Pieces of the Tapestry

The horrendous journey from Covena in Lithuania, she made with her widowed mother, a younger brother and two older sisters, was a tale told many times. Books have been written about the heroic pioneer women who sailed on ships like the Mayflower, to face a new raw unknown country, but our mothers were no less heroic. They left a country where they also were despised for their religious beliefs, and set sail for America the "golden land," with no more then the clothes on their backs and sacks of Kosher food for the trip.

At Ellis Island, they were met by their own pathfinders; two older, stylishly dressed daughters, who had come to America first. They were working together in a dress factory in Philadelphia, and managed to save enough money for passage to America for their mother and siblings.

It was a cold winter day when they finally climbed the three floors to their new home on a street that was no more then an alley. As they had ridden in the horse drawn trolley down the cobblestone streets, they knew for sure they were not paved in gold.

My mother, never seemed able to sew a fine seam or use the sewing machine. She claimed she had been cursed by being born left handed, so did not join her four sisters in a hot loft on Arch street. My grandmother's cousin found this fourteen year old girl a job at a cigar factory, rolling cigars by hand. There she remained until, at twenty-three, she finally consented to marry my father.

Her escape from the smells and rough sounds of the factory came at night when she went to school. Here, like so many of the young *greenies* she struggled with English. Her tongue grappled with the spoken language, as her left hand fought against the written word. The teachers also felt the left hand was a curse and tried to force her to use her right hand, which made her script even worse. However she was good at adding columns of numbers, and loved learning to read. She had been taught by her mother to read Yiddish and Hebrew. With English, she could learn to be a real American.

My mother was very imperious and looked down at her in-laws as not being refined. My grandfather was a tall handsome man, with a full neat brown beard, who may have looked like a scholarly rabbi but was a mere humble shoemaker. Poppa's mother, was a beautiful woman, I have been told, but did not keep her house as clean as my mother thought she should. So Momma came visiting not only with gifts of food, but always bought her mother-in-law a new tablecloth and apron as well.

It seemed to me as if deep down in my mother there was a hot spring that bubbled up; a dynamo that kept her in constant motion. I can see her standing outside in the winter painting the window frames and entry door of one of the many little houses we lived in. Growing up we were always rootless. Momma moved us from one area of Philadelphia to another, then up and back from Virginia, still seeking her *golden land*. In the summer, wherever we were if there was a plot of ground, she would plant flowers and a few vegetables. In the winter she cleaned, fighting off a horde of germs. She seemed to make a friend in every new neighborhood, but never any real friendships.

Momma's greatest pleasure was getting dressed and taking the bus into town and wandering around the Five and Dime store, buying little inexpensive things like button earrings or nail polishes that my father would paint on for her.

She was never really a hardy person. When I was in my twenties one doctor said she was anemic, and told my father to go to the local brewery for brewer's yeast for her to drink. Years earlier she was diagnosed as diabetic; wound up in the hospital a few times until she learned to give herself insulin, and watch her diet. She never really complained, kept any pains she felt to herself, worked with my father in the shoe store; and enjoyed her grandchildren.

♍︎♒︎♋︎■♌︎♏︎

Were we ever suspicious there was anything really seriously wrong with Momma? It was only when I was going through the soup tureen that she kept on the dinning room table, which never held soup but cards, bills, notices, that I found an appointment card. It was for mother to see a Dr. Harold Seliger for an X-ray.

"What's this Momma? Why did you have an appointment with a Dr. Seliger? How come you never mentioned it? Did you keep the appointment?"

"No, it wasn't important."

"If it wasn't important why were you supposed to go, and who was it that set it up?" My voice must have raised an octave or two, which made my mother angry.

"Everything's your business. If you must know, when I was on Market Street two weeks ago I got dizzy and fell. Okay?"

"No it's not okay. Did you get hurt? Did they take you to the hospital? Why didn't you say anything?"

She closed her lips, and would not say another word. My father when confronted, shrugged his shoulders and shook his head. "You know your mother, she never said anything. She came home as usual, made dinner, then went to bed."

I called my sister, and she knew no more then anyone else. I called her doctor, and he was as puzzled as the rest of us.

It seemed that, from that point, our roles were exchanged. My sister and I became the parents, and our mother became our child to love and take care of. She finally admitted to pains, for which her neighborhood doctor did no more then give her pain pills. Finally she went with my sister to a specialist recommended by a cousin. The doctor's suite of offices was located in a dark old building on Rittenhouse Square. It was as dire looking as the doctor himself.

The doctor brutally said, "You must go in the hospital right away. I think it's cancer."

As they stepped out of the office, my mother faced my crying sister and ordered her to go home, "Lisa will be coming home from school and you should be there. A sixteen year old girl shouldn't come home to an empty house."

"Momma," my sister cried, "come I'll take you home."

Later my sister told me, between tears and laughter, that our mother looked down at her and coldly said; "You go home, I've got things to do. I need to buy a new bathrobe, and nightgown, and a little toilet water, for the hospital."

She left my sister crying at the bus stop, and only stopped to warn her to stop crying or people would think there was something wrong with her. "And don't you dare say anything to Poppa. I'll tell him when I get home." With her head held high she headed down the street.

Her long, painful journey began. To the very end she fought her terminal illness like a soldier on a battlefield. From the hospital she went to stay with my sister, as my father could not close the store to take care of her. My sister was having marital problems, so went out to work. My children were young. The oldest had just started school, so it was difficult for me to make the trip to my sisters every day. I told my father that she had to come and live with us.

It was during one of the crises that made up each day that my mother told me, "What would I have done without you?" Was it need, or had my mother finally learned to love me?. She enjoyed being with the two little girls, and now and then she recognized the goodness of my husband.

She made many trips up and back to the hospital, as she grew weaker, and lost much blood. The doctor tried experimental medications which I dosed out, keeping a chart of when, how much, and her reaction. I had a running battle with this cold doctor, who insisted she needed to be hospitalized more times then I was willing to release her to his care. I argued I would take care of her myself, for I felt he was using my mother as a test case, and was doing things when she was in the hospital that only made her condition worse.

It had been a cold snowy winter. My husband was doing a lot of traveling for his job; the girls both came down with the measles, and I had succumbed to the shingles. I was feeling overwhelmed and caught up in a morass of self pity. Perhaps if we could survive these last few bleak months of winter, spring would bring renewal for us all.

That evening Momma's doctor made a surprise visit to the house. He loomed over me, threatening, cajoling. What would I do here alone if my mother started hemorrhaging? I called my father and he told me to arrange for her to go back to the hospital.

Sick, and in pain myself, I was unable to visit her for about a week. When I finally felt well enough to go, it was to find her beyond hope. The women in her room told me she cried that since she was so sick, I had abandoned her.

"Nora," Momma cried when she saw me, "I have my socks on, take me home."

I escaped to the lady's room, and cried on the shoulder of the little nurse who had taken care of my mother through so many bad times.

After washing my face, I went into her room and held her hand, "Of course Momma, I'm going to take you home."

I called my father, asking for his approval, which he gave very reluctantly. When the doctor came with his assistant that afternoon, I held a conference with him out in the hall and said I was taking her home.

Pieces of the Tapestry

He was horrified, "If that was my mother I would never give up hope." I knew then that he was using us.

"She is not your mother, and she is no longer my mother, she is my child, and I can not see her suffer any longer."

He walked away from me, while his young assistant put his arm around my shaking shoulder. "You're doing the right thing, take her home, there is nothing we can do."

The next day, Momma was back home, at my sisters. This my father insisted on. I made her a lunch of all the things she liked, but knew she could not eat. That afternoon I brought our two girls over, and my mother seemed so alive, so alert. I knew that we had done the right thing. My brother and sister-in-law and their two girls came to visit. Her oldest granddaughter sat beside her, while my father held her hand. That night she took a turn for the worst, and what the doctor threatened happened. By dawn she was gone.

Momma died as she lived, knowing the path she must take; and we who loved her, let her go, with dignity and love.

⚭

SONGS MY MOTHER SANG
by
Eleanor Freemer

My mother sang as she wielded her broom,
moving like a dancer from room to room,
sweeping away cobwebs that clung to the walls,
fishing under beds for old shoes and dust balls.

She sang, "*Hello Frisco*" and "*Whose kissing her now*,"
as she scrubbed out the sink with a His or Her towel,
then polished the spigots until she could see
the sun kissed shore "On the Isle of Capri."

She needed no audience as she dusted a shelf,
in her crackly voice she sang just for herself,
or a hymn to the Lord as she kneaded her bread,
with a flour like halo circling her head.

Sometimes I catch myself singing an old time song,
and I can hear my mother's voice singing along;
from a shadow in a corner I smell her perfume,
I feel her breathe beside me as I move around my room.

"All alone, I am all alone," I softly croon
"All alone by the telephone," she takes up the tune,
as we sweep up the cobwebs and waltz through the hall,
we weep once more for the lovers, "After the ball."

)(

Pieces of the Tapestry

Tears of winter's heart,
Fall as crystal songs from clouds,
Cover sleeping earth.

-Elizabeth Bowers-

A COLD PASSING
by
Elizabeth Bowers

While my weary eyes strain to take
One last look through the windowpane,
To see once more the mulberry tree make
The change from autumn amber to winter plain;
Within my worn and used up body I can feel
That winter time has come to claim my flesh,
And free my soul so it can heal
In some safe haven where it shall mesh
With other entities of like consciousness;
Blossoms of the once yellow and orange flowers
Now brown with rot, blow loosely around,
Whipped by the wind, yet enhanced by its powers,
Symbolizing the freeing of my soul, no longer bound,
As the cord is severed from this decomposing mound.

Pieces of the Tapestry

Cantaloupe skies, death
To stars and dreaming raindrops,
Pray for breathless earth.
⸸

-Elizabeth Bowers-

PENCILING IN
by
Helen Tulis

When Dad died, I found so many things he had kept.
I found forty or fifty pencils, all bundled together,
Carefully tied with an old rubber band;
The shocking blue pencil was near the common
orange colored one,
many of them stamped #2.
Right next to those was a silver cross pen,
sleek and new looking.
Inside the bundle of pencils lay one stamped, "Delta."
Another pencil advertised Johnson's Cabinet shop,
long out of business.
The one labeled university simply meant any university;
while another navy blue pencil had the name of a church.
The one I liked best said, "With a warm heart, I quiet you."
That described Dad the best.

Dad saved many things, though he was not stingy.
Mom found an old wallet of Dad's;
all our pictures were in it, as if time had stood still.
Photos were vintage 1945.
The plastic inserts were even held together with tape,
So dad's treasures would not fall out.

Pieces of the Tapestry

My sister found Dad's old shaving brush,
Bought in New York City in 1921,
Another sister found Dad's father's prayer shawl,
Folded neatly inside his prayer sack,
which lay in his dresser drawer.

When my grandchild visited me on Sunday,
she rummaged through the desk drawers,
looking for pencils for school.
Sure enough, she found the shocking blue pencil
that my father had saved.
"It's pretty," she said delightedly.
"You may use it," I remarked.
"I like blue," she told me.
Then I told her about her great grandfather and the multitude of pencils.
She looked up at me and said, "He was nice."

⋇

Pieces of the Tapestry

Sweet honesty takes
Last breath at sun's rising, in
Pasture land of faith.
※
-Elizabeth Bowers-

FAITHFUL SERVANT
by
Elizabeth Bowers

"Hello. Be strong ... in the love of God," Daddy greeted me when I picked up the phone that Sunday afternoon. "I heard ... there were several tornadoes in the Atlanta ...." There was a long pause. "Are you and your family ..." Another pause. "All right?" Daddy's speech was very slow and disjointed.

It was the year that Corazon Aquino was elected president of the Philippines and President Reagan began down-sizing the United States Government. A year before then, my husband, children and I had moved from our long time home in Carson, California, to a place that Martin Luther King spoke of in his "Let freedom ring," speech.

"Hi Daddy. We're all right but you don't sound so good. The tornadoes were somewhere in Cobb County. We live in Stone Mountain. That's in Dekalb County, quite a way from there. But Daddy, I can hear in your voice that you're not all right. Have you been to see a doctor lately?" I hoped my tone hid well, the shock I felt at hearing what I suspected might be serious illness in Daddy's voice.

♍ ♒ ♋ ■ ♑ ♏

Whenever mother nature started acting up anywhere within a hundred miles of where I was, Daddy would forget that I am a grown up woman with two children and a husband. Predictably, he would call frantically to inquiry as to my safety. That is probably because of the time when the Atlantic Ocean made its way into our living room. Until the day I finally drift off into that sweet bye and bye that Daddy always preached about, I shall remember that terrifying experience.

It happened just about a month after Daddy had preached about Astronaut John Glen's spectacular four-hour and fifty-five minutes cruise in outer space aboard the Friendship VII. When the order to evacuate came, I was at my best friend's house on the other side of town studying for midterm exams. She and I were much too busy trying to figure out the square root of Pi, and minutes of arc, to be bothered with what was being said between songs on the radio.

I suppose if on my way home; I had not been so preoccupied with trying to memorize the Spanish version of Mark Anthony's speech, to the Roman populous after the assassination of Julius Caesar; I would have paid more heed to the eerie emptiness around me. I only half noticed boarded up store fronts and sidewalks empty of people. A few army jeeps rolled by, but I paid them no mind, and I wasn't bothered by the absence of the usual rush hour traffic.

I was glad that Mommy was not at home when I arrived. It was still Spring break, a time when she had millions of unpleasant, boring chores for me to do like changing the paper in the kitchen cupboards and scraping the wax build up off the kitchen floor. After studying so hard for so long, all I wanted to do was to stretch out under the covers and sleep like Rip Van Winkle. I poured myself a glass of milk, heated up a large cinnamon bun over the gas pilot in the oven, then went upstairs to my room.

The lights went out just as I was getting undressed. I went to the big double window adjacent to my bed, and peeked out. No lights were on anywhere that I could see. It was early dusk, so I didn't worry. I took the two angel candles that I had rescued from the Christmas box, off my dresser, and set them on my night stand, wishing I'd bothered to pick up the pack of matches I saw on the sidewalk in front of Miller's Grocery Store. Then I settled in under a thick layer of blankets and my yellow bedspread and shut my eyes.

When I awakened, I was surprised to see filtered sunlight streaming in through my bedroom window. I had slept through the night. The milk and cinnamon bun were still on my night stand, untouched, next to my two angels. Silence was as thick as the earth's core. I took a deep breath of fish scented air and realized that something was terribly wrong. Frightened, I climbed out of bed and raced to the window. I peered out upon brown waters surrounding houses as far as I could see. Dancing beams of light bounced off roof tops that stood like ice burgs in the middle of the Atlantic. My stomach began to hurt as I realized my predicament. I backed away from the horror before me and raced from room to room calling out for any signs of life. No one was upstairs. I started down the stairs to look but was stopped by mud-brown ocean. It was all the way up to the middle of the stairwell. I was all alone, trapped in the cold, damp house without heat or electricity.

It was a good thing that I hadn't gulped down my milk and cinnamon roll before I went to sleep because they and the water in the toilet tank, were all I had to sustain my body.

By daylight, I continued to study for my midterms. During those cold, dark nights, I bolted my bedroom door shut and huddled under the covers, repeating the '23rd Psalm' to myself a hundred times and 'The Lord's Prayer' at least twice that many times before dropping off into fitful sleep. Every time I wanted a peanut butter sandwich and a bowl of store-bought chicken noodle soup really badly, I pinched off a tiny piece of cinnamon roll and washed it down with a single swallow of milk.

Two days later, just when I was certain that I was headed up stream on a row boat into that sweet by and by, I heard the sound of Daddy's footsteps outside my bedroom door. "Daddy, come in. I'm in here," I called out, relieved.

"My blessed Hope! Praise the Lord," Daddy cried, as he swung the door wide open. "He has stayed the hand of the tides that pulleth in. Thank you Lord for empowering me with the strength of Your saving right hand."

♍︎♒︎♋︎■♑︎♏︎

I thought about my phone conversation with Daddy for about a half hour before picking up the receiver and calling him back. When I finally did call back, Mommy answered the phone.

"Something's the matter with Daddy," I told her. "He called me a little while ago and he kept fading out like he couldn't remember what he wanted to say."

"Oh, don't worry. Nothing's wrong with your father. He was complaining about pains in his chest just last week. I took him to the doctor. The doctor couldn't find a thing wrong with him," Mommy assured me. "He works too hard ~ evangelizing from one church to the next ~ spreading the gospel. I keep telling him, its time to hang up the collar. What he needs is a good rest."

"Well then make him rest," I ordered. "I don't care what the doctor says, Daddy is not well."

The next week, I got a call from my sister Charity, who lives in Hinesville. "We have to go to New Jersey right away," she told me. Daddy is very ill. Martha found him unconscious, slumped over the bench in the back yard. She said his feet had swollen so badly that his shoes had ripped wide open. He's in the Presbyterian Hospital. He wants us all there.

The muscles in my stomach tightened up the way they did that day when I looked out of my bedroom window and saw that our front yard had become a part of the Atlantic Ocean. "Oh God! I knew something was terribly wrong when I talked to Daddy last week. I could hear it in his voice. Mommy said he was just tired, but something inside me knew better."

In one week it would be Halloween. I'd already bought the decorations and ordered the cake for the big Halloween party my daughter Trinity, planned to host in our basement for her eighth grade class. Besides, it was the start of the school year. My son Johnnathan had to study for the SAT test next week. I couldn't take the kids with me. I didn't know how long I'd be in New Jersey and I didn't want them to miss any school. My husband Henry, was in the middle of a crisis at work and so I got on the plane for New Jersey by myself to try and save Daddy, as he had saved me more times than I care to report.

I didn't feel like I was being powered by the saving right hand of God on that fateful flight to Newark Airport. As if stopping at every airport along the way wasn't enough up and down motion, we hit every air pocket known to God. My stomach shook with each one. The Man sitting next to me talked the whole time about the cruelties inflicted upon

Pieces of the Tapestry

him during his youth by his dead sister whose funeral he was going to attend the next day in Camden; and the heavy-set old man in front of me kept on passing gas. I was terrified for Daddy. I prayed silently to myself for him as I listened to the tearful droning of the angry, bereaved man sitting beside me.

♍︎ ♒︎ ♋︎ ■ ♑︎ ♏︎

Nothing could have prepared me for that moment when I entered Daddy's hospital room and stood before this wonderful, faithful servant of God. "Hi Daddy," I said as cheerfully as I was able.

He looked at me with dead eyes as though I were someone he was seeing for the first time. "Ruth. What are you doing here? I thought you were in Springfield." Daddy rolled his head to one side and closed his eyes as though asleep.

"Daddy I'm not Ruth. Look, this is me ~ Hope," My eyes were scratchy. Daddy had confused me with his brother's oldest daughter who used to baby-sit my brother, sisters and me when we were little. I wanted to cry but dared not.

A brown skin man, with raven hair slicked straight back with a ton of grease, walked into the room. Judging from his white jacket over dress-paints, I deduced that he must be the attending physician.

"The good Reverend has lost forty six percent of his lung capacity, and his kidney functioning is rapidly deteriorating. We've run all the standard tests and we've come up empty. So far, we don't have a reason for his condition." The doctor pulled out his stethoscope and listened to Daddy's heart. "We're going to have to run more tests," he told us.

Daddy's hair had always been off-black. Now it was dull white wool. His usual rich chocolate, smiling face was creased with black pain lines and he seemed more child-like than I must have been the day he pulled my head from between the wooden spokes of the banister leading from upstairs to the front room of our house in Absecon. I wanted to cradle him at that moment, as he had cradled me the day he took me to the hospital to have the orange crayon removed from my noise. Instead, I massaged his legs with a soothing ointment and read the passage to him out of the Bible about "*Well done, my good and faithful servant.*"

Several days later, the Doctor called us into the hospital lounge. "The Reverend is suffering from a disease called Systemic Lupus

Erythematosus. He is in a life-threatening flare. We've administered immunosuppressives and several other drugs; but so far, nothing we have given him has had a positive impact. Tomorrow if things don't improve, we are going to have to start him on dialysis."

"What is this Lupus. I never heard of such a disease," Mommy screamed at the Doctor.

The doctor put a comforting arm around Mommy's shoulder. "It is an autoimmune disorder. In essences, the Reverend's body is attacking itself. His immune system has mistaken his lung and kidney tissue for diseased tissue and is working hard to wipe them out. He will die if we cannot correct this situation." The doctor's look was sober.

"Why didn't you know this before," Mommy cried, pulling at her hair like a bird pecking mites off its feathers. "Last week you told him there was nothing wrong. He just needed rest. Now this. Why?"

The doctor dropped his head. "Most of the reported cases of SLE, as it is called for short, have been women between the ages of thirty and forty. The Reverend is sixty-seven. He doesn't fit the common profile. I'm sorry. I just didn't suspect it." The Doctor's look was like a little boy caught swimming naked in the duck pond.

Once I knew a woman who had Lupus but I had never bothered to ask her what it was. All I remembered about it was that you had to either stay out of the sun all together, or wear big sun-hats and use a lot of sun block. It was inconceivable to me that a man who had been such a good and faithful servant to God all the days of his life, could be struck down by a disease usually reserved for women of childbearing age. It was too absurd to be taken seriously.

♍︎♒︎♋︎■♑︎♏︎

Daddy was sitting up in bed, his head resting against a stack of pillows, when we returned to his room. Daddy and Mommy had obeyed the Lord's command to *"be fruitful and multiply,"* exceedingly. God had blessed them with twelve healthy children. All of us stood obediently around his bed, except for my older brother Aaron, who was off in some foreign county on assignment looking out for American interests.

Daddy was alert and called each of us by our correct names. Then he puffed out his chest and began preaching to us as though it were a Sunday morning. "Little children, be good to one another, as the good

Pieces of the Tapestry

Lord told you to be. Keep on getting understanding and always do right by everybody. Then when you make it to that sweet by and by, God will smile and look you straight in the eye and say, well done my good and faithful servant."

It struck me as funny that Daddy still thought of us all as little children. I was forty-two; and Matthew, the youngest one of us, was a grown man of twenty-six years. It was useless to argue with Daddy about such things, particularly at that moment. I was just so glade that he seemed back to normal.

A nurse came into Daddy's room with his food tray, and very politely waited until after the service, before setting it at his bedside. After Daddy finished his sermon, everyone left the room except Mommy and the nurse, and me.

"Now Reverend, we have some nice mashed potatoes and chipped beef for you tonight. You have to eat it so you can get strong," she cooed like a deranged child.

"Take it away," Daddy ordered. "Bring it back in the morning. I'll eat it then."

"Daddy, please eat it for me. I'm going to stand right here until every last drop is down your throat," I coaxed, using the same words and tone Daddy had used so many times to me when I was a little girl.

Daddy smiled at me, then went to work and cleaned his plate. "There now; are you happy?"

I talked to Daddy about the future. "Come to Stone Mountain for Thanksgiving. Johnnathan and Trinity haven't seen you since last summer. Mommy, you come to. I'll fix a big turkey and we'll have home-made peach ice cream like you used to make.

I stayed with Daddy that night until he fell asleep. The next morning my brother took me to the airport. I flew back to Stone Mountain, thinking all was well with Daddy.

♍︎♒︎♋︎■♑︎♏︎

It was October 30, 1986. I had a lot of things to do to get ready for Trinity's big Halloween party the next day. After she and Johnnathan left for school, I gave the house a good cleaning, then went to the beauty shop and got my hair done. When I finished with that, I went to the book store and picked up a book Johnnathan needed to help him prepare for the SAT, which he would be taking on November 4. Then, I did my grocery shopping and returned home to begin the long process of making party favors.

My hands were sticky with the makings for candied apples when the phone rang. I gripped the receiver in my chin and laid it down on the counter; then positioned my ear and mouth to hear and speak. "Hello. Can I help you?"

"Hope, Daddy died this afternoon at about 1:30," I heard Charity say. "They had to put him on the dialysis machine because his kidneys had stopped functioning all together. When they took him off, he went into cardiac arrest and died." She stopped talking and sobbed softly.

I was in a state of shock. Why did I leave him? I was so angry with myself for rushing back home. Maybe if I had stayed, Daddy wouldn't have died. My sister and I cried together over the phone until we had both used up all our tears. Then I whispered away from the mouthpiece, "Well done, my good and faithful servant." I was sure God was saying these words to Daddy at that very moment.

)(

Pieces of the Tapestry

Loblolly Pine stands
Tall as sweet maple in warm
Season of slow wind.

♓

-Elizabeth Bowers-

MEMORIES
by
Eleanor Freemer

Come, I'll tell you what Yom Kippur was
for me when I was a young girl
like you, thirteen, fourteen, years old;
living for the first time
in a Jewish neighborhood,
the first time feeling Jewish
from the bones out.

Jewish did not mean being Orthodox
like your family is now,
or like my grandmother of
blessed memory was
A stranger to me, an old woman;
dried out
    like a peach,
    that sits
    in the sun too long;
    casting off a sweetish smell
    from her soft wrinkled fuzzy cheeks
    like old sour wine.

Pieces of the Tapestry

My grandmother,
I see with a child's eyes,
a red shatel perched low on her forehead,
a widow longer then she had been a wife,
wearing a widow's shiny black satin skirt
that reaches down to rest modestly on
the tips of her black laced up shoes.

It drapes her round extended stomach
which I believe was molded into
shape from the eight living children she bore
and the others she never brought to term
but never forgot.

My grandmother was only young
in the stories my mother told of her.
It was hard for me to believe
she was ever young.
Did she ever tell me a story
or sing a Yiddish song,
or give me a kiss?
I can't remember.
Would I have remembered if she had?
Only in a brown cracked
picture does my grandmother rock me on her lap.

When I was five she came to visit
where we lived like expatriates in Virginia.
I was ashamed to tell
my friends, who came to stare
at this ancient creature from an
alien world, she was my grandmother.
No English came from her toothless
mouth. My mother was angry
at my disrespect; my lack
of love for this black clad
woman my mother loved, who only

Pieces of the Tapestry

frightened me.
My grandmother died on erev Rosh Hashanah
and was buried quickly on the holy
of holy days.
I had never encountered death before.
My cousins, where my grandmother lived,
did not seem to feel her lose.
We huddled together in one large
feather bed, giggling, until
we heard the crying began.
Her daughters wailed,
a lament that shook the little brick house.
The wind beat hard fists against the walls.
The rain cascaded down the windows onto
the flooded streets.
A holy good woman had left
this earth, and at age eight,
I did not feel regret, only
fear for my mother.

We lived in the shadow of the
Valley of Death every year,
while mother sobbed reading the
Yizkor service by the light
of the Yartziet lamp she burned
during both holidays.

The war years, when my brother was away
Momma seldom went to Shule.
She faced God alone in the house,
while my father and I sat on the
hard folding chairs at the Shule
where Poppa bought a ticket every year;
a ticket to pray.

Yom Kippur ~ September ~ Indian Summer;
the folding chairs complain, cry

Pieces of the Tapestry

out, another quaking voice added to the
morning prayers as we stand, then sit
in the quiet of the morning.
The room holds the warm
breath, the tears of Kol Nidre night.
Under the heavy prayer shawl,
my father's shirt already clings to
his back.

Flies, first one then another,
like the congregates file in
for Yizkor a buzzing stirs around the room.
Windows stand open, catching
noise and dirt from the busy street,
more then any vagrant breeze.
"Please mister, what's the page?"
The page and line is found,
only to be lost again and again
throughout the day. Lost amid
the myriad of prayers; lost
in the pleas for mercy; for
forgiveness; for promises to
do better in the new year.
We are all lost in our
own needs, own thoughts.
We are thirsty, for solace,
for a sip of water, for some
answer to why we are here, this day
year after year, frightened, by the
words we read.

The Rabbi, like a prophet,
a Jeremiah encased like a holy vessel
of white, pours scorn on all
those who come to seek God
on this one day of the year.
His white beard trembles as he

Pieces of the Tapestry

scolds the housewives; with their work worn hands,
and tired eyes for shopping
on the shabbath; for breaking
the holiness on the day God gave
them for renewal and rest.
They fear Yom Kippur; they should
fear the all mighty's wrath, and
curse for destroying the peace of
His Shabbath.
How can they come to plead
for health, and pernusis,
on Yom Kippur, then cheat
and curse their fellow man
the following day?

The day wears on, heat bakes
down on the ancient roof;
the smell of lemons and cloves
competes with the smelling salts.
More sit head bent over the blurred words,
then rise on their weakened legs;
the young congregate on the sidewalk outside
flirting, talking, making plans for when the
sun goes down.
Like the swarming flies, they group
and regroup, walk from one little Shule
to another, young servicemen on leave
fill their parents eyes, their love;
their prayers are all for them.

Things I remember, how can I explain?
Questions the grandchildren ask,
the joy the pain the life in the city
when I was a child.
They laugh at my stories.

)(

Pieces of the Tapestry
CLOSING THE GAP
by
Helen Tulis

You extinguished the fire of mind,
When nothingness surrounded you;
But embalmed your soul in the early hours
Before your intellect closed up shop.

Yet the memory of your being my friend
Becomes the healer of my pain,
As I relive our tumultuous kinship,
Skidding through the ebb and flow of seasons;
I see white winters when you lent me your gloves
And wonder if spring will ever come again.

May brought forth your roses
For me on Mother's Day.
Your garden rendered plump tomatoes,
We shared together for lunch.
Through you, I had a glimpse of another world,
Silent and peaceful, with only sounds
Of you turning the pages
Of the evening newspaper.

You extinguished the fire of your mind
When nothingness surrounded you;
Because you were a man of class,
Genteel, austere and steely.

You were New England bred,
Endowed with honor and dignity,
Overshadowing our cultural and age differences,
Yet orchestrating our lives with quiet reassurance.

)(

Pieces of the Tapestry

River of swimming
Souls is life to rocky shore,
Fruit of vine of peace.

♆

-Elizabeth Bowers-

THE WARM WATER POOL
by
Helen Tulis

When Dad died, Mom began to complain that her right leg hurt. On days when she had shopped, washed the kitchen floor and prepared her meals, she said, "Oh! I can't move with this leg."

I usually answered, "But Mom, look at all the work you do. No wonder you can't move."

Months went by. After hearing Mom complain repeatedly, we three daughters took her to the orthopedic surgeon. He suggested that she have knee replacement surgery. Mom told the doctor, "Oh, no. I wouldn't do that. Not at my age."

The doctor then suggested to Mom, "Well, let's try something else and see if that doesn't help your situation. Now, you won't get well, but you can strengthen your leg muscles and ligaments. Here is what I want you to do," he said. "Go downstairs to the rehabilitation center in this building. Let the physical therapist show you the warm water pool. That is where the group does water aerobics. Now, they have what you have ~ arthritis."

"So, doctor, would this help? Must I go in the water?" Mom inquired.

"That's exactly what I want you to do. Exercise. Exercise three times a week. They have a health specialist and that teacher will show you everything you need to know. I'll write you a recommendation, saying I want you to go to water exercise classes," the doctor added emphatically.

My ninety year old Mom looked down at her knee, which the doctor had just examined. She sighed as she noticed her leg, with the crocked thigh bone. "Well, there's nothing he can do. He can't make me a new leg. I'll have to listen and try to do what the doctor says."

Soon Mom was enrolled in the Tuesday – Thursday classes at the rehabilitation center of the hospital. At first, when I took Mom to her class, she walked very slowly, reluctant to go. Then, when she approached the large dressing room, she pulled the curtains apart and peered in. Since Mom also had muscular degeneration, she could barely see anything, as there was very little light in the room.

After I helped Mom undress, she pulled her old bathing suit out of the canvas bag she had brought. As she sat down on the cold bench, she shrieked, "How come it is so cold in here? You could catch pneumonia."

I quickly put a towel on the cold bench. Mom moved onto the towel, still trying to put on her old bathing suit. Not wanting to criticize her bathing suit, which I think was about eight years old, I looked away. Then, when Mom finally tried to stand up, she almost fell, because putting weight on her leg made her unstable. I put my arms out in time and just caught her, as she stood more upright.

"You see. You see what happened? I worked so hard all my life that I overworked standing on the cement floor in the store. You be sure to take care of yourself. See you shouldn't end up like me, a cripple," Mom warned me.

Finally, Mom put on her bathing suite and tried to walk down to the pool, leaning on her cane with one hand and hunching over towards me with the left side of her body. We walked very carefully over the tiled floor, making sure we took small steps. I didn't want Mom to fall. I didn't want to fall either.

We almost got to the door leading to the pool. Mom turned and said, "Oh, I forgot the jacket. I need that little jacket because it will be cold when I come out of the water."

Even though we were only a few feet away from the dressing room, I hurried, because I had a fear of my mother falling. I ran down the space between the shower room and the dressing booth, found the jacket, and dashed back. "Whew," I breathed. "Mom is still standing and she is okay."

We both meandered down to the pool. I introduced us to Jennifer, the exercise specialist, and hung up Mom's jacket and cane. Mom sat down on the bench on the side of the pool, but did not go further. All the other people had already taken their places in the pool. Mom looked around, but did not talk.

Finally, I asked her, "Mom, don't you want to go into the pool like the other people?"

"I don't want to, but the doctor says I must." With that remark, she made her way down the entrance to the pool. Once inside the water, she stood like a little lost child, hanging on to the side. Mom barely moved when Jennifer announced the exercise. Instead, Mom remained in the corner of the pool, swinging her legs to the music that was being played. Even when the others stretched out their arms in accord with the leader's directions, Mom merely motioned, not getting fully involved in the activities. Once, she turned around to see if I was still there, but Jennifer had motioned for me to leave the pool area. I only saw Mom through the glass window of the door and she kept turning around, looking for me. I saw her kicking her legs in the water as the leader demonstrated for the group; then, I walked slowly away from the door, praying that Mom would finally do all the exercises like the others did. I kept hearing her voice repeating, "Well, the doctor can't make me a new leg, so I'll have to do what he says." I wondered if Mom would really do what the doctor ordered.

We returned a second time to the rehabilitation pool area. Mom put on her bathing suit, held on to me, walked with her cane to the pool area. This time she said, "You go. I'll be okay."

Though I was not reassured by her remark, I asked, "Are you sure, Mom?"

Mom had turned to follow the others into the pool where the group heard music as they listened to instructions by the physical therapist. Soon they began their forty-five minutes of exercising. When I looked back through the glass door, I saw Mom holding on to the bars on the side of the pool while she lifted her arms up into the air in tune to the music.

Quietly, I thought, "Thank goodness. Mom is trying to follow the others. Good."

At the close of the period, I returned to take Mom into the dressing room to change. "Did you like it today?" I asked.

"It's all right. We had another instructor. She is better than the first one," Mom decided.

"I'll bet this will get better and better for you, Mom," I assured her.

"It makes you a little tired. I am not used to it; but it also makes you hungry to do all that exercising," she replied.

"Good. Then, let's go to lunch," I announced. "Fix your hair Mom, and let's put on a little lipstick," I suggested as we passed the mirrors near the dressing room.

"I never liked lipstick. But if you insist, I'll do it," Mom complied.

Several days went by before we again returned to the rehabilitation center. This time, Mom walked ahead of me as she approached the entrance. "You have to hurry or they start without you," she said.

"Really?" I asked.

"Sure. This is a regular class. The teacher won't let you in if you are late. Come on." Mom pulled me as she took bigger steps, still holding on to her cane as we entered the building.

As soon as Mom changed into her bathing suit, she carefully walked down to the pool where she said, "Hello," to the ladies in her group. Then, she folded her towel, took off her white jacket top, waded into the pool, and took her place with the others awaiting the opening strains of the music. As soon as all the other participants joined the group, Mom watching the class members, began raising her arms. Soon she was swirling with them through the water, kicking her legs rhythmically and exercising her fingers individually.

With this flurry of activity, I knew Mom was still filled with spunk and zest for life. That afternoon, I asked "What did you think of class today? Was it fun?"

Mom answered spontaneously, "To tell you the truth, I don't see why you don't do exercises like I do. Everybody should do it to stay healthy."

When I realized that Mom had become an advocate of physical fitness through her water aerobics, I became convinced that she would survive.

)(

Pieces of the Tapestry

Begging ivy weeps
On blood soaked soil, ridiculed
And hated by time.

-Elizabeth Bowers-

DEATH OF LAUGHTER
by
Helen Tulis

Death of laughter comes from thoughtlessness
That parches the heart,
Simmering it to an agonizing fever,
Until not even goodness invades its tissues;
And the heart is forever closed to life.
It remains dried out and leathery,
Yet wanting to be watered and cooled
By the comforting feel of aloe
Dripping into its dying cells
By someone who cares.

Pieces of the Tapestry

Anagram insights,
See the flower of my soul
Through winter's window.

⚹

-Elizabeth Bowers-

BEGINNINGS
by
Eleanor Freemer

    Our lives are like train trips. Listen, hear the clickety clack of the wheels as they hug the cold steel tracks, sending off fiery sparks as we speed through our days, and our nights. Too fast we ride under long dark tunnels, over narrow bridges that span across an empty sky. We soar up into sun drenched heights, then plummet to low plains before we reach our terminus.
    The miles speed by; scenes from childhood, sights barely remembered are marked by our faces pressed against the cold glass. Yesterdays, todays and tomorrows have no demarcation in the dark.
    The suitcase beneath our feet is packed with mementos we have collected along the way, but tucked in between the folded tissue paper are gifts given to us by past generations. The passengers who have come and gone, left us with a sign of their presence, bits of wisdom, sadness and joy. Ghosts of the past hover over these seats, the aroma of a perfume they wore or the smell of tobacco that clung to their hands and clothes. Reaching between the cushions we find messages scribbled on bits of paper, or a wrapper from a once favorite bar of candy.
    Sometimes standing on the platform breathing in the air that feels so familiar as it touches our hair and face, tears come to our eyes. We try to escape from memories that are too painful to carry around. So we change trains, try a different route, but alas, we are still burdened with our old baggage that keeps weighing us down.

Pieces of the Tapestry

My journey started on August 2, 1925, in Philadelphia, Pennsylvania. My parents were Stanley and Frances Rosenheck, proprietors of a small family shoe store on Orthodox Street. They were also parents of Leah ten, and David six, when I entered their lives.

Memories, where do they begin? Are they mementos of things we actually felt, smelled and saw, or do they spring forth from having listened to the same stories so many times, that we say, "Oh yes, I remember that."

What is my first memory? I see myself, a little tot of two or three standing on a chair beside a big black stove. My father, with a wooden spoon in hand, hovers over a pot of cocoa. He stirs and sings:

"*Up up a little bit higher,*
Say Babe the moon is on fire.
Come Josephine in my flying machine.
Away we go, good-bye."

Like magic, at that point in his song, the brown milk rolls to a boil. With a grand flourish my father lifts the pot up, and pours the hot bubbling drink down into my waiting cup.

My poppa, he was the hero of all my earliest memories. You'll not find his likeness depicted as a Galahad or Lancelot in storybooks. He was no tall shinning knight out of King Arthur's court. Poppa was the peasant, not the prince. He was a short solidly built man, not taller then five feet seven, or eight. In old sepia pictures taken of him as a young man, his hair was light brown, his nose straight and broad like his mouth; uncompromising and stubborn, they dominated his round full face. In those brown photos you could not see the startling deep blue of his eyes that smiled warm and lovingly below his dark thick eyebrows. Those blue eyes were a gift he gave to me alone, of his three children

Poppa was the one who kissed away the pain and tears when I was hurt. When I had a minor part in an elementary school play, he would be the one to take me, and stay to cheer me on. As we made our way home, hand in hand, under the cold evening stars, Poppa would point up to heaven and tell me I was his star.

My father lived for the day. He looked forward to a happier tomorrow, but never turned around to re-exam the past. His childhood, or his life as a young man was never discussed. I blame myself for not probing, questioning him about when he was young.

Pieces of the Tapestry

Poppa would sit with me at the kitchen table; the Jewish Forward spread out like a table cloth. There he would read aloud in Yiddish articles about Jewish American heroes whose names never appeared in my history books at school. Wetting his finger he would always turn last to the Bintel Brief. These letters were the fore-runners of the modern day Dear Abby columns.

What did I know about my father and his family? Poppa never shared with us the journey he and his family made before reaching America. All I know was that he was born in Poland. His parents were William and Malke Rosenheck. His father had been a shoemaker, and Poppa and his two brothers and two sisters had at one time lived in St. Petersburg Russia.

Even in his later years, when we spent so much time together, Poppa never mentioned the years when he was young and growing up, living and working in Philadelphia. Those years of his life remained behind a locked door. After my mother passed away, a friend also recently widowed asked my father to take a trip to Russia with him. Poppa's answer was, "No, I've been there."

I doubt when his friend came back that Poppa ever asked him about where he had been and what he had seen. My sister Leah, said she could not even get him to go see "Fiddler on the Roof." My father was stubborn, he had his priorities, and the past was not one of them.

"You are a special child," Momma once told me, as I sat with her at the kitchen table playing with my own piece of dough. It soon resembled gray clay, unlike the loaves she pounded, kneaded and braided into challah for the shabbath. "After you were born Poppa came and picked us up from the hospital in a brand new car. For you Libbie, Poppa bought a model T."

I am sure it was not for me that my father bought this marvelous conveyance. He bought it hoping to please my mother. She had been angry and sick through the entire nine months of this third and unwanted pregnancy. I was a monstrous child, weighing in at ten pounds at birth; colicky and blotchy, with a round red face.

"Oh how you cried, day and night, perhaps you were hungry. I had no milk to feed you, nor the strength to pick you up. How else could we have brought you home, I was so sick." Momma shuddered, reliving again that unhappy time in her life.

Pieces of the Tapestry

Years later I understood that she was already suffering from diabetes, an illness that was finally diagnosed when I was in Junior High School. At age thirteen I was old enough to travel to the Graduate Hospital where I attended classes on diet and how to plan healthy menus. I struggled to design meals that would be approved by the Tartar like dietitian, even though they never were put into use at home. Mother was in the hospital where the medical staff brought her sugar under control and taught her how to inject the insulin into her thigh.

Momma must have fussed with my father over this extravagant purchase of the car. I don't remember hearing my sister or brother ever talking about excursions or outings in that fabulous vehicle. The car must have gone the way of the mythical griffin, for whenever we went visiting, we went by public transportation.

My father struggled with me, a toddler, and a shopping bag full of hot goodies from our kitchen. My mother would pack up shoe boxes of food in the morning to be eaten at our destination; also snacks for us to nosh on during this arduous expedition. My father would boost me up the high steps onto the clattering trolleys that jerked up and back with each stop and start. My brother or sister would grab my hand to keep me from falling as we searched up the aisles for seats together.

Sometimes we would have to climb steep steps to the elevated cars. There we waited for the train, standing on the platform that perched on rickety legs like an aerie, over the shopping center on Frankford Avenue. I would tightly close my eyes, afraid to look down. Clinging to Poppa's free hand, I would imagine the wind swirling around me, blowing me away. I saw myself gliding down to the pavement, then rolling away like a page from a discarded newspaper.

Before leaving the house mother would admonish us, "I don't want you falling into the house crying you're hungry. You ate before we left and we will wait until everyone is served."

However, children being children, no sooner did we walk into the front door, than we wailed, "We're starved. When are we going to eat?." Things never change.

Watching the Oscars and seeing clips of the first talking movie stirred up the memory of seeing my first motion picture. I must have been no older then three when our parents took us to the movie house on Frankfort Avenue to see Al Jolson. We not only saw him, but heard him sing that tear gusher, "Sonny Boy." To insure the success of this undertaking the movie theater presented a vaudeville show. Two young people came whirling onto the huge stage on roller skates with a dummy like figure that they flung up and back.

I must have been all of three years old when I sensed the tug and pull of my parents lives. They were two good people who should never have been married to one another. My mother and father were like the ant and the grasshopper. Momma believed that through hard work, and saving for the future, they would have that good future. Poppa felt that worrying about tomorrow was fine, as long as it did not interfere with having a bit of entertainment and enjoyment today. If all our todays were being sacrificed for tomorrow, Poppa argued, how could we be assured that there was going to be a tomorrow to warrant so much struggle? Momma believed you had to take your chances; one had to have faith. Poppa was a cynic.

However one of the sacrifices they made along the way to becoming successful Americans, was the strict observances of Orthodoxy; the ways of their parents in Europe. The shoe store was kept open on Saturday, and only closed for Rosh Hashanah and Yom Kippur.

In our house my father never conducted a Seder, and I don't remember attending one until we moved to Virginia where we joined my Aunt Hilda and her family one Passover. My father, never one for a drop of schnapps, drank more glasses of wine that evening then he was used to. After the fourth glass he became very lively. I can still see his flushed face, his eyes bright with an extra glint, as he lifted his glass, and in a rich baritone voice began to sing. It was not a song from the Haggadah, but a Russian drinking song from a George Gershwin movie called "The Song of the Flame." It was the highlight of the evening. "One little drink makes me bolder." Poppa had no head for any type of alcoholic drink. To my delight, we were unable to make it to the ferry, and spent the night in my Aunt's house.

Momma always lit Shabbath candles, kept kosher, and David and I were expected to attend Saturday morning services and Sunday School. Mother, herself, seldom went to Synagogue, even on the High Holidays. She filled me with an awful dread on Yom Kippur. I can still see her sitting at the kitchen table, her head covered, bent over her prayer book;

Pieces of the Tapestry

the Yartziet (memorial) candle flickering its light on her tear stained face, as she sobbed through the Yizkor prayer.

Yet the house always tasted and felt like a Holiday. My Mother was a wonderful cook. The traditional dishes flowed from her stove and oven. The aromas filled every corner of any house we ever lived in.

On Yom Kippur my father would be gone for the day. He would leave in the morning before I awoke. Poppa would take the trolley, and El to the Temple on Broad Street. There he would listen to some great guest Cantor who would lead the liturgical music. To Poppa, even Yom Kippur should be enjoyable. He did not believe that God meant you to suffer through services lead by a mumbling old Hazan (cantor). One attended services to be uplifted, right to the gates of heaven, guided by the voices of Angels. Momma ranted and raved at him for his frivolous waste of money, when he returned to break the fast with us.

Their battles were always fought in Yiddish. I guess they did not want me to understand what was being said. It was not necessary for me to know the words, the tone, the expressions on their faces, were more articulate then any words. My brother and sister were both in school during these pitched battles. I was usually the only witness and survivor in this no man's land. Every time my father grabbed his hat and left, I would cry hysterically thinking I would never see him again.

Once, the door closed behind him, with a wild clarion from the brass bell nailed to the top of the door, quiet settled like dust in the store. My mother would calm down and give me a quick hug. She would assure me my poppa would be home before it was my bed time. "He will be here to make you cocoa Libbie and put you to bed."

Then, with me trailing behind, she would get busy rearranging the stock. Momma would give me a rag to dust off shoes that had been hidden in boxes for too long. She would set them out on a table near the front door, and with a thick black pencil, carefully print on a piece of cardboard, "For Sale." While she swept and I dusted, her ears would be attuned to the bell. She hoped it would announce customers coming in to buy, thus proving she was a better salesperson than Poppa. While we worked together, she sang, "I wonder who's kissing him now" in her high piping voice. Momma didn't really wonder who was kissing him now, Momma knew exactly where he had gone. Poppa would be heading toward the trolley that would take him to Strawberry Mansion, seeking succor in the bosom of his family.

They were a kissing family. No matter which sister or brother he would visit, Poppa would be greeted like a long lost traveler. He would be embraced, plied with tea and cake, and emotional talk, unrestrained in the absence of Poppa's haughty wife. His eldest sister's house seemed to bulge with people any time of the day. Beside her eight children, landsmen, friends, neighbors, cousins, collectors from some Yeshiva in Jerusalem would find their way to her door. Everyone was welcomed and fed. His eldest niece was not much younger then my father, and remained his closest friend until she died. If she was not at the house he would walk to her apartment that was down the street from her mother. There they would talk and laugh until he was fortified by love and ready to face Momma again.

Poppa could never say "No" to his family. I can now see why Momma would become upset when his sister would come to buy shoes for the eight children.

One of the younger nieces always commented, "Oh Uncle Stan, you have so many pairs of shoes."

Momma would mutter under her breath, "We did have so many until you all came in."

Poppa could never charge them for anything they needed, unlike his oldest brother Martin, who also had a shoe store. Martin made it clear that business was business, family or not Momma would point this out to my father, who would turn away from this criticism with, "I'm not Martin."

That was the problem. Poppa was not like his oldest brother, who was shrewd in the ways of business and money. His wife, a tiny round pretty woman, was his queen, and his five children grew up believing themselves royalty. Only Robin, the oldest daughter always helped in the shoe store. All five girls had an aristocratic air about them, that annoyed many of the other cousins. They were always referred to as the "Rosenheck girls," as they never seemed to mix with the rest of the family. They could have all been related to my mother rather then my father.

I remember when I was about ten or eleven, living on Wilmot Street. Saturday afternoons I would walk over to their store on Kensington Avenue to take elocution lessons from Terry who was the youngest.

These lessons took place only in the milder weather, for it would have been too hard to walk that distance in the cold. I would recite my poetry as I walked across the wide streets; dodging trolleys that ran up and down the avenue below the elevated cars that dominated the sky line. Frabbot's Dairies was one of my landmarks. I knew I was near the business section once I passed the dairy. Next came the square with its benches under the trees, and sidewalks dominated by children on skates and girls with jumping ropes.

Terry conducted her lessons, for paying customers, up in her bedroom. There I too, would pay my twenty-five cents, and recite what I had memorized from the week before. With emotionally charged language and actions, I performed.

Terry was our David's age, but to me she seemed so much older and more sophisticated. She had black curly hair, and dark eyes that squinted into an oriental slit like her mother's. When she smiled her strong white teeth were separated in the front like almost all the Rosenheck's.

My Aunt Jesse would never give me a snack when I would be on my way home again. I was treated like all the little girls who came on Saturdays and paid their twenty-five cents to learn proper diction from my cousin Terry.

My father never changed; he never learned to be like Uncle Martin. If he had he would have been wary of his youngest brother, my Uncle Sam. Sam exasperated my mother the most of all my fathers' family.

"What does he want now?" She would yell when he came into the store with his warm smile and gentle manner. Momma knew he was always trying his hand, unsuccessfully, in a new kind of business, and it would cost us money. When he decided to peddle shoes, along with his magic polishing clothes, he felt free to help himself to my fathers' stock with no more then a thank you. Poppa would shake his head and say, "Sam will pay when he's able."

Sam never paid my father. He either forgot, or the money went into a different undertaking.

Poppa's compassion was meted out also to his poorer customers. As the neighborhood declined where he had his last business, Poppa would always have some special sale price shoes for his poorer customers. The mothers would come in with their rag tail army of children conceived by a variety of fathers who never seemed to pay for their upkeep. His Black customers cried when my father died at the age of eighty-five, although he had long retired from his business. They told my sister, who had become owner of the little store, that Poppa was truly like Jesus, who also died after the last supper (the Seder).

Mother, uneducated except for basic English courses she took when she first arrived in America, searched for some outlet, some way to work off the terrible frustrations that moved her like un-controlled atomic energy. She thought about the long summer ahead, when she would be cooped up with us children in our home over the shoe store. One summer she decided she would find some way to take us all away to Atlantic City. There David could have plenty of fresh air, sunshine and sea air that would stir up his lagging appetite.

David had a bad experience the year before I was born. Mother seldom spoke of this tragedy, but it gave her cause to guard and protect him more then ever. David was her whole life. He was a quiet, boy with a warm, winsome smile. He could hide within the pages of a book, where adventure awaited without causing him or mother any pain, worry or aggravation. However, one day while playing in front of the store he was jumped by a huge monster of a dog. He was so badly frightened that he would not speak, and shook at the sight of any stranger as if electricity was surging through his skinny body. No doctor could help him One even suggested sending him away to a special hospital. Mother was determined that he could be cured. As a last resort she asked advice from her mother, who was wise in the ways of old world cures, and curses.

My bubah arranged for my mother and dad to take David to see a wise man, a mystic, named Label, who lived in a small house in South Philadelphia. Momma was told to bring an egg, which Label broke on David's head. While my father, held mother's hand tightly, they watched as Label, silently, studied and prayed, over their only son. When he was through, he made a blessing over David, cleaned him off, and told Momma and Poppa to take him home; he would be well within a week. My parents left tzduka (charity) for the old man. By the next week, David was back to normal.

Was it because of this early experience that my mother had a special place in her heart for my brother, the fear of losing him?

After David and Leah were both married, and being the only child still living at home, I felt that there would be a more binding relationship between my mother and myself. I hoped that she would show me more affection then when I was a child. I guess I expected too much. Coming home from work one day, I walked into the kitchen where Momma was busy preparing supper. The first thing I saw when I looked at her was a coat of petroleum jelly glistening on her eyebrows and lashes, covering her eyes.

"Momma, what happened?" I cried out, "What happened to your face?"

Tears poured down her ravaged cheeks, an accompaniment to the tale she told. She had gone to light her gas oven with a match when there was a flash of flame. The front of her hair, her eyebrows and lashes were singed. She had thrown a dish towel over her head, always cool in an emergency, then spread petroleum jelly on her face.

"And all I could think of was my David hearing the news, and having to say Kaddish for me," Momma cried.

I stood there silently looking at my crying mother. I wanted to run up and throw my arms around her, but was immobilized by a heaviness in my legs, I was overcome by a feeling of utter rejection She had given not one thought of my finding her. It was always David; he would always be first with her. Yet I felt no resentment towards my brother; for I too loved him very much.

Well, for whatever reason, my mother decided to rent a large house at the shore that summer of 1928. She had seen some of her sister-in-laws spend the summers running a rooming house, and could not imagine that she could not do the same thing even better.

Mother was never strong, but with her Herculean determination she could accomplish anything. I don't remember this particular summer. All that I can tell you is what was told to me.

With Leah as her helper, Momma scoured, swept, and arranged bedrooms, and she set up the kitchen to be shared by the women who came for a *rest*. These kitchens were called *kouch leffels* cooking spoons, because pots, pans and stirrers were their weapons. Momma's weapons were cleanser and scrub brushes. Her enemy was the sand that invaded the house, on bare feet, shoes, and bathing suits. The sand left its grit; like bird's droppings on the floors, beds and the bath tubs. No one felt clean all summer long. The families brought their own linens and towels, that

Pieces of the Tapestry

they rinsed out in the big wash basins down in the basement, to lug up and hang in the sunny back yard. This, they did for the children.

I am sure that if any of Papa's nieces or nephews wanted to move into one of Momma's precious rooms, they would have to pay the going rate. She was not the philanthropist. Momma's business was not an ongoing charity.

At three I was sent to the beach with a shovel and pail when the days were sunny, to be watched over by my brother David. Mamma was constantly tired, frustrated by the slovenly woman and their bratty children. Even financially this undertaking was not a success. Who could she blame, whom could she complain to? This was an undertaking that she had entered against my fathers will, so we waited for the summer to be over.

The end of summer in Atlantic City was marked by the Miss America Pageant; and mother, like the rest of the city, looked forward to this event. Someone gave mother tickets for seats on the reviewing stand. Relaxed, happy, free from her chores for one day, with her children beside her, she waited for the parade to begin.

The bands strutted down the boardwalk, and the beauties in their daring bathing suits rode by in the rolling chairs, throwing kisses and waving brightly at all the spectators. I grew restless. I was not happy. Not one band that passed played the one song I was waiting for.

"I want to go home," I cried, "take me home right now."

"Now what's the matter?" my mother asked angrily. "Look at all the beautiful girls. Come on, clap your hands to the time of the music." She told me, showing me how.

"No," I said stubbornly, "If they don't play, '*Ain't She Sweet*' I'm leaving." I stood up, to be pulled down by Leah,

"Listen, hush, hear that." My face broke into a big grin. I clapped my hands and sang along with the music. "*Ain't she sweet see her walking down the street, I ask you very confidentially ain't she sweet.*" They made my day.

My father came to take Leah and David back, while Momma and I stayed a little longer. She was pushing me along the boards one day, stopping to look in the store windows, when in a photography shop, a picture caught my eye. There we were, our family caught by the camera, as we were walking along on the boards. All I saw was my father. I screamed and cried until my mother stepped into the store and bought the picture. I cradled it in my arms until Momma put it safely away when we went back to Philadelphia.

The picture still hangs on the stairwell wall going down to my basement. How aristocratic we look; Poppa in a snap brim hat, and overcoat; Momma in her seal skin coat trimmed in fox; a cloche on her head to match, tee strapped shoes and clutching a black bag. Leah bare headed, her curly hair blowing in the breeze, clutched the fur collar of her coat. David wore a cap and high socks up to his knickers. I had on a velvet hat, and a matching velvet coat. My face was all screwed up in a scowl from the sun shining in my eyes. How precious this picture is now. It is the only one I have of the whole family, when we were young, but not so gay.

After our adventure in Atlantic City, mother was quiet, as if mulling over what she would do next. So the next summer, she took me and went to Portsmouth Virginia to visit her sister Hilda.

We went by bus, which is all I remember of that time. I was terrified, sitting by the window as the bus plowed up and down the mountain roads. I felt as if we were being hurtled into a void. All I could see were the tops of trees whose roots clung desperately to their perch in order not to drop down into an abyss, taking us along. This was worse then looking down from the elevated cars. I cried and whimpered with fear, nothing my mother did could calm me down until we finally arrived at the bus station in Portsmouth, both of us exhausted.

After we safely arrived back home, plans were made and executed for us to move to Virginia. So ended one phase of our lives. For me this was the first lap in our journey of discovery into our personal history.

)(

Pieces of the Tapestry

Dove, reverse the way,
Chart a new course for wild wind
And sowers of seed.

※

-Elizabeth Bowers-

GREETING SEASONS IN THE CEMETERY
by
Helen Tulis

    The past seven years of my life have been colored with various sounds and sights in the Greenwood Cemetery. I have visited my father's grave-site once a month, usually on the first of the month since he died December 1, 1986. Oftentimes, I have felt that my car has found its way to the cemetery automatically, having memorized the route itself.
    Beginning in autumn, the leaves fluttered almost blanketing the car as it approached the gates of the cemetery. The drying leaves, splattered onto the pavement, and remained still as the tires rolled over them. The brownish dead leaves managed to slip underneath the tires, causing a screeching sound as I drove onto the narrow road leading to section "G" where my father was buried.
    I could feel the wind blowing gently as I made the swerve around the huge building-like tombstone, centered, and used as my marker at the opening of one lane. I followed the permanent sign marked "Funeral" with its arrow pointing towards section "G."
    The narrow road leading to my father's grave was filled with potholes. I thought, "Why can't they repair these holes? They are ruining my tires." Today there seemed to be more potholes since it had rained so much the past two weeks.
    As I tried to restrain tears that were already dampening my face, I suddenly heard the loud siren of the emergency 911 vehicle. It had turned

Pieces of the Tapestry

down the road outside the gates of the cemetery, yet the loud sound prevailed. I was barely able to hold on to the steering wheel, as my mind jumped into reverse.

I immediately screamed, "Dad, Dad," recalling an earlier incident during my father's illness.

As I took the ball of Kleenex out of my pocketbook to wipe my eyes, I reminded myself of a close call Dad had. His nurse had given him medications on an empty stomach, which prompted him to have sudden pains near his heart. We had called "911," which blasted its siren as it came speeding to our house. At this very moment, I could envision the emergency team trying to help Dad. More tears oozed from my eyes, dribbling down my face, making it barely possible to find the grave-site, as I became shaky and stunned.

Wintertime in the cemetery is often scary. The leafless black limbs of the tall trees barely move. They are naked and often look like short railroad tracks going nowhere. Even the tombstones look shorter as if they grabbed hold of the ground and sunk in to keep from being cold.

One day in the middle of winter, when it was much too cold to open the car window, I drove to the cemetery. The holly bushes, snuggling up to one another, fit like a puzzle in between the fir trees along the paths. The patches of grass, in places, were very green looking, as in a new grave-site. Most of the huge expanse of lawn contained straw-colored grasses. A couple of fake flowers, having been placed on someone's grave, had now blown away; lying in the middle of the lane. The satin ribbon, with which the flowers were decorated, was dirty and smudged; having been driven over by cars entering the lane.

Finally, I found my father's grave-site. I checked on the miniature Japanese myrtle tree that I had planted on Dad's birthday. I had worried that it had been too cold for that little tree. Relieved, I discovered it was fine, and looked protected with the adequate amount of pine straw at its base. I found myself talking with Dad, bringing him up-to-date on all the news about the family. Before I left, I said, "Kaddish." Bending down and kissing the bronze stone was also a part of my monthly ritual. Then, I promptly looked for pebbles to place on the bronze stone, marking that I had visited.

I repeated, "This pebble is for Mom. This one is for me Dad, and this one is for my two sisters. I love you Dad."

Pieces of the Tapestry

When I drove out of the cemetery, I could swear I heard the trees saying "Come back again. Come back." They knew I would as I always returned on the first of the month.

♍ ♒ ♋ ■ ♑ ♏

During springtime, the cemetery is usually decorated with tiny flags for Veterans Day. The grass is green and smooth looking. This year, when I drove inside the gates, I was in an uplifting mood. Maybe it was because the sun was out. Maybe it was because I did not have to work and could spend more time at my father's grave-site. A soft breeze was blowing. New leaves were appearing on the trees. I could even see the mixture of dark and light green colors, dressing up the limbs. Several graves were adorned with wreaths, mingled with pastels of yellow, pink, and blue.

I looked around. I did not see anybody. Again, I was the only visitor in the cemetery. As I approached the plot where my father is buried, I began saying the Kaddish, the Hebrew prayer praising God. Kneeling down closely to the bronze marker to read the inscription, I repeated, "A good name endureth forever."

I heard a horn blowing. Startled, I turned in the direction of the sound. "What is that?" I said out loud. "Gosh, that horn is loud. This is a cemetery," I called out.

I looked up and saw a lady waving her hand from the window of a black car. She yelled, "Come here for a minute."

"Whom did you want? Me?" I shouted.

Cautiously, I approached the car, standing a few feet away from the window. Since I did not know the lady, I purposely stood a distance away.

Still draping her arm out the window, she said, "Don't stay in here too long. Don't hang around here too long by yourself."

I looked at the lady, wondering why she said this to me. "Why? What happened?"

"You know, a few weeks ago, they had a rape here. I don't come in here without this gun. You see?" She slid her hand gently over a silver gun in the black leather holster, lying beside her on the seat.

Pieces of the Tapestry

Hesitatingly, I added, "Well, this cemetery can be a lonely isolated place at times." I thought to myself, "I usually am the only person around."

"You just do your business and get on out of here," the middle aged lady advised.

With that, I turned around and went back to my father's grave-site. I just cried out, "Dad, I've got to go. I've got to go because it is dangerous for me to be here all alone. Please forgive me. I love you Dad," I said as I knelt down and kissed the bronze marker. I dashed up the slight incline, jumping into my car, tears streaming down my face.

As I turned the ignition on, drinking my own tears, I tried to comfort myself saying, "Dad understands. Dad understands. I know." It was no use. I became angry, throwing my pocketbook on the car floor, and yelling out, "You can't even visit your own father's grave in peace any more. I hate this. It's not fair." Wailing and crying, I touched the gas pedal lightly.

As I drove slowly towards the huge iron gates of the cemetery, I saw the sun glistening on the jade leaves sprouting on the bushes. Even in the distance, the breezes were blowing the tiny American flags seen dotting the various tombstones.

I heard the trees whispering, "Come back again. Come back again." They knew I would, as I always do on the first of every month.

)(

Pieces of the Tapestry

Foxes run wild through
Sunken fields of dying moss,
Breezes to their tails.

✷

-Elizabeth Bowers-

THE GHOSTS OF PASSOVER PAST
by
Eleanor Freemer

Is it sacrilegious to say I don't like Passover; that I never liked Passover? My sister and I talk. I ask her, "Tell me something nice about Passover, something happy."

She shakes her head and laughs. "Something warm, maybe like chicken schmaltz. Grivens. One year, when I was little, I remember going to Aunt Julie's house right before Passover. I was always hungry, and looking for something to eat. I saw some cut up golden squares near the sink. Uncle Harry saw me standing there, and said, 'You can have some. It's good candy.' I grabbed a piece and put it in my mouth. While he laughed, I spit it out as fast as I could. They were pieces of chicken fat waiting to be rendered." she sighed. "But who knows better then you what a terrible tease he was."

"How awful," I shivered, "but that was so typical of him. I hated him, and that nasty dog of his. When I was sick with the measles, Poppa would come into our darkened bedroom at night, and read to me from the Big Little Fairy tale Book. When he read the story of Rumplestitlskin, I pictured that sly little man looking like Uncle Harry, that hunched back gnome with cruel jokes and tricks."

"Well," my sister continued, "I loved emptying out the big crate of dishes Mama kept on the back porch. They were special, the gold bank

Pieces of the Tapestry

around the edges, the sprigs of flowers in the center of each plate and round the cups. Remember the blue cups, so delicate, almost translucent; they made drinking tea a party."

Our brother joined us on the low chairs, stretched out his stockinged feet, and softly reminisced about the Sedar we had with our Tante Millie, the only Sedar that I remembered every going to. My aunt and uncle with their eight children, and Momma's bachelor brother lived in that large rambling house. With the five of us, it was a rollicking crew.

Poppa had a little too much wine, and stood up with a full glass and sang, "One little drink makes me older and bolder."

We all agreed. Poppa was never a drinker, so even one glass of wine was more then he could handle.

♍ ♒ ♋ ■ ♑ ♏

This was April 1973. These were the middle days of Passover, and we were sitting Shiva for our father who had died suddenly the week before after the first Sedar. So we spoke of other Passover's and Poppa.

With our parents in the shoe business, we never had a Sedar in our house. Easter and Passover usually fall in the same time slot, so our parents were busy in their store selling black patent leather shoes for other children's holidays. Although my mother prepared all the traditional dishes, often my brother and I ate a lonesome meal. My sister as a teenager was expected to help out in the store in those busy times.

Growing up we always lived in predominately gentile neighborhoods, which was pure torture. There I would sit in the lunchroom choking over a hard-boiled egg and matzo, while my classmates teased me with their spectacular chocolate creamed filled eggs. Easter, I stood out as different, Jewish, a Christ Killer. I didn't know what that meant, but I knew no one in my family ever killed anyone.

I had my first formal date with my then future husband during Passover. It was only a miracle that we saw each other again. While I sat alone watching "*The Prince of Foxes*," he was sitting and moaning in the men's room suffering with the matzo runs.

Later that evening, I cried to my mother, how can I go out with a man whose Hebrew name was Pesach, when our Pesach date was such a fiasco. My mother smiled wisely and said it was a good sign. She and my father had become engaged on Passover.

Pieces of the Tapestry

Joel's mother, since his father died, just made a dinner for his sister and her family, and our small family on the first night of Passover. Although his father had been very Orthodox his children were very liberal. His mother had to be satisfied with blessings over the matzo and wine.

When our two girls grew older, I tried to have some religious ceremony for Passover. I acquired Haggadahs for us all to read, but the girls became bored, and my father who retired after my mother passed away, would be three pages ahead of us.

One Passover, we celebrated with our youngest daughter and her new husband, who had become very religious. They had married a week before Passover, and I tried to make it as perfect as I could for them.

Another Passover we flew to Israel to be with our eldest daughter and her family. They lived up in Neve Yaakov where the stars and bright moon guided us through the quiet cold windy streets to the apartment where we were staying after their Sedar. We were able to gaze over the rise of hills, where during the day Arab shepherds still herded their sheep, and saw the lights of Jordan twinkling in the distance, in competition with the stars in heaven.

One memorable first night I sat with our one day old granddaughter Sarah, sleeping across my lap. As I lit the Memorial candle for my father, I pleaded with him to be an emissary to God for this new life.

Seven Passovers later our whole family gathered to celebrate what we knew would be Sarah's last birthday ~ last Passover. I was angry with God. I was angry with my father. How could he, who had loved his grandchildren so much, let this happen? In my eyes he had been a tzadik. Why could he not plead with God for this young soul?

Each Passover I say to my husband, "Let's go away, take a cruise, join our friends in the Catskills." Each year I make Passover, we spend the first night with our youngest daughter, her husband and their children. We delight in the way the older grandchildren read from the Haggadah. Finally as the night overcomes them, we watch as one by one their heads droop down among the fallen petals from the flowers that decorate their table.

Pieces of the Tapestry

God has given us a fountain of strength to bear the unbearable. He will help us through many more Passovers, where I'll clean and cook and set the table; listen to the voices of our children and their husbands, our grandchildren, and a chorus of loving voices from the past. I will work, and tears, unbidden will salt the hard boiled eggs, and mingle with the bitter herbs. I can not divorce the past from the present. Still, I will never render chicken fat, make grivens or really love Passover.

)(

Heart of bleeding lamb
Cries out to souls of lost sheep,
Deep in pine forest.

✸

-Elizabeth Bowers-

WINGED FLOWER
by
Elizabeth Bowers

In the dark of winter's first night,
Comes the summons to take flight;
And I make haste, like a winged flower
Dressed in shimmering colors of light,
To fly out from the lost reality of flesh,
And glide gently through a remembered place
Filled with sweet warmth of spring's breath,
Kissed by the tenderness of a healing shower;
To commune with dazzling flying gems
And sip sweet nectar until summer's last light.

✸

Pieces of the Tapestry

KOLK
by
Eleanor Freemer

They came from a town called *KOLK*
these old men, embraced by their
yellowed prayer shawls,
lying deep and silent in this
plot of holy ground.

Their siddurs',
edges curled up
from a thousand dampened fingers;
letters washed out by tears
from eyes that had no need
to see the words,
now share this resting place,
this haven in a new world cemetery,
embraced by a broken gate
whose sign reads in faded Yiddish,
KOLK

These sleeping souls
are all that is left
to testify that they once lived
in a place whose name was spoken
only among themselves.
No oral or written testimony
bears witness to what they saw,
or felt or feared.
In life, as now in death,
they silently engulfed themselves
in their huge wool tallithsm.
Together, they beat their breast,

Pieces of the Tapestry

crying out a prayer to HaShem
a Kaddish for those who sleep
somewhere in *KOLK*.

The tiny *KOLKER* Shule
where my father worshipped is gone.
Gone too is the pungent smell
from tobacco stained fingers
that wrapped the tiffilin
around arms that embraced their torah
across foreheads where memories were
stored of graveyards
that overflowed with family martyrs.
A place of too many graves
for too many who perished
in the distant shtetel of
KOLK.

My father, his young comrades,
believed a man must have a dream,
must live, marry, beget
leave behind a Kaddish
for their soul's sake.
So they left this town
taking with them only the name.
Leaving behind a marker that reads,
KOLK

Today Poppa, I stand here and
say Kaddish for you, and for
those who never made the journey.
What can I tell our young,
who are our future, about our past?
I cannot talk of the lost years
of which you never spoke.

Pieces of the Tapestry

We your children, grandchildren
great-grandchildren, now seek markers,
resting places, a shtetle no longer there.
We search among broken head stones
for our beginnings.
Where are the maps to show us the way?
Where are the sages to tell us their story?
Where are the candles to bless the night?
There are no answers.
The earth is silent.
It keeps its secrets of
KOLK.

Poppa your thumbprint is on me.
Your eyes gaze out from your grandchild's eyes.
Your voice echoes from my grandchild's lips.
That is all we have.
How can I tell them of our past?
I can only whisper the name
which means nothing to them,
Just a word written in faded Yiddish,
swinging on a cemetery gate.
KOLK.

א

SONG OF REASSURANCE
by
Helen Tulis

A muffled silence dangled loosely
over a darkened street,
abandoning the stale winter mist,
with dreaded stillness
hanging perilously onto my body,
enveloping it into a shroud,
as the glare of the lamp evaporated.
Silence is the desolate tune
of memories of the departed
who whisper songs of quiet reassurance,
nurturing a generation along a stony path,
marking the route with indelible reminders
Of dignity, ethics, and brotherly love,
Rendering the perfect piece of tapestry.
Women with threads dipped in golden prose
paraphrased quotes, hued and circled into a rainbow
that blends into messages, trumpeted from the righteous
who were once outspoken,
now exalted,
and never silenced.

⚸

Pieces of the Tapestry

Breeze of first night, like
Clouds rushing through stormless sky,
Leaves no sacrifice.

҉

-Elizabeth Bowers-

EXIT LANE
by
Helen Tulis

Mrs. Fu, my Chinese neighbor, paced back and forth in her driveway. She checked the small garden beginning her daily trek around the cul de sac. Though Mrs. Fu exercised throughout the year, I only saw her in the mornings about 9:00 a.m. Steadying herself at the turn of her street, Mrs. Fu rounded the entire complex, counting steps as she went along. Everyone living in the complex had already departed for work when Mrs. Fu appeared all bundled up in her wine colored sweat suit.

She was a chunky woman, who weighed about 170 pounds. She appeared to be carrying extra fat for her five feet of height. Her smooth looking yellow brown complexion reminded me of cooking oil, as her face glistened in the wintry sun. Mrs. Fu had six children, all married. All six children had children, totaling six grandchildren for Mrs. Fu.

She was quiet and very shy. Perhaps it was because she feared her English was not acceptable. On the other hand, Mr. Fu spoke English very well.

Mrs. Fu's Chinese mingled with her English when I asked her, "How are you today?"

She mumbled back to me, "Oh, he working." This meant she thought I asked about her husband. Mr. Fu was an engineer, who had gone to work about eight o'clock in the morning.

Trudging down the block and hiding in her sweat suit and jacket, Mrs. Fu continued on her walk which was a daily routine. I wondered,

Pieces of the Tapestry

"How many months has she been walking around here?" Suddenly, I realized it had been at least six months that I had observed her routine. Though her pace had quickened, she still dragged her heavy feet as if something were holding her back. But, I did notice that she had lost weight.

One evening I met Mr. and Mrs. Fu in the neighborhood grocery store, shopping. I nodded and said, "Oh, hello. Good to see you both."

Mr. Fu took the initiative and answered, "Fine. We fine."

The next day was a windy day. When I looked out the back door, I saw Mrs. Fu, walking again. "Boy," I thought, "She is going to be so skinny. Look at me. I'm still overweight."

By now, Mrs. Fu had rounded the bend and was returning to her house.

I felt guilty. I asked myself, "Why is it that the Chinese lady has such discipline and I don't?" After consulting with myself, I remarked, "You had better start exercising yourself, lady. You're overweight, too."

A couple of weeks passed and I did not see Mrs. Fu. I was concerned, but felt sure that she would be around. Sure enough, later in the day, I saw her as she stalked down the street, as if she were counting her steps. She quickened her pace when she saw me.

I approached her and asked, "How are you?"

She looked at me from her side glance and answered, "Oh, he fine." Again, Mrs. Fu thought about her husband. Of course, they were very close, having been married about forty years. Even when they worked in the garden, they did chores together. Mr. Fu raked while Mrs. Fu tended to her flowers and plants. On one occasion, I saw them through the kitchen door. Together, they prepared their evening meal with rice, leeks onions and peppers. They always entertained their grandchildren together. Mr. Fu played "catch" while Mrs. Fu showed the younger grandchildren how to cook. Then they all came outside.

In early spring, after two months had passed, I realized I had not seen Mrs. Fu. "I wonder what happened?" I said to myself. "Well, Mrs. Fu has lost all that weight. I suppose she doesn't need to walk. No, I bet she went to visit her son in California or maybe Mr. Fu found an engineering job elsewhere. No, they probably went to China for a visit. They have relatives over there," I laughed to myself for all my speculations. "Mrs. Fu once told me her daughter no longer lives here. She lives in Virginia.

Pieces of the Tapestry

"That's right. That's where Mrs. Fu is. She is in Virginia." I was satisfied with that conclusion.

♍︎ ♒︎ ♋︎ ■ ♑︎ ♏︎

It remained quiet around the house of Fu. I saw no grandchildren visiting. No one worked in the yard. The flowers Mrs. Fu cared for on her porch, looked tired, almost dead. I went to work and did my chores, thinking, "How nice, to visit your children out of town. Mrs. Fu is having a vacation in Virginia."

Another month passed. About sunset one evening, as I swept the back patio, I saw Mr. Fu stop his blue car right in front of me. I was so surprised to see him that I ran around to his side of the car and asked, "How are you? How is your wife?"

"Oh, she die a few months ago," Mr. Fu declared sadly. "I alone now," he added quickly.

I almost asked, "What will you do now?" I held myself back, because I knew what Mr. Fu would do. He would cook, tend to the garden, and play with his grandchildren.

"What happened to Mrs. Fu? Why did she die?" I inquired.

"Oh, my wife, she have asthma long time. Sick a long time. She could not breeze," he answered, "Long time."

Turning away after I had offered my condolences, I began to think, "So this is it? And I never did get to know Mrs. Fu. I'll bet she was a good cook. Maybe I could have learned some new recipes. But, now, what's the use? Gone."

Several months later I saw Mr. Fu as he began to drive out of his driveway. Seeing me walking by, he stopped his car, cracking his window on the driver's side. I said, "How are you doing? What are you doing? Working?"

"Oh, I no work much. Just have children here from Houston now."

"That is wonderful," I said.

"Maybe you help me. I do breezing exercises. Last week I climb Stone Mountain in 51 minutes ... breezing," he smiled.

"Gosh," I thought. "What is he saying?"

"You know, my uncle, granfadder give me lessons in dis exercises ... breezing. I write a book. Make cassette," Mr. Fu tried to explain.

Pieces of the Tapestry

Taking out an envelope from his glove compartment, he showed me figures of deep breathing exercises. I finally caught on to what he meant. He was referring to breathing exercises. "That is wonderful," I said, trying to give him some encouragement to finish explaining to me.

"I seventy-one and I breeze like a fifty-one to go Stone Mountain," he added.

"I know no Henglish, so maybe we write a small book on breezing the old Chinese method," Mr. Fu suggested.

"Well, sure, maybe we can get together when you have time and talk about it," I replied, smiling.

"Maybe nes week when children go home, we do dis in Henglish. Your Henglish better than mine. You help write book. We make money," he joked.

"Breathing exercises?" I thought about all the knowledge he wanted us to put in a book to make money. I turned away with a sad wave of my hand, thinking to myself, "Sure Mr. Fu, maybe someday we'll talk about it. Humph! Breathing exercises! It's too late for poor Mrs. Fu."

⚹

Pieces of the Tapestry
Cherry spiced tales of Rosemary summer's thyme, give Blessings to sweet sage.

✻

-Elizabeth Bowers-

THE VISITOR
by
Eleanor Freemer

Momma went away for two weeks every summer. When we lived in Philadelphia she made a trip to Aunt Jessie in Virginia; and when we lived in Virginia, she traveled back to Philadelphia to see her mother. It was the summer we were living in the apartment below Mrs. Topper's, that when Momma left, the girls moved in.

Leah was sixteen and Poppa's' lieutenant in charge of the house, Michael and me. She was in High School and the kids at Maury High were considered fast. Leah worked hard to obtain a sheen of sophistication to keep up with them. However, when Momma wasn't home, I sort of cramped her style as she had to take her six-year-old sister with her wherever she went. Poppa was wiser then we thought. That was his way of insuring that both of us kept out of trouble.

It seemed that no sooner had Uncle Sam driven Momma to the bus station that Sunday morning in his sporty two seater with the rumble seat in the back, that our next door neighbor was knocking on the front door.

"Can I speak to your Momma?" she asked, looking down at me as I opened the door, acting as if she hadn't seen Momma with her suitcase just leave the house.

I shook my head, "Momma isn't here."

"Then may I speak with your Poppa?"

"Poppa," I yelled out, not wanting to leave my post. She had never been in our house before and I didn't know whether it was wise to invite her in now.

Pieces of the Tapestry

Mrs. Kaplan was a thin sharp faced woman, who always wore a large white bib type apron tied around her middle like a sack of flour. It never looked really clean, or very dirty. It merely announced to the world that she was the proprietor of the meat and grocery store down on Church Street.

Poppa, always the gentleman, lead her back into the kitchen that was still as clean and bright as Momma had left it that morning. Mrs. Kaplan, a business woman, wasted no time on small talk, came right to the point as graciously as she was able.

"Mr. Bernstien, I know your wife is out of town, and I should have asked before she left, but the situation just arose, and I know she would have helped if she could."

Behind her back I shook my head, "No," at Leah, knowing Momma would never help this woman who was ready to snare Poppa behind her back into some ploy for her own good.

"My niece who is staying with us from New York, invited some friends to spend the week with us. Three girls came in just this morning, just like that, expecting me to put them up. I have no place for them." Her gnarled fingers reached out helplessly.

"You know how young girls are," she looked at Leah with a false smile, "I didn't know they were coming until they landed on my doorstep this morning. Shirley, my niece, said she was just joking when she told them to come on down. She never, as God is my witness, thought they would take her up on it." She played with the ends of the sash from her apron, a woman in a real quandary.

"Maybe you could find room for two. You said your wife is gone for the week. Perhaps your son could move in with you and the girls could have his room. I, of course will pay you for your inconvenience." She clenched her teeth as though in pain.

Poppa shook his head and said "I'll think about it. I'll let you know a little later today." He walked her back to the front door, a baffled look on his kind face that seemed to say, "Why me? Why now?"

Leah tried to play it cool, but she was really interested in the girls from New York. She had seen the niece who sat on the front porch swing sipping cokes and wearing what looked to be real silk dresses. Mrs. Koladine's son Abraham, who was home that summer from Med school in Baltimore, invited college friends over to entertain her, but they had nothing in common with her. So she swung and swung looking real bored. Perhaps the girl friends would liven things up, and even carry Leah along on the current of excitement.

Michael and I tried to talk Poppa out of it. Michael didn't want to lose the privacy of his bedroom. Leah was already in there stripping the linens from the bed and taking things out of his dresser to put in boxes that had been stored in the wood shed out back. "It will be fun, she kept repeating like a cheer leader. You'll see. And how nice the extra money will be. Momma will be proud of us."

I knew better. Momma would hate having strangers in her house if she were home or not. Momma would yell and carry on when she found out. Leah tried to assure me she wouldn't find out. What about the money? Poppa would take care of that.

By the afternoon, through sheer will power, Michael was out of the room, and the three girls were in. There was only a double bed, but how the girls would manage, wasn't my problem, I was told.

Strange smells like cigarettes and perfume, came from the room as soon as they moved in. Even Poppa was not allowed to smoke in the house.

"Frances is the one smoking," Leah said

I couldn't even guess how she knew since she was standing next to me on the other side of the closed door.

Shirley soon joined them behind the closed door. A record player materialized from someplace playing "*Have you ever seen a dream walking?*" Laughter and loud talk swelled within the confines of the room, ready to explode. By eight o'clock, when I was ready to go to bed, the music stopped, the door opened and the four girls emerged like under an exotic cloud. The dresses were short, the heels were high and jewelry sparkled on their ears, on their skinny arms, around their throats. Their eyes, cheeks and lips outshone the brightness of the jewels. They posed at the door of the kitchen and asked Leah if she would like to go with them.

Poppa's hand pressed tightly against Leah's full shoulder. "No," he answered for Leah.

We heard their loud giggles as they skipped down off the porch to a waiting car. The driver gaily twirled the key to the front door in her hand.

It was very late at night or early in the morning when they came back into our house emitting the same giggles they had left with. I nudged

Pieces of the Tapestry

Leah who lay beside me in the bed we always shared and whispered, "They're home."

She pretended to be asleep but I knew she wasn't. I was also sure I heard a man's voice, and I knew it was neither Poppa or Michael.

The next morning when Poppa got up early to get ready to go to the store, I could hear him fussing when he went into the bathroom. The room was draped with their lingerie dripping into the bathtub. I followed him into the kitchen while he made breakfast and his face was gray from lack of sleep and worry. "This wasn't a good idea at all. Girls like that should be home with their mothers. I don't want Leah to get ideas from them. It is very bad."

As he poured himself a cup of coffee, the door bell rang. His hand shook as he put it on the table. I was at his heels as he lumbered to the door to see two big policemen and another big burly man standing there.

"Mr. Bernstein, may we come in?" It really wasn't a question for they were in the house before Poppa could even answer. "We understand you have three young girls staying with you over night?" The emphasis was on young, as if Poppa had kidnapped them like the Lindbergh baby.

Poppa's throat was dry but he was able to answer "Yes. A neighbor who is a friend of the girls asked us if we could take them in for the night."

Michael and Leah came to join us.

"Did your neighbor tell you the girl's parents didn't know where they were and called the FBI to find them?"

Poppa shook his head. "No."

I don't think he really knew who the FBI was. I sure didn't.

"Where are the girls?" The burly man's tone was sharp.

Leah lead them to the door. They stopped and the big plain dressed man banged on the door. Not a sound came from the room He banged again, harder.

The door opened slowly and one eye peeked out from the other side of the door. "Yes?"

"Open up. We came to talk to you."

The door opened and closed behind the three men. Cries were heard from the girls, then the men walked into the kitchen and said they would wait until the girls got dressed. They would be put on a bus and their parents would be waiting for them at the station in New York.

Pieces of the Tapestry

Poppa put up more coffee. The stern faced man said he hoped Poppa's two girls never did a trick like that ~ just pack up and leave home without telling anyone where they were going.

Soon they all left the house much more subdued then when they came yesterday. The smell of their perfume lingered, even though the windows had been open all day and all night. To Leah's delight, they had forgotten all their fancy underwear drying in the bathroom.

Mrs. Koladine's niece soon went home too, but Mrs. Kaplan never gave Poppa any money for his trouble and she never walked into our house again.

♍︎♒︎♋︎■♑︎♏︎

"Well, did anything exciting happen while I was gone?" Momma asked when she arrived home that Friday.

"No. It was the same old thing. We survived. We sure missed you a lot though," Leah said.

"Well I'm glad to be back home," Momma said.

♓︎

Pieces of the Tapestry

CROWS
    by
Eleanor Freemer

Like Chasidim they come
all clad in black
suits and hats,
bowing their backs
down in prayer to Ha-Shem
in a congregational gathering
twice daily on my front lawn,
to sing mincha and ma'arivh in the evening,
then shachareit at dawn.

From where do they come,
swirling around like a cloud
of ebony feathers in constant motion
and where do they go after their devotions,
these wanderers, these aliens, unwanted
unloved, noisy crows?

Life is so hard when you're chased
like a thief from yard to yard,
a leaf blown by the wind,
washed by the rain, dark like a shadow,
black as pain.

Black ~ black is a mystery
black is so strange,
but Ha-Shem made them black
and they never can change
to look like a robin or a royal blue jay,
they wear their black proudly
day after day.

Pieces of the Tapestry

Are they Chasidic souls incarnated,
intoxicated with religious fervor,
dancing on my grass each morning,
each night as if possessed by a Dybbuk
who will live forever in these birds,
these crows?
Only Ha-Shem knows.

As a mere woman I hide
Inside behind my curtains, and watch
as they raise themselves high
to fly to the very reaches of heaven
on those powerful wings, where they sing
psalms of praise to our Father, our King;
"Hallelujah, Hallelujah,"
for the whole world to hear;
"Hallelujah! Hallelujah! Hallelujah! Amen!"

)(

Pieces of the Tapestry

Memories, like dry leaves, ride winds of changing times When streams become ice.

-Elizabeth Bowers-

INITIALS I.B.
by
Helen Tulis

The lining of Dad's winter coat had an embroidered emblem with his initials detailed with flowers and scrolls. I loved the satin smooth feel of it. When he bought a new overcoat, Mom took the initialed emblem off and carefully stitched it to the new lining. I thought, "My, it is aristocratic to have your initials sewn on your coat lining." When Dad died, my sister Barbara took that initialed patch. She wanted to be aristocratic too.

About a year or two after Dad died, I was in his house and picked up a history book about Polish Jewry. As I turned the pages, a bookmark fell on the floor. I started reading it though it was upside down. It said, "Property of Ivan Bernstein," above Dad's address. I was positive it was Dad's handwriting, because I could clearly recognize it. I was so astonished that Dad had inscribed this bookmark and I read it repeatedly. "Property of Ivan Bernstein," as if anyone would steal a bookmark. I simply replaced the bookmark inside the book and put the book down.

On the back porch, I noticed a plaque of a chicken carved out of wood. I felt that I had seen that before. I touched the small gold key nails. I asked Mom, "Where did you get this?"

"Oh," said Mom, "don't you remember? You gave to Dad on one of his birthdays."

As the back porch light shone just right, I could read the inscription on the wooden chicken. It said, "Gift from daughter Helen, February 2, 1970." I thought to myself, "Dad made sure he identified everything."

When I got home that evening, I thought about Dad's initializing personal possessions. I opened the drawer where I kept Dad's black gloves. "I'm going to see if Dad's initials are in these gloves," betting that I would not find I. B. But, sure enough, I looked on the inside of the gloves and there stood the two letters, capital letters, "I. B." Yet, I was sure Dad did not think anyone would steal his black gloves. I looked in my closet at the notebook Dad had given me when I started college. That would have been a perfect spot for my own initials, I decided. Why hadn't I put my initials there? With so many girls in the dorm, someone could have stolen that notebook. I treasured it. "Should I write my name in it now? It is never too late," I thought.

Dad had initialed all his possessions because he treasured them. He liked owning something. He wanted to make sure he knew from whom these gifts had come. In Poland, as a youth, he never owned anything. Even the house in which he lived, his parents did not own. His grandfather owned that house. Dad once told me a story about the house in Lask, Poland. To attend school there, you had to pay taxes on a house. So, Dad's grandfather, Herschel, told the tax collector that he owned only one side of the house and Dad's father owned the other half. In this way, Dad was allowed to attend school. Ownership was important.

I began to notice that Dad initialed things he owned, even gifts. In a desk drawer, I saw a leather initial I had made while I was in camp. On the reverse side, I saw Dad's initials. Even letters sent to me by Dad had an ending like this: "Your Dad, I.B." When my two sons gave Dad a gift, I could expect to find identification marks on those, too.

Once, on the high holiday Rosh Hashanah, I had hurried to reach for the special holiday prayer book. I kept it in the breakfront, so I could always find it in a hurry, even though it had a white cover. I was thinking, "This year won't be any happier than the last year, because Dad is not with us." I sighed, grabbed the white prayer book and was off to the synagogue.

As the Rabbi was giving his sermon towards the end of the services, I thumbed through the prayer book, stopping on the first page. I glared at

Pieces of the Tapestry

the inscription on the inside cover: "A Happy Yom Tov this year and every year, from your parents, Rose & Ivan." Dad had initialed his wish for my happiness as he had inscribed the prayer book. Dad cherished Judaism and me. At that moment, I looked up with teary eyes and I heard the Rabbi say, "L'Shono Tova" (Happy New Year).

א

Pieces of the Tapestry

Tomorrow's seedlings
Sleep in gentle roots of thyme
And morning glory.

)(

-Elizabeth Bowers-

ANNIVERSARY
by
Eleanor Freemer

They're all talked out;
what more is there to say
then hello, good-by, have a good day.
She basks in this silence,
like a cat in the sun,
for as long as he's with her
her life is not done.
He's her friend, and companion,
and yes still her first love,
they fit snugly together;
a cool hand in a warm glove.
She laughs, he looks up,
they smile, and don't find
that it's a mite bit boring
to read each others mind.
They still eat side by side
and share the same plate,
a habit that started
on their very first date.
Tomorrow, as today,
they will still share the same bed
with the same feather pillows
under their heads.

)(

Pieces of the Tapestry

Cantaloupe skies, death
To stars and dreaming raindrops,
Pray for breathless earth.
⚸

-Elizabeth Bowers-

SOUGHT BY THE LIGHT
by
Elizabeth Bowers

Deeper, deeper I flow in warm heart of
Sweet circle of brilliant yellow light that
Summons me, compels me to go above
Time ~ space, to a place where once I was at
On another occasion; different path
That lead to the spot where the entrance now,
As then, is where I feel only the bath
Of warmth that is poured by sweet light; but how,
I do not know or care to give a thought.
Unconscious of physical self, I am
Floating and drifting, my essence is sought
By light energy, as it were a dam
Sucking up waters of life as they flow;
Where it shall lead, I do not really know.

⚸

Pieces of the Tapestry

Butterfly gardens
And ginger lilies herald
Thyme's turning of leaves.

♓

-Elizabeth Bowers-

DEATH DECIDES
by
Helen Tulis

Death is seriously taken
When a parent dies.
It tails us, designing our finish lines,
Secretly planning a rendezvous,
Sharpening its game call "gotcha."
At the beginning of mid-life
A cluster of fame or fortune surrounds us,
We cling to recognition in a highlight of fervor;
Yet death lurks in a shallow harbor,
Pretending to give us a second wind
To accumulate our possessions,
While all along, it hovers like a midnight sky.

To take flight or remain calm and review?
Do nothing or work in a frenzy?
No matter.
Death decides when gotcha begins
And its stiff whip clutches us in silence.

♓

Pieces of the Tapestry

Skies in secrete worlds
Of Spring gorges and meadows,
Show me to myself.

⟊

-Elizabeth Bowers-

BRIDGING DEATH
by
Helen Tulis

Bridging death,
Burning bridges,
Tears extinguished
and
Night replenished;
Mid-life erased,
Time stands still;

Burning bridges
Harboring devotion,
Embellishing moments,
Bonding cultures;
Creating a tapestry
In a tribute to love.

⟊

Pieces of the Tapestry
NIGHT
by
Elizabeth Bowers

Before the night came,
I had no awareness of being me;
But then a thought rolled over that
Set into urgent motion a powerful flow,
Like a mighty stream rushing out to sea;
It took shape as night upon a
Solid sphere of earth and sky.

And in the night came I,
Into an awareness of being me,
When motion turned to urgency and
Forced a change in speed.
A fiery passion filled my depths,
As all that I was rotated about,
Through shadowless orbits of nothingness.

Out of the night came I,
Rotating freely through liquid places,
Like night and purple horses, and roads
Lined with pink and blood red trees;
Shadows of formless dreams did dance
About me in coalescing streams of
Constantly changing rates of motion.

Out of the night came I,
As though upon a purple mount, dashing
Into a place filled with wind and light;
Not a sound did I make as I roamed
Through shadowless paths of nothingness,
Where even dreams keep their silence,
And nothing made a sound back at me.

Pieces of the Tapestry

Out of the night came I,
With a sack full of dreams I found,
When once I did run freely through
A place where nothing is substantial,
Not even the smallest part of me;
Thoughts are all that churn about
In that shadowless realm of invisibility.

Into the light came I,
And stood in a place created from
A single thought that lingered and
I became the thing itself that danced;
The ever-expanding spark that ignites
The passions of the whole of life and,
Fires the ever-expanding dream of creation.

)(

Index By Author

HAIKU VERSES
(First Lines, in order of appearance)

by: Bowers, Elizabeth

9	Rose sun shine down on
13	Lost baby breath blows
27	I am hope's passion
31	Butterfly sings tale
37	Dancing rock sing loud
38	Wings of love spread wide
39	Cypress leaves wink at
50	Sunshine in my heart
51	Threads of season's light
54	Broken sky holds gleam
58	I walk in peaceful
62	Sweet Source of wind and
66	Midnight road, lead me
68	Impatient's spirit
73	Black bird, at first light,
74	Garden of faithful
76	Hold tight to thriving root
81	Flax blows in threatening
93	Sparkling waves entice
119	Cold Wind steals my light
125	Sun, shine on flowers
128	Clouds to earth's call come
134	Golden sun gives strength
136	Bluejay sings good day
151	Tangled rainbows stuck
155	Soft motion of spring
158	Star dust born on winds
159	Rohdea, lost in shades
162	Dreaming woodlands hold
174	Season of wisdom
176	Lilies sleep in time
180	Weak branch draws life from
184	Lamb of shinning peace
204	Sunshine keeps its sweet
207	Nightingale, sing your song
208	Diamond lights midnight
213	Soul of morning star
214	Heavenly waters
217	Rain upon the rue
218	On wind blown sand, stands
170	See the flower of
173	Sparrow digs for joy
215	Season of change sneaks
225	Skylark in great day
231	Dark root stores promise
233	Winter hides fallen
243	River of sunny
241	Transforming currents
247	Shadow of death hides
249	Angry wind roars
257	Grisly death rides crest
263	Summer's spider weaves
270	Tears of winter's heart
273	Sweet honesty takes
281	Loblolly pine stands
287	Rivers of swimming
292	Anagram insights
291	Begging ivy weeps
304	Dove, reverse the way
308	Foxes run through wild
312	Heart of bleeding lamb
317	Breeze of first night, like
321	Cherry spiced tales
328	Memories, like dry
332	Cantaloupe skies, death
333	Butterfly gardens
334	Skies in secrete worlds

Bowers, Elizabeth

Tapestry, *Introduction*
Child of My Heart, 12
Kara's Path, 13
Love, The Master Thread, 38
Pacific Reflections 39
Sweet Morning, 50
On My Mountain, 57
When Ivy Dances, 56
Essence of Love, 56
Ode To A Monarch Butterfly, 61
Beautiful Black, 73
Season of the Hawk, 74
One Water Way, 93
Cantaloupe Sky, 127
Daddy's Pitchfork, 128
Shaky Peace, 143
Taking a Chance, 155
Witness, 173

I Hear You Maya, 176
Morda, 184
Judgment, 207
Aloneness, 213
Greet Wide Ocean, 214
Pain, 217
Ready for That Great Day, 225
Questions, 231
Woman Heed The Call, 243
Toward the City of Light, 245
Song Birds in A Season Of Rage, 256
Caught in a Wedge, 257
A Cold Passing, 270
Faithful Servant, 273
Winged Flower, 312
Sought By the Light, 332
Night, 335

Freemer, Eleanor

We Women Cry in the Bathroom, 10
Hoardings, 11
Life, 26
The Survivor, 27
Spring Cleaning, 54
The Game, 58
Love Food, 66
Priorities, 77
Second Chance, 81
The Kiss, 125
The Pinochle Player, 136
Marge, 144
The Lesson, 145
Mirror, Mirror on the Wall, 148
Colorblind, 148
Knots and Stitches, 149
In The Company of Women, 152
What Am I Doing Here?, 159
Marooned, 169
Research, 170
Me, 175
Kosher is Kosher?, 180
Restless, 183
Fireflies and Rain, 199
Rachel, 200
Our Son, 208
The Jacks Players, 219
Old Men-Old Women, 233

The Bell of St. Nikos, 234
A Front Porch, 238
January, 248
The Last Journey, 263
Songs My Mother Sang, 269
Memories, 281
Beginnings, 292
The Ghosts of Passover Past, 308
Kolk, 313
Crows, 326
Anniversary, 321
The Visitor, 321

Tulis, Helen

Strawberries, 22
On Vapor Flies The World, 22
Conversations with my Dad, 23
Plumb Down to Earth, 31
Countessa For a Moment, 51
A Real Butterfly, 62
Talking About Miracles, 68
Real Memories, 80
Donna's Room, 119
The Hanukah Gift, 134
Wonderment, 141
A Second Thought, 158
The Return, 168
The Monologue, 169
Mom, 195
Change of Seasons, 215
Multi-Colored Playground, 241
Good Timing, 242
The Big One, 249
Penciling In, 271
Closing the Gap, 286
The Warm Water Pool, 287
Death of Laughter, 291
Greeting Seasons in the Cemetery, 304
Song of Reassurance, 316
Exit Lane, 317
Initials I. B., 328
Death Decides, 333
Bridging Death, 334
Bowers, Tulis, Freemer
Fear, -162--

NOTES

NOTES

Pieces of the Tapestry

ABOUT THE AUTHORS

Elizabeth Bowers received her Master of Arts Degree from Lindenwood College, St. Charles, Mo., and is a graduate of the Institute for Children's Literature. She draws upon past involvements as a business woman and a community activist, as well as her experiences as Bill Bowers' wife and Edward and Carla Bowers' mother, to breathe life and character into her stories and poems.

ℋ

Eleanor Freemer is a prolific writer. Her works are rich in the passion, humor, and insights she has gained through participation in long standing customs. Her stories and poems have appeared in numerous Jewish and other publications.

ℋ

Dr. Helen Tulis is widely recognized as an experienced Gerontologist, and innovative educator. Holding degrees from Syracuse, and New York University, Helen has been honored as a Teacher of the Year. Her work has been recognized by the National Endowment for the Humanities.

ℋ

ORDER FORM
PIECES OF THE TAPESTRY

☺ YES, SEND ME: ____ COPIES OF *PIECES OF THE TAPESTRY* at **$19.96**/copy.

(Please Print or type)
NAME_____
Street_____
City_____State_____
ZIP_____Phone (____)_____
All personal information is confidential

☺ YES SEND _ Additional ordrs/gifts may be included on a separate sheet of paper.

AS A GIFT: ____ COPIES OF *PIECES OF THE TAPESTRY*
ISBN: 0-9644473-0-4

SEND TO_____
Street_____
City_____
Zip _____Gift From_____

My check or money order in the amount of $_____, is enclosed.

Make your check or money order payable to ADEPT PUBLISHING ASSOCIATION, Inc., and mail to : PO Box 87
Pine Lake, Georgia 30072-0087

Pieces of the Tapestry

Pieces of the Tapestry

Pieces of the Tapestry

Pieces of the Tapestry

Pieces of the Tapestry

Pieces of the Tapestry

Pieces of the Tapestry